The Detroit School Busing Case

LANDMARK LAW CASES

&

AMERICAN SOCIETY

Peter Charles Hoffer
N. E. H. Hull
Series Editors

For a complete list of titles in the series go to www.kansaspress.ku.edu.

JOYCE A. BAUGH

The Detroit School Busing Case

Milliken v. Bradley and the Controversy

over Desegregation

UNIVERSITY PRESS OF KANSAS

© 2011 by the University Press of Kansas
All rights reserved

Published by the University Press of Kansas (Lawrence, Kansas 66045), which was
organized by the Kansas Board of Regents and is operated and funded by Emporia
State University, Fort Hays State University, Kansas State University, Pittsburg State
University, the University of Kansas, and Wichita State University

Library of Congress Cataloging-in-Publication Data

Baugh, Joyce A.
The Detroit school busing case : Milliken v. Bradley and the controversy
over desegregation / Joyce A. Baugh.
p. cm. — (Landmark law cases & American society)
Includes bibliographical references and index.
ISBN 978-0-7006-1766-1 (cloth : alk. paper)
ISBN 978-0-7006-1767-8 (pbk. : alk. paper)
1. Milliken, William G., 1922– — Trials, litigation, etc. 2. Detroit (Mich.). Board
of Education. 3. Michigan — Trials, litigation, etc. 4. Bradley, Ronald — Trials,
litigation, etc. 5. National Association for the Advancement of Colored People.
Detroit Branch — Trials, litigation, etc. 6. Discrimination in education — Law and
legislation — United States. 7. Discrimination in education — Law and legislation —
Michigan — Detroit. 8. Busing for school integration — Law and legislation — United
States. 9. Busing for school integration — Law and legislation — Michigan — Detroit.
I. Title.
KF228.M55B38 2011
344.73'07980977434--dc22
2010038986

British Library Cataloguing-in-Publication Data is available.

Printed in the United States of America

10 9 8 7 6 5 4 3 2 1

The paper used in this publication is recycled and contains 30 percent postconsumer
waste. It is acid free and meets the minimum requirements of the American National
Standard for Permanence of Paper for Printed Library Materials Z39.48-1992.

To my parents,

the late Reverend Jeff Baugh and Mrs. Ella Jones Baugh,

and to all who work for justice, freedom, and peace

CONTENTS

The course of enforcement of desegregation in the United States was not straight or smooth, as school boards colluded with local authorities in massive resistance to the plain sense of the Supreme Court's ruling in its landmark *Brown v. Board of Education* (1954) decision. Bit by bit, after nearly two generations of litigation, schools in the country moved toward integration. The equitable means for this — the injunctive relief federal district courts fashioned for children of all races — often depended on complex busing plans, as "white flight" from integrated schools in some districts had effectually resegregated their school systems. Busing within school districts was approved by the High Court in *Swann v. Mecklenburg* (1971), but what about busing within a larger region that included urban and suburban, multicounty and multidistrict schools? If the right to be upheld was an education in integrated schools, how far did the busing remedy reach? *Milliken v. Bradley*, the case at the center of a tortured Detroit resegregation tale, answered that question.

Joyce Baugh has not only written here the definitive account of *Milliken*, she has lived the story in a way that gives a special authority and depth to her account. Growing up in South Carolina at a time when school integration was finally gaining acceptance, when she traveled to Ohio as a graduate student, she was surprised to discover the de facto segregation of northern schools. Hired as a faculty member at Central Michigan University, she found that the Detroit story, so powerful and poignant, was news to her students.

The events in Detroit made up only one chapter in a much bigger story reaching back to the earliest days of the new nation. In swift and sure strokes of the pen, Baugh's first chapters trace the malign impact of racialism from those days to the time that Detroit sought to bus some of its schoolchildren beyond the city limits to the almost entirely white schools in the nearby suburbs. She reminds us that even after the Civil War ended slavery, segregation was not limited to the South, but it also was a way of life in the North, including Michigan. Even when, in 1867, the state outlawed segregated schools, Detroit's school board resisted the new law — shades of the Jim Crow South.

Baugh has combined her personal insight, thorough scholarship, and mastery of the details and doctrines of school desegregation to bring the Detroit case to life. She interviewed counsel representing both sides in the case, pored over school board minutes and records, and sat down to talk with the reporter who covered the events as they unfolded. Her account of the federal district court judge whose mind was changed by the evidence and whose courageous decision, if honored by the High Court, might have fulfilled *Brown*'s mandate, is truly moving. Her chapters on the Supreme Court deliberations and the doctrinal impact of the decision in *Milliken* are heart-rending. She also spent time with the federal district court judge who closed the litigation in 1989 and gained from him additional insights into the process and the meaning of the litigation.

What emerges from this book is Baugh's empathy for all the people in the story, giving their claims fair hearing. And when she writes that "more than thirty-five years after the first *Milliken* decision, urban education remains in crisis," who can doubt this judgment? Politics at the local level, mirrored by politics on an increasingly conservative U.S. Supreme Court, had drawn a line over which a more equitable vision of right and wrong could not cross. In summing up the contemporary landscape of education in Detroit, Baugh notes that "the school district remains plagued by high dropout rates, declining enrollments, ballooning deficits, high superintendent turnover, financial scandals and corruption, and public disputes among school board members." The poverty of the city, in part enabled or at least accelerated by *Milliken*, has impoverished the education it can offer its children. Surely that is a wrong that law should have righted.

In the fall of 1969, fifteen years after the Supreme Court's decision in *Brown v. Board of Education*, I entered the fifth grade at Dorchester Terrace Elementary School. This was the beginning of school desegregation in Charleston, South Carolina. From first through fourth grades I had attended Murray Hill Elementary, an all-black school. Very little conflict accompanied black students' entrance into the formerly all-white elementary school, although the formerly all-white high school to which students from my community and other nearby black neighborhoods were assigned did experience some degree of turmoil. Eight years later, in August 1977, I enrolled at South Carolina's Clemson University, where in 1963 another Charleston native, Harvey Gantt, had become the first African American student.

After completing my undergraduate degree at Clemson, I went to graduate school at Kent State University in Kent, Ohio, beginning in January 1982. There I learned about the political and social climate in northeastern Ohio, including the extent of racial segregation within the public school systems, especially in the Cleveland area. Based on what I had been taught about race relations while growing up in the South, I had expected these schools to be well integrated. That they were not was a great surprise to me.

I noticed similar patterns after arriving as a faculty member at Central Michigan University in 1988. As I began to I teach my Constitutional Law: Civil Rights and Liberties course, I found that while my students had heard of *Brown* and school segregation in the South, they knew nothing about similar problems in the North generally or about *Milliken v. Bradley* specifically. This was particularly striking, since so many of them came from the Detroit metropolitan area (both the city and suburbs). Most attended public schools that were overwhelmingly white or black, but they seemed to have no idea why this was so. Suspecting that this was true for students in other major metropolitan areas, as well as for the general public, I came to realize just how significant *Milliken* really is.

Telling the story of *Milliken* is not an easy task; this is a complex case with interesting origins, characters, and many twists and turns. The book is organized into seven chapters. Chapter 1 discusses the significance of *Plessy v. Ferguson*'s "separate but equal" doctrine, the NAACP's successful legal strategy to overturn it, and the Supreme Court's major school desegregation cases in the first decade after *Brown*. In Chapter 2, I provide a history of race relations in the Detroit metropolitan area, setting the stage for understanding how Detroit became central to the conflict over northern school desegregation. The initial focus of Chapter 3 is the impact of *Brown*, including federal enforcement of the decision, along with patterns of school segregation in the North, with particular emphasis on Detroit.

Chapter 4 describes the specific events that led to the lawsuit being filed in federal district court, followed in Chapter 5 by an examination of the proceedings in the district court and court of appeals. Chapter 5 also recounts the political and social atmosphere surrounding the case as it unfolded in the lower courts. Chapter 6 follows events as the case reached the Supreme Court and was decided there. This includes an extensive discussion of the briefs, oral arguments, and written opinions. Finally, Chapter 7 covers the aftermath of the Supreme Court's decision, including reactions to the ruling, events occurring after the case was remanded to the federal district court, its impact on educational opportunities for students in Detroit and other metropolitan areas, and a discussion of later Supreme Court school desegregation cases.

Many people deserve recognition for their assistance and encouragement as I worked on this book. Paul Dimond, a member of the NAACP legal team, wrote a compelling account of his experience litigating *Milliken* and other desegregation cases. He was the first person I interviewed, and his insights and suggestions helped propel me in the right direction. William Grant, former education writer for the *Detroit Free Press*, had a unique vantage point as the only reporter who followed the case diligently. I very much appreciated the perspective he shared in our interview, as well as the numerous articles he wrote before, during, and after the case. William Saxton, attorney for the suburban districts that challenged the metropolitan remedy, also provided valuable information, both in his reflections of the case and by loaning me a substantial set of documents, which included key excerpts from the trial transcripts, important motions, and other exhibits. His generosity saved me valuable travel and research time. I also interviewed federal district judge Avern Cohn, who eventually closed the case; he also provided useful documents, including his complete file on the proceedings from the second round. In addition, he spearheaded a four-part series on *Milliken* that was published in 2008 and 2009 in *The Court Legacy*, the journal of the Historical Society for the United States District Court for the Eastern District of Michigan.

I also wish to thank the staff at the Manuscripts Division of the Library of Congress, who helped to facilitate my research into the collected papers of Justices Harry Blackmun, William Brennan, William O. Douglas, and Thurgood Marshall, along with the NAACP files on *Milliken*. The reference staff of the Park Library and the Clarke Historical Library at Central Michigan University also provided helpful assistance. Michael J. Klarman and Paul A. Sracic, who carefully reviewed the manuscript, made numerous suggestions that helped me sharpen and improve the final product. I am grateful to Peter Charles Hoffer and N. E. H. Hull, the editors of the Landmark Law Cases & American Society series, for including this project in the series and especially to Michael Briggs, my editor, for his patience and encouragement from start to finish.

I appreciate the insights of members of the Social Ethics Seminar, a group of scholars who have studied and written about racial justice issues for more than thirty years, especially Warren Copeland, who commented on early drafts of parts of the manuscript. Thanks go also to colleagues in the Department of Political Science at CMU and to Thomas R. Hensley and Christopher E. Smith, who have collaborated with me on previous research projects on the Supreme Court and civil rights and liberties, for their words of encouragement and moral support.

Finally, words cannot express adequately my gratitude to Roger Hatch, my husband, for patiently serving as a sounding board and a superb proofreader and informal editor of this manuscript.

From *Plessy* to *Brown*

The Rise and Demise of "Separate but Equal"

> The object of the [Fourteenth] amendment was undoubtedly to
> enforce the absolute equality of the two races before the law, but,
> in the nature of things, it could not have been intended to abolish
> distinctions based upon color, or to enforce social, as
> distinguished from political, equality, or a commingling of the
> two races upon terms unsatisfactory to either. . . . If one race be
> inferior to the other socially, the Constitution of the United
> States cannot put them upon the same plane.
>
> JUSTICE HENRY BROWN, MAJORITY OPINION IN *PLESSY V. FERGUSON* (1896)

Justice Brown's majority opinion in *Plessy v. Ferguson* (1896) helped to legitimate Jim Crow, a system of racial subjugation in the South that lasted for nearly a century. This period of American history was marked by rigid, government-imposed racial segregation in nearly every aspect of life. As a result of *Plessy*, the so-called "separate but equal" doctrine was established, a legal concept that would take a carefully planned litigation strategy, several Supreme Court decisions, a Civil Rights Movement, and a federal civil rights law to fully overturn.

"Separate but Equal": The Legalization and Perpetuation of Jim Crow

Plessy concerned the 1890 Louisiana Separate Car Act, which required "equal but separate" accommodations for blacks and whites in railcars. Individuals who violated the law were subject to criminal penalties, outraging Louisiana's black community. During Reconstruction, the state legislature actually had passed a law *forbidding* segregation in railcars, but the Supreme Court had struck it down as an interference with

Congress's power to regulate interstate commerce (*Hall v. DeCuir*, 1878), even though the statute applied only to railway operations within the state. Louisiana was not the only state with a law requiring segregation on the railways. Florida passed the first one in 1887, followed by Mississippi (1888) and Texas (1889). The Supreme Court upheld the Mississippi law over claims that it interfered with interstate commerce, but, as Richard Kluger noted, "the Court ducked the more profound question of whether Negro passengers had to submit to such state-imposed segregation and ride in separate cars."

New Orleans blacks and Creoles formed the Citizens Committee to Test the Constitutionality of Louisiana's Separate Car Law. The group's challenge was supported by railway companies, who also objected to it; having to establish separate cars increased their operational costs. The Citizens Committee and the companies arranged to have Homer Plessy arrested for refusing to move to the "colored" section of a coach. Plessy, a very light-skinned man, was classified as "colored" although he was seven-eighths white and could "pass" for white. At his trial, Plessy was pronounced guilty of violating the statute.

Taking his case to the Supreme Court, Plessy claimed that the law was unconstitutional under both the Thirteenth and Fourteenth Amendments. By a 7-1 vote, the Court rejected both claims. Justice Brown's majority opinion held that the Thirteenth Amendment did not apply because it was meant only to forbid actions that reintroduced slavery. Furthermore, Brown concluded, the Louisiana law did not violate the Equal Protection Clause of the Fourteenth Amendment because that clause was not meant to abolish all distinctions based on color or to guarantee social equality. As evidence, he argued that laws forbidding interracial marriage "have been universally recognized as within the police power of the State" and that the "establishment of separate schools for white and colored children . . . has been held to be a valid exercise of the legislative power even by courts of States where the political rights of the colored race have been longest and most earnestly enforced." Brown relied explicitly on an 1849 Massachusetts Supreme Court decision, *Roberts v. City of Boston*, which upheld the authority of the Boston school committee to require separate educational facilities for black and white children. (This case is discussed in more detail in Chapter 3.)

In a solo dissent, Justice John Marshall Harlan criticized the majority for affirming the power of states to deny civil rights to citizens because of their race. In the dissent's most frequently quoted passage, Harlan wrote: "Our Constitution is color-blind, and neither knows nor tolerates classes among citizens. In respect of civil rights, all citizens are equal before the law." Harlan's dissent was particularly notable because he was a former slaveholder and avid supporter of slavery.

Although the words "separate but equal" did not appear in the opinions, judicial sanction of Louisiana's "equal but separate" accommodations law helped to ensure state passage of additional Jim Crow laws. In the aftermath of *Plessy*, state-ordered segregation pervaded every aspect of life (and death) in the South: transportation, schools, water fountains, telephone booths, hospitals, cemeteries, and a host of other public accommodations. Even textbooks for schoolchildren had to be stored separately. Presumably, these laws were valid as long as the accommodations provided were equal, but in most places this was not the reality.

The Jim Crow system was undergirded by disenfranchisement, sharecropping, economic reprisals, physical threats and violence from individual citizens and the Ku Klux Klan, and, ultimately, lynchings. Despite the dangers, African Americans resisted this racial caste system, as a case decided three years after *Plessy* illustrates. It involved segregation in the public schools in Augusta, Georgia. In *Cumming v. Board of Education* (1899), at issue was the school board's decision to close a public high school for blacks while at the same time providing a high school for whites. A group of black parents contended that because state law required "separate but equal" school facilities, the white school should be closed until a comparable one was opened for black children. A unanimous Court, however, did not apply its own doctrine and refused to invalidate the board's decision. This time, Justice Harlan accepted the segregation policy, concluding that the plaintiffs had not proven that the board decision was based on racial malice. To the contrary, he apparently was persuaded that the board actually was trying to assist the black community. The black high school could accommodate the increasing number of black primary school students, and there was insufficient funding available to build another school.

Nearly a decade later, a challenge to segregation in higher education met a similar fate. In *Berea College v. Kentucky* (1908), the Court upheld a state law that required separate classes for students who were being educated in institutions that taught both blacks and whites. Berea College, a private, religious college, had been racially mixed since its founding in 1859, and the trustees asserted that the state illegally impaired its charter through the law requiring blacks and whites to be taught separately. In a 7-2 decision, the majority ruled that the state was free to limit the college's rights because the school functioned as a corporation that owed its charter to the state. The Court also noted that the state did not prevent the college from teaching both races altogether; it merely prohibited them from being taught in the same space at the same time. Justice Harlan dissented, describing the statute as "an arbitrary invasion of the rights of liberty and property guaranteed by the Fourteenth Amendment against hostile state action."

The Court was also forced to address the question of whether segregation laws applied to racial or ethnic groups other than blacks. At issue in *Gong Lum v. Rice* (1927) was the application of Mississippi's school segregation laws to children of Chinese ancestry whose families had lived in the state's Delta region since the 1870s. In many of these communities, Chinese children had been permitted to attend white schools, but when Gong Lum tried to keep his nine-year-old daughter, Martha, enrolled in the white school in Bolivar County, he met stiff resistance. The trial judge ruled in his favor, but he lost his appeals at the state level.

Gong Lum, concerned about the inferior conditions of the "colored" schools, went to the Supreme Court. He requested that his daughter not be classified as colored so that she would not be sent to colored schools, but a unanimous Court rejected his plea without even hearing oral argument in the case. Chief Justice Taft held that no argument was necessary because "we think that it is the same question which has been many times decided." Citing federal and state cases upholding racial segregation in public schools, Taft said the decision to exclude Chinese children from white schools was within the discretion of the state in regulating its public schools. He concluded: "Most of the cases cited arose, it is true, over the establishment of separate schools as between white pupils and black pupils, but we can not think that the question is any different or that any different result can be

{ *Chapter 1* }

reached . . . where the issue is as between white pupils and the pupils of the yellow races."

———

Charles Hamilton Houston, Thurgood Marshall, and the Development of a Legal Strategy to Overturn *Plessy*

In 1909, the National Association for the Advancement of Colored People (NAACP), an interracial civil rights organization, was founded in response to a devastating race riot in 1908 in Springfield, Illinois. During the riot, two blacks were lynched, four white men were murdered, and seventy other persons were injured. Richard Kluger notes that it took nearly 5,000 members of the militia to restore order, and afterwards, "more than 2,000 blacks . . . fled the city in terror — a principal goal of the rioting ringleaders, none of whom was punished." The national headquarters for the NAACP was in New York City, but local branches sprang up in communities across the country, including in the South. Much of the NAACP's initial effort was focused on an antilynching campaign, including a push for federal legislation to impose stiff penalties against participants. (Despite the efforts of NAACP officials and others, no federal antilynching law ever was passed.) The NAACP focused its attention on other civil rights issues as well, and, under the leadership of Charles Hamilton Houston, it eventually became the primary organization that worked actively to end the "separate but equal" legal doctrine.

Charles Hamilton Houston was born in Washington, D.C., in 1895. His father, one of about two dozen black attorneys in private practice in the city, also taught part-time at the law school at Howard University. His mother, trained as a teacher, found more lucrative work as a hairdresser and seamstress. After graduating Phi Beta Kappa from Amherst College in Massachusetts, Houston returned to Washington, where he taught school for two years before serving from 1917 to 1919 in a segregated army during World War I. Genna Rae McNeil, Houston's biographer, explained that his experiences with Jim Crow during the war led him to the study of law as a means to change that system and work for racial and economic justice. Houston had observed a black officer being court-martialed for following orders. Houston also had been deemed unqualified to lead white field artillery soldiers, and his life had been threatened by a lynch mob of enlisted men.

Houston graduated from Harvard Law School in 1923. He studied constitutional law under future Supreme Court justice Felix Frankfurter and was the first African American to make the prestigious *Harvard Law Review*. After law school, Houston returned to Washington, joined his father in private practice, and accepted a teaching position at Howard University Law School, which provided legal education on a part-time basis. In 1929, after being appointed dean of the law school, he worked diligently on two missions. First, he sought to improve the school's academic standing in the field of legal education, in part by transforming it from its part-time status to offering a full-time curriculum. This change would assist in his second, larger purpose: to bring together talented students and faculty in order to mount a legal assault against Jim Crow and the pernicious "separate but equal" doctrine.

Houston became well known in the civil rights community for his activism and legal acumen, and he served as counsel for criminal defendants in cases sponsored by the NAACP during the early 1930s. In 1935, NAACP officials appointed Houston as full-time special counsel to direct a litigation strategy for battling Jim Crow, with segregation in education as the starting point. This strategy had its origins in a report prepared for the organization in 1931 by Nathan Margold, a white Harvard Law School graduate, with funding from a left-wing foundation known as the Garland Fund. Houston carefully studied the Margold Report and used it to develop a two-stage attack. During stage one, the goal was to compel states to make their elementary and secondary schools equal, the idea being that this would prove so expensive that states might be forced to abandon their separate and unequal practices. To that end, Houston made a film documenting the unequal conditions in black and white schools in the South.

Stage two would move to an attack on segregation itself. Efforts initially would be concentrated on segregation in graduate and professional schools, for two main reasons. First, because white public universities excluded blacks from these programs and because no comparable programs were provided in black colleges, black students had no opportunities for postgraduate education in Jim Crow states. Second, Houston believed that entrance to graduate and professional schools by a small number of black students would be less threatening to whites than would be the wholesale desegregation of elementary and secondary schools.

Houston's strategy was based on his understanding of how the legal system operates incrementally, according to precedent, with slow, rather than abrupt, change. He implemented this strategy with the help of his cousin and fellow Harvard Law School graduate, William Hastie, along with attorneys Houston had trained at Howard, including James Nabrit, Leon Ransom, and, most famously, Thurgood Marshall, who in 1939 succeeded him as NAACP special counsel. At that point, Houston generally left the education cases to Marshall and others, while he focused on other matters, particularly discrimination in labor unions and employment.

Pearson v. Murray and the Teachers' Salary Cases

Marshall worked closely with Houston on one of the earliest cases, representing Donald Murray, an Amherst College graduate, in 1935. Murray had applied to law school at the University of Maryland in December of 1934, and, despite his qualifications, his application was rejected because of his race. A trial judge ruled in Murray's favor, ordering his admission. To the surprise of many, a state appellate court upheld the ruling (*Pearson v. Murray*, 1936), on the basis that Maryland was providing a legal education for whites but nothing for blacks. The case ended when the state decided not to appeal.

During the late 1930s and early 1940s, NAACP attorneys, along with their local counterparts, brought cases in state and federal courts challenging disparities in teachers' salaries in various communities in several southern states. They enjoyed some success, with some cases resulting in negotiated settlements to be enforced by court orders and others leading to school board policies requiring equalization in salaries over a prescribed period of time. Marshall successfully litigated the first cases in 1938 and 1939 in Maryland. Other cases were initiated in Virginia, Kentucky, Alabama, Arkansas, Florida, Georgia, and Texas, but these efforts proved more difficult. By 1945, the

NAACP began shifting away from the salary cases. According to Mark Tushnet, an expert on the NAACP's litigation strategy, the salary cases "did increase the cost of maintaining a dual system, but not so much that segregation became a severe financial burden." The financial consequences were limited in part because school boards began using "merit pay" systems, which ostensibly were neutral but "happened to pay almost all African-American teachers much less than almost all white teachers."

———

Laying the Groundwork for a Frontal Assault on *Plessy*

Even as the teachers' salary cases were making their way through the courts, Houston began laying the groundwork for an eventual attack on segregation itself. In *Missouri ex rel. Gaines v. Canada* (1938), he continued the effort against segregation in higher education. The case involved Lloyd Gaines, president of the senior class at Lincoln University, Missouri's all-black institution. Gaines had been denied admission to Missouri's all-white law school because of his race. University officials offered to pay his tuition to attend law school in any neighboring state that would admit blacks. Or, the state contended, a black law school could be created at Lincoln. Missouri's Supreme Court ruled in the state's favor, but by a 6-2 vote, the U.S. Supreme Court reversed the decision. The majority held that Missouri's denial of Gaines's admission to the law school was unconstitutional and that paying for his legal training elsewhere did not constitute equal protection of the laws. "By the operation of the laws of Missouri," Chief Justice Hughes wrote, "a privilege has been created for white law students which is denied to negroes by reason of their race." Yet Hughes did not require Gaines to be admitted to the University of Missouri Law School; creating a separate law school for blacks would suffice. Within a year, the state legislature opened Lincoln law school, located in a building that housed a hotel and movie theater in St. Louis. A class of thirty students enrolled, but Gaines was not among them. Instead, he earned a master's degree at the University of Michigan; he then disappeared and never was heard from again.

Ten years later, the Court reaffirmed the *Gaines* ruling in *Sipuel v.*

Oklahoma State Regents (1948). Ada Sipuel's parents had moved to the small town of Chickasha, Oklahoma, from Tulsa, where one of the worst race riots in American history had occurred in 1921. Sipuel was valedictorian of her class at the all-black school in Chickasha, and, after graduation from the Colored Agricultural and Normal University at Langston, Oklahoma, she applied to the College of Law at the University of Oklahoma. The president of the university determined that she was fully qualified for admission, but he concluded that under the Oklahoma constitution and state laws she could not be admitted because of her race. The Oklahoma Supreme Court upheld the trial court's dismissal of the case. In a brief per curiam opinion, the U.S. Supreme Court reversed that decision and ordered the state to provide Sipuel with a legal education "in conformity with the equal protection clause of the Fourteenth Amendment and provide it as soon as it does for applicants of any other race." Shortly after, the state regents created the Langston University College of Law, which was "to convene in the basement of the state capitol building, with a student body of one, access to the state law library, and a faculty consisting of three lawyers, who would continue their private practices." Sipuel refused to attend the new "law school," but the Supreme Court rejected her additional appeal, which argued that the state had not provided an equal facility.

The "separate but equal" question was not addressed in Ada Sipuel's case, but two cases handed down on the same day in 1950 — *McLaurin v. Oklahoma State Regents* and *Sweatt v. Painter* — indicated that this doctrine was on shaky ground. *McLaurin* began just as Ada Sipuel's case was wrapping up. At the age of sixty-eight, George McLaurin applied to the University of Oklahoma to earn a doctorate in education. After his application was rejected, a federal district court ordered him to be admitted. Once McLaurin entered the university, every aspect of his life there was segregated because state law required that instruction be provided "upon a segregated basis." For McLaurin, this meant that in the classroom he was required to sit behind a rail with the sign, "For Coloreds Only"; in the library he had to study at a separate desk; and in the university cafeteria he had to eat at a separate table. McLaurin returned to court to protest this treatment, but the court found no constitutional violation.

When the case reached the Supreme Court, the justices unanimously held that the treatment accorded McLaurin was an obvious violation of the Fourteenth Amendment. Despite permitting him to attend the school, the state's restrictions "impair and inhibit his ability to study, to engage in discussion and exchange views with other students, and, in general, to learn his profession." In placing these conditions upon McLaurin, the state "deprive[d] him of his personal and present right to the equal protection of the laws."

NAACP attorneys had begun working on *Sweatt v. Painter* before *Sipuel* was decided. Heman Sweatt, a black postal worker from Houston, applied for admission to the University of Texas Law School. After the law school denied him admission solely because of his race, a state court ruled that this action constituted a denial of equal protection, but the court would not order that he be admitted because the state was proceeding to establish a law school in Houston for black students. Meanwhile, a temporary, makeshift law school was created in Austin, near the state capitol and the University of Texas.

This school "consisted of three small rooms in a basement" and three part-time instructors who were new faculty members at the Texas law school. It also included a limited library collection and access to the state law library at the capitol. Sweatt refused to apply, alleging that the education to be provided by the black law school would be far inferior to that offered at the regular law school. When the state courts ruled that the two law schools were essentially equal, Sweatt sought review in the U.S. Supreme Court.

In another unanimous decision, the high court ruled in Sweatt's favor. The Court, however, refused to reexamine the "separate but equal" doctrine, despite being encouraged to do so by Thurgood Marshall, Sweatt's attorney. Instead, the justices focused on the "equal" part of the doctrine and concluded that the law school for blacks was by no means equal to the University of Texas Law School, in both tangible and intangible ways. In terms of tangible factors — number of faculty, variety of courses, availability of law review, and volumes in the library — the regular school was far superior. "What is more important," Chief Justice Vinson wrote, "the University of Texas Law School possesses to a far greater degree those qualities which are incapable of objective measurement but which make for greatness in a law school. Such qualities . . . include reputation of the faculty, experience of the administration, position and influence of the alumni, standing in the community, traditions and prestige." While this case, like *McLaurin*, did not explicitly address the constitutionality of segregation itself, it implicitly raised the question of how much longer "separate but equal" could withstand challenges.

The Role of American Foreign Policy in the Battle against Jim Crow

In addition to the legal precedents provided by *Sweatt*, *McLaurin*, and other cases, the NAACP team and civil rights activists were aided in their efforts to overturn *Plessy* by international affairs. Scholars have written about changes in the political environment wrought by American involvement in World War II and the nation's Cold War fight against communism. The image of black veterans returning from fighting Nazi racism and anti-Semitism abroad, only to be subjected to racial violence, inequality, and injustice when they returned home, led other nations to accuse the United States of hypocrisy. Consequently, by the mid-1940s, officials in the State Department were arguing that the system of segregation was harmful to American foreign policy, especially in competition with the Soviet Union for the allegiance of largely nonwhite Third World nations. This concern prodded the Justice Department to begin filing amicus curiae briefs in support of the litigation brought by NAACP attorneys. (Amicus briefs, also known as "friend of the court" briefs, are submitted by those who are not parties to the case but who have a particular interest in the case or who may be able to provide important additional information.)

In 1948, Justice officials submitted a brief in an important case concerning restrictive covenants in housing (discussed in Chapter 2), followed a year later by a brief opposing segregated dining cars on interstate trains. Amicus briefs from the federal government also were submitted in the *Sweatt* and *McLaurin* cases and, ultimately, in *Brown v. Board of Education* itself. The brief for *Brown* highlighted the potentially positive impact that a decision striking down school segregation could have on American foreign policy:

It is in the context of the present world struggle between freedom and tyranny that the problem of racial discrimination must be viewed. The United States is trying to prove to the people of the world, of every nationality, race, and color, that a free democracy is the most civilized and most secure form of government yet devised by man. We must set an example for others by showing firm determination to remove existing flaws in our democracy.

The existence of discrimination against minority groups in the United States has an adverse effect upon our relations with the other countries. Racial discrimination furnishes grist for the Communist propaganda mills, and it raises doubts even among friendly nations as to the intensity of our devotion to the democratic faith.

It was in this political context, then, that Marshall and his team would mount a direct attack on "separate but equal."

Brown v. Board of Education: The Demise of "Separate but Equal"

With *Sweatt* and *McLaurin* behind them, in 1951, NAACP attorneys began preparing the litigation concerning segregated elementary and secondary schools. They decided to take cases from five communities to the Supreme Court. These cases were consolidated, with *Brown v. Board of Education*, from Topeka, Kansas, listed first. The others were *Briggs v. Elliott*, from Clarendon County, South Carolina; *Davis v. County School Board*, from Prince Edward County, Virginia; *Gebhart v. Belton*, from Delaware; and *Bolling v. Sharpe*, from Washington, D.C. Although the five cases were argued together, the Court made a separate ruling in the District of Columbia case because the Equal Protection Clause of the Fourteenth Amendment applies only to states; thus, the segregation in the District of Columbia was challenged on Fifth Amendment due process grounds.

The five cases dealt with laws either requiring or permitting segregation in public schools. The cases were argued twice, first in December of 1952 and again in December of 1953. When the cases initially were argued, the Court could not agree on whether to go beyond its decisions in *Sweatt* and *McLaurin* to overrule *Plessy*'s "separate but equal" doctrine itself. The justices decided instead to hold the cases over until the next term, and the Court ordered the parties to address a series of questions regarding the history of the Fourteenth Amendment, including whether it was intended to end segregation in education. In September of 1953, Chief Justice Vinson died unexpectedly and was succeeded by California governor Earl Warren. President Dwight Eisenhower had told Warren a few months earlier that he would consider appointing him to the high court should a vacancy arise, but Eisenhower was not thinking of the position of chief justice. The president's consideration of Warren was based on his perception that the governor had been primarily responsible for swinging the California delegation behind Eisenhower's candidacy on a critical procedural issue at the 1952 Republican presidential nominating convention. After Vinson died, Warren made it clear that he wanted that seat and Eisenhower, although hesitant at first, conceded.

President Eisenhower proved to be less supportive of civil rights efforts than his predecessor, Harry Truman, had been. As a result, the Justice Department, which had submitted a brief in support of the NAACP's position at the earlier stage of the case, had to press President Eisenhower to agree to submit a brief in the second round. This second brief was less clear on the question of whether the Fourteenth Amendment was meant to outlaw segregation in public schools.

After the cases were reargued in December 1953 with Warren as chief justice, it still was uncertain whether the Court was ready to overrule "separate but equal." But five months later, on May 17, 1954, a unanimous Court ruled that the laws regarding segregation in public schools violated the Fourteenth Amendment's Equal Protection Clause. Chief Justice Warren wrote the opinion, and, as was learned later, he had worked diligently behind the scenes not only to assure unanimity but also to persuade his colleagues not to file any concurring opinions. Warren wrote that the history of the Fourteenth Amendment was inconclusive as to whether the framers intended it to prohibit school segregation. He then noted that public education when the amendment was adopted in 1868 was quite different than in 1954. "In the South, the movement toward free common schools, supported by general taxation, had not yet taken hold. . . . Even in the North, the conditions of public education did not approximate those existing today. The curriculum was usually rudimentary; ungraded schools were common in rural areas; the school term was but three months a year in many states; and compulsory school attendance was virtually unknown."

These cases forced the Court to determine whether segregation itself was unconstitutional, because officials in some states had begun to make noises about increasing funding to make the schools substantially equal as a way to maintain segregation. As a result of the numerous cases being brought, state officials promised to equalize buildings, curricula, and teacher qualifications and salaries. Addressing this issue, Warren stressed that the justices could not return to 1868 when the Fourteenth Amendment was adopted or to 1896 when *Plessy* was decided. "Public education," he declared, must be considered "in the light of its full development and its present place in American life throughout the Nation." He characterized education as probably the "most important function of state and local government" because it was the "foundation of good citizenship" and prepared children for "later professional training." Furthermore, a good education was considered to be necessary for success in life, and, he concluded, if the state provides educational opportunity for its citizens, it must be provided to all on an equal basis.

Warren looked next to the social science evidence that had been presented by the NAACP team concerning the negative effects of enforced racial segregation on schoolchildren. Asserting that black students were deprived of equal educational opportunities by these segregation policies, Warren wrote: "To separate them from others of similar age and qualifications solely because of their race generates a feeling of inferiority as to their status in the community that may affect their hearts and minds in a way unlikely ever to be undone." Consequently, he concluded: "Separate educational facilities are inherently unequal."

Warren's citation of sociological studies in the opinion became the subject of heavy criticism by members of Congress, legal scholars, and other social scientists. Abraham Davis and Barbara Graham asserted that the Court likely would have reached the same result in *Brown* even if social science data had not been introduced. They noted that the lower courts in the South Carolina and Virginia cases determined the testimony from social scientists to be "irrelevant and unproven" and that the Court invalidated the segregated system in Washington, D.C., without the presentation of social science evidence. Davis and Graham attributed the outcome of *Brown* to several factors, including "logic, history, precedents, the Constitution, the spirit of the times, prevailing concepts of justice, and the ideological orientations of the Justices."

Criticisms of the decision notwithstanding, the NAACP's litigation strategy finally had come to fruition: the infamous "separate but equal" doctrine no longer was a valid precedent. Questions remained, however, about the manner in which public schools would be desegregated. The Court ordered the parties to submit arguments for when and how desegregation should proceed, and, one year later, in *Brown v. Board of Education II* (1955), the justices provided an initial answer. NAACP attorneys had encouraged the justices to implement desegregation immediately or, at the very least, to set firm deadlines for state compliance with the ruling. By contrast, the states' attorneys pressed the Court to delay implementation indefinitely, due to widespread community hostility to the decision.

In another unanimous opinion, the Court remanded the cases to the lower courts where they originally had been heard, with instructions for those courts to supervise the implementation process. The rationale was that each school system would have unique problems that would be solved best by a court in close proximity. In deciding whether the school districts were acting in good faith, the lower courts were to consider problems related to administration, physical facilities, transportation, personnel, and the drawing of school district boundaries and attendance zones. In taking these problems into consideration, the school boards were to be required, nonetheless, to make a "prompt and reasonable start" toward full compliance with the ruling.

Despite the Court's attempt to establish a feasible, reasonable implementation strategy, many state and local officials resisted. Furthermore, four words in the opinion — "with all deliberate speed" — permitted these officials to drag their feet in implementing *Brown*. The opinion also ensured that the Court would continue to be faced with school desegregation litigation.

Reactions to the Rulings

It is difficult to overstate the levels of outrage and anger that the two *Brown* decisions provoked, particularly in the South. Southern governors, legislators, and other public officials vowed to fight any attempts to desegregate their schools and to engage in "massive resistance" to preserve their way of life. State legislatures passed "interposition" and "nullification" statutes, claiming that state laws requiring segregation took precedence over federal court decisions. State compulsory education laws were repealed, and "freedom of choice" plans were adopted, plans that were doomed to fail because the existing racial antagonism guaranteed that few blacks would choose to attend all-white schools and vice versa. A few states passed laws authorizing the closure of their public schools, and public funds then were provided in some instances to open segregated private academies for white children.

In March of 1956, senators and representatives from eleven southern states introduced the "Southern Manifesto" into the *Congressional Record* of the United States. It was signed by seventy-seven members of the House and nineteen from the Senate. It characterized the Court's decision in the *Brown* cases "as a clear abuse of judicial power" that was "contrary to the Constitution," and these legislators pledged "to use all lawful means" to reverse the decision. The document concluded: "In this trying period, as we all seek to right this wrong, we appeal to our people not to be provoked by the agitators and troublemakers invading our States and to scrupulously refrain from disorder and lawless acts."

School Desegregation after *Brown*

Whether or not the legislators who signed the Manifesto were sincere in urging their constituents to refrain from violence, other officials used claims of impending violence as justification for delaying desegregation. One highly publicized effort from Little Rock, Arkansas, went to the Court for resolution. The school board had developed a very limited plan to allow nine black students to attend Central High School beginning in 1957. Governor Orval Faubus, however, ordered the state's national guard to prevent the students from entering the school, claiming that riots would result. A district court forced Faubus to withdraw the guard, and President Eisenhower reluctantly agreed to send in federal troops to protect the "Little Rock Nine." In the middle of the school year, because of continuing hostilities, the school board asked the district court to withdraw the black students from

Central High and to delay any further desegregation for two and a half years. The district court granted the request, but the court of appeals reversed that decision, so the school board appealed to the Supreme Court.

After calling a special summer term in late August in order to make a decision before the beginning of the next school year, in *Cooper v. Aaron* (1958), the justices refused to allow claims of ensuing violence to permit delay in implementing the plan. A brief per curiam opinion on September 12 affirming the appeals court decision was followed by a formal opinion on September 29. Although sympathizing with the plight of the school board and acknowledging the board's good faith efforts at desegregation, the Court ruled that "the constitutional rights of [the black children] are not to be sacrificed or yielded to the violence and disorder which have followed upon the actions of the Governor and Legislature." Government officials would not be permitted to evade the command to desegregate, the justices said, whether through direct or indirect means.

Various states, nevertheless, continued to develop schemes to avoid desegregating their schools. By 1964, ten years after the initial *Brown* ruling, the Court had grown weary of these evasive tactics. In *Griffin v. County School Board* (1964), the Court declared that there had been "entirely too much deliberation and not enough speed" in school desegregation efforts. The case arose because in 1959, after closing its public schools, the county provided financial assistance for white children to enroll in all-white private academies. The black community then refused the county board's offer to set up a similar scheme for black children, preferring to fight for integrated schools. In 1961, a federal district court ordered the county to stop funding the private schools, and the following year, the court ordered the county to reopen the public schools. The county sought review in the Supreme Court, and the Court unanimously affirmed the district court ruling. "Whatever nonracial grounds might support a State's allowing a county to abandon public schools, the object must be a constitutional one, and grounds of race and opposition to desegregation do not qualify as constitutional."

As the federal courts continued to supervise school desegregation cases in the South, northern communities began their own struggles against segregated schools. One of them was Detroit, Michigan, where efforts by civil rights activists resulted in a landmark Supreme Court decision in 1974. *Milliken v. Bradley*, the most significant school desegregation case since *Brown*, had far-reaching implications. The next chapter examines the political, social, and economic environment in Detroit in preparation for telling the story of this landmark case.

CHAPTER 2

Metropolitan Detroit
From Boomtown to Ticking Time Bomb

"Our nation is moving toward two societies, one black, one white — separate and unequal." This provocative conclusion from the February 1968 report of the National Advisory Commission on Civil Disorders — also referred to as the Kerner Commission, after its chairman, Illinois Governor Otto Kerner — poignantly described conditions in urban America in the mid-to-late 1960s. President Johnson had created this commission to investigate the causes of the civil disorders that rocked nearly 150 cities in 1967, including Detroit. Many occurred in urban communities in the North, Midwest, and West — areas that had not been targeted by the traditional southern Civil Rights Movement. Although numerous civil rights activities had occurred in communities outside of the South from the 1940s through the 1960s, the most publicized efforts were those directed at eradicating Jim Crow segregation and disenfranchisement in the South. The system of Jim Crow reflected racial separation required by law, known as "de jure" segregation. After passage of the Civil Rights Act of 1964 and the Voting Rights Act of 1965, leaders from the southern movement joined forces with their counterparts in the North to address racial discrimination and inequality there. While there previously had been segregation laws in many northern states, by the mid-1960s, most of the North was characterized by what was termed "de facto" segregation. This refers to racial separation that exists in fact but is not created by specific statutes nor enforced by statutes or judicial decisions.

Alan Anderson and George Pickering detail the efforts of the Chicago Movement to address de facto segregation in the city, which they later refer to as the "metropolitan color line." "In the North . . . the issues were different. Legally mandated segregation and discrimination had been mostly eliminated by midcentury, but the color line continued in the form of segregated and inferior schools and housing for blacks and in black poverty and unemployment. This *de facto* segregation was not legally mandated, but many of its major causes were legally sanctioned." Anderson later contends that the distinction between de facto and de jure segregation was largely unhelpful, given the role of public officials in creating and preserving both housing and school segregation in northern communities. Specific examples of this will be discussed later in this chapter and in those that follow.

At the time of *Milliken*, and indeed for many years previously, Detroit, like Chicago, reflected the metropolitan color line. Historian and Detroit native Thomas Sugrue carefully documents the development and perpetuation of this color line. Sugrue argues that the urban crisis in Detroit was not the result of the 1967 rebellions, as conventional wisdom has suggested, but rather stems from events of the 1940s through early 1960s. He notes that white flight from Detroit to the suburbs began during the post–World War II period, long before *Milliken* was decided. Sugrue discusses the interrelationship of three simultaneous forces as the primary explanation for the economic, social, and racial crises that have afflicted Detroit (and many other major cities): (1) the loss of thousands of good-paying, secure industrial jobs, (2) the persistence of employment discrimination, and (3) intractable racial segregation in housing. Understanding the interplay among these three factors provides insight into the social, economic, and political climate in the Detroit metropolitan area in the years leading up to *Milliken*.

Detroit, like other northern cities, had attracted thousands of southern African Americans seeking to escape their status as second-class citizens under Jim Crow segregation and disenfranchisement. During World War I and the first "Great Migration," hundreds of thousands of black Americans left the farms of the South to find better opportunities in northern cities like New York, Philadelphia, Chicago, Cleveland, and Detroit. As Table 2.1 indicates, from 1910 to 1920, 525,000 southern blacks migrated to northern cities, followed by another 877,000 in the following decade. While the numbers declined during the Great Depression, they rose again even more dramatically during the period between 1940 and 1960, with nearly 1.5 million black migrants arriving each decade. Not surprisingly, the black population in northern cities increased significantly between 1950 and 1970. In Detroit it increased from 16 percent to 44 percent in that period.

Table 2.1. Migration of Southern Blacks to Northern Cities, 1870–1970

1870–1880	71,000
1880–1890	80,000
1890–1900	174,000
1900–1910	197,000
1910–1920	525,000
1920–1930	877,000
1930–1940	398,000
1940–1950	1,468,000
1950–1960	1,473,000
1960–1970	1,380,000

Source: U.S. Census Bureau

Here is what census data show about the black population percentage of several northern cities during this period:

	1950	1970
Chicago	14	33
Cleveland	16	38
Detroit	16	44
Philadelphia	18	34

These increases were the result of black migration into the cities, combined with white flight to the suburbs. Although many black migrants to these cities did find new economic opportunities unavailable to them in the South, they also faced discrimination in employment and housing. In addition, changes in the economy in industrial states and cities made it difficult for many to gain a foothold in their new communities.

———

Employment Discrimination and Economic Decline

In the 1940s, African Americans in Detroit gained access to industrial jobs, mostly in semiskilled and unskilled positions. These employment gains resulted not only from wartime production demands, but also from the postwar economic boom, efforts by the National Association for the Advancement of Colored People (NAACP) and the United Auto Workers (UAW) to promote equality in the workplace, and President Franklin Roosevelt's Executive Order 8802 mandating nondiscrimination in war industries. Although blacks gained access to some jobs, they did not experience equality in their employment. Job discrimination was "widespread but not universal," with large variations from workplace to workplace. According to Sugrue, due to practices across various industries — automobile manufacturing, steel making, machine tool production, retail work, employment by the city government, and construction labor — a "dense and tangled web of forces . . . kept blacks, in the aggregate, entrapped in Detroit's worst, most insecure jobs." Black workers also were subjected to ugly acts of racial harassment and degradation. One involved the Ex-Cell-O Company, a major machinery manufacturer. In 1951, nearly all of its white employees walked off the job to protest the fact that one skilled black worker had been offered a position in an all-white department.

Racial discrimination in employment advertising and by employment agencies also had an impact. Prior to passage of the state's Fair Employment Practices Law (FEP) in 1955, race-specific job listings were commonplace, including those placed with state agencies. Detroit's black workers fared little better with private agencies, many of whom listed jobs in the yellow pages as "Colored" and "White." Similar labels appeared in newspaper ads, particularly those for small employers.

As the economic crisis in 2008–2009 demonstrated, the importance of the automobile industry to Detroit cannot be overstated. In the decades before *Milliken*, not only was it the largest employer in the city, but it also was the largest employer of blacks. The black percentage of auto workers increased from a mere 4 percent at the start of World War II to 15 and 16 percent in 1945 and 1960, respectively. In the automobile industry, racial discrimination was most prevalent in the skilled trades area, where apprenticeship programs often excluded blacks and seniority rules worked against them.

The steel industry and city employment were the other best employment arenas for blacks, but, again, job segregation was the norm. In the steel industry, blacks were concentrated in unskilled and semiskilled jobs, while black city employees were confined to unskilled work, transportation jobs, low-level clerical work, and primary education. Blacks found the fewest opportunities in the chemical industry, small automotive plants, machine and tool companies, breweries, retail sales, and the building trades/construction industry.

The exclusion of fully qualified black electricians, carpenters, and masons from unionized construction jobs was particularly significant. Their only alternative was to be hired as day laborers for a fraction of the wages paid to their union counterparts. This "casual labor" market (referred to locally as the "slave market") required them to gather at major intersections in certain neighborhoods to wait for work. The work was unpredictable, short-term, and strenuous, and there always were more potential workers available than jobs. Consequently, there often were large numbers of black men on the streets during the day, many of whom drank alcoholic beverages as they waited for work. One consequence of these images of unemployed or underemployed black men drinking and hanging out on street corners was the reinforcement of negative racial stereotypes. This undoubtedly helped spur the resistance of some whites to school desegregation, especially suburban residents whose only visual references to black people were these stereotypical images.

Detroit may have been a boomtown in the 1940s, but by the end of the decade, a long period of economic decline had begun, with the city hemorrhaging thousands and thousands of good-paying as well as entry-level manufacturing jobs, which previously allowed thousands of working-class Detroit residents to enjoy a decent standard of living. Census figures show that the number of manufacturing jobs declined from 338,400 in 1947 to just 204,400 in 1958 — a drop of nearly 40 percent. As workers were laid off, relocated, or dismissed, the ripple effect on the local economy was tremendous. Local businesses closed as their customers no longer had adequate incomes to purchase the goods and services they offered. Vacant homes, shuttered factories, and abandoned storefronts and restaurants marked the city's steady decline.

Sugrue cites automation as the "most important force that restructured Detroit's economy after World War II." As automated assembly lines were instituted in manufacturing plants, manufacturers were able to increase worker output and reduce their labor costs. Although automation was a nationwide phenomenon, Detroit-area workers were particularly hard hit because many of the very labor-intensive engine production jobs were located in Detroit area plants. In addition, heavy automation by General Motors and Ford helped to drive independent automobile manufacturers as well as parts suppliers out of business.

Next to automation, plant location decisions by the "Big Three" automobile manufacturers contributed to Detroit's economic decline. During the 1940s and 1950s, Ford, GM, and Chrysler closed, downsized, and relocated numerous plants. New facilities were built not only in small- and medium-sized cities in other states, but over twenty new plants were built in the Detroit suburbs.

Once the Big Three shifted their production facilities out of the city, other auto-related companies also left — machine tool companies, metalworking companies, and parts manufacturers. Also contributing to the economic difficulties were complaints by business owners about taxes and strong unions and a shift in the 1950s of federal military spending away from states in the Midwest and Northeast to the Sunbelt states.

The effects of the economic downturn were dramatic and far-reaching. Older workers were hit extremely hard, particularly those whose plants were closed or who did not have sufficient seniority to transfer to plants in other areas. Their work experience in heavy industry did not provide them with the necessary skills for newer jobs. Many workers, black and white, with little education and few skills could no longer look to the entry-level manufacturing jobs that had provided a means to move up the economic ladder. The elimination of these types of jobs, in conjunction with racial discrimination, was especially devastating to Detroit's black residents. As a result, countless numbers of them became part of the "long-term unemployed." Summing up the devastation created by the economic deterioration, Sugrue pointed to the closed and abandoned factory buildings, blocks of boarded-up stores and restaurants, burned-out and empty homes in formerly middle-class and working-class neighborhoods, and trash-filled vacant lots.

Working-class and middle-class whites who had adequate resources and skills moved to the suburbs. As the census data show in Table 2.2, the white population in suburban Detroit grew from 732,000 in 1940

Table 2.2. Detroit Suburban Population, 1900–1970

	Total	White	Black
1900	145,000	144,000	1,000
1910	148,000	147,000	1,000
1920	312,000	308,000	4,000
1930	609,000	592,000	17,000
1940	754,000	732,000	22,000
1950	1,167,000	1,106,000	61,000
1960	2,092,000	2,015,000	77,000
1970	2,668,000	2,591,000	97,000

Source: U.S. Census Bureau

to 1,106,000 in 1950 and to 2,015,000 in 1960. The number of black residents living in the suburbs throughout this same period was very small—22,000 in 1940, 61,000 in 1950, and 77,000 in 1960. Those whites who remained in the city grew angrier and more frustrated. White flight in the 1950s led to a city that became "poorer and blacker," characterized by fiscal distress due to disinvestment and the departure of much of its tax base. In this environment, concerns about housing and neighborhood boundaries took on added proportions.

Racially Segregated Housing

Racial conflicts over neighborhoods and housing did not begin with economic decline in the late 1940s, however. From the mid-nineteenth through the early twentieth centuries, Detroit's black residents generally were not tightly concentrated in all-black neighborhoods. They often lived in the same neighborhoods as recent white immigrants, although perhaps on different streets. The turning point was the first Great Migration, from about 1910 to 1930. The large influx of black migrants was alarming to many whites in Detroit, as it was to white residents of other northern cities. Douglas Massey and Nancy Denton note the hardening of white racial views, the increasing use of terms such as "nigger" and "darkey" in northern newspapers along with unflattering stories about black crime and vice, and an upsurge in racial violence.

Table 2.3. Population of Detroit, 1910–1970

	Total	Black	% Black	Others	% Others
1910	465,766	5,741	1.2	460,025	98.8
1920	993,675	40,838	4.1	952,837	95.9
1930	1,568,662	120,066	7.7	1,448,596	92.3
1940	1,623,452	149,119	9.2	1,474,333	90.8
1950	1,849,568	300,506	16.2	1,549,062	83.8
1960	1,670,144	482,229	28.9	1,187,915	71.1
1970	1,511,482	660,428	44.5	851,054	55.5

Source: U.S. Census Bureau

A second period of increased migration of southern blacks, along with white migrants, beginning in World War II, put tremendous pressure on the local housing stock. (See Tables 2.1 and 2.3.) The wartime production boom in Detroit had created unprecedented job opportunities, as the Ford Motor company and other automobile manufacturers shifted their production from cars to military hardware, airplanes, tanks, and other vehicles. Sugrue declares, "Almost overnight, Detroit had gone from one of the most depressed urban areas in the country to a boomtown, a magnet that attracted workers from all over the United States. . . . Between 1940 and 1943, the number of unemployed workers in Detroit fell from 135,000 to a mere 4,000." While the boom was good news for workers, there simply was not sufficient housing to meet the new demand. The shortage was particularly acute for black residents.

OSSIAN SWEET

One early Detroit example of racial violence in 1925 involved Ossian Sweet. Sweet, a prominent black physician, had purchased a home in an all-white neighborhood. When a mob of several hundred whites tried to force his family to move out, several shots were fired from the home occupied by Sweet and several relatives and friends; one of the mob participants was killed. Subsequently, Sweet, his wife, and nine other relatives and friends were charged with murder. The NAACP hired Clarence Darrow, the famous defense lawyer, to represent the defendants. The trial produced a hung jury, and the state subsequently decided to prosecute the defendants separately, beginning with Sweet's brother. He was acquitted by an all-white jury, and charges against the others were eventually dropped. Despite the acquittal, this incident was a clear harbinger of the widespread racial conflict and violence to come.

STEERING

Segregation and discrimination also aggravated racial tensions, producing numerous conflicts, particularly related to housing. Despite improvements over life in the Jim Crow South, most blacks in Detroit were confined to lower-paying, less secure jobs, so they lacked resources to purchase homes, and very little reasonably priced rental housing was available. But those who did have the financial means nevertheless faced other barriers in the housing market, especially the discriminatory practices of the real estate and banking industries, as well as policies of the federal and local governments. Real estate agents refused to do business with black clients, practicing a policy of "steering" blacks and whites to neighborhoods strictly defined by race, and they encouraged white homeowners to place restrictive covenants on their properties to avoid selling to blacks. The Detroit Real Estate Board adopted its national association's Code of Ethics steering policy, which commanded that real estate agents would "never be instrumental in introducing into a neighborhood a character of property or occupancy, members of any race or nationality, or any industry whose presence will be clearly detrimental to real estate values." This policy, originally enacted in 1924, was amended in 1950 with the specific reference to race or nationality deleted, but it was clear that the meaning continued to be the same. Agents who violated racial covenants, the steering policy, and other discriminatory practices supported by their national and local boards faced the wrath of white customers and other agents.

RESTRICTIVE COVENANTS

Restrictive covenants became an important tool for ensuring residential segregation after the Supreme Court invalidated local segregation ordinances in a 1917 case, *Buchanan v. Warley*. Here the Court held that the government had violated the Fourteenth Amendment rights of property owners to dispose of their property as they saw fit.

Restrictive covenants became a means to get around the Fourteenth Amendment, as these were private contractual agreements among property owners specifying that the buyer and seller not sell or lease property to blacks, and sometimes other groups, for a designated period of time. Provisions in the covenants called for enforcement by courts if they were violated, and the agreements generally took effect after a specified percentage of property owners in the relevant community signed on. In 1926, the Supreme Court dismissed a challenge to a restrictive covenant in a Washington, D.C., case, *Corrigan v. Buckley*. Justice Sanford's opinion relied on the ruling in the *Civil Rights Cases* (1883), in which the Court held that the Fourteenth Amendment did not authorize Congress to legislate against private discrimination but was limited to discrimination involving "state action." In refusing to strike the covenant in *Corrigan*, Sanford concluded, therefore, that private individuals were not prohibited "from entering into contracts respecting the control and disposition of their own property." For the next two decades, federal courts enforced restrictive covenants in other cases from the District of Columbia, and several state appellate courts also utilized *Corrigan* to uphold restrictive covenants against challenges.

The issue of restrictive covenants went before the Supreme Court again in 1948, in *Shelley v. Kraemer* and *McGhee v. Sipes*, companion cases from St. Louis, Missouri, and Detroit, respectively. In the lead case, the Shelleys, an African American couple, purchased a home in a white neighborhood, not knowing that the home was covered by a restrictive covenant that had been operating since 1911. The covenant restricted property owners from selling to blacks or to persons of the "Mongolian race." Two months after the purchase, the Kraemers sued to prevent the Shelleys from taking possession of the home. The trial court refused to enforce the agreement because it did not have the requisite number of signatures, but the Missouri Supreme Court ordered that it be enforced. In the Detroit case, Minnie and Orsel McGhee, a middle-class black couple, bought a house in a white neighborhood in northwest Detroit. Shortly thereafter, they received a letter from their neighbor Benjamin Sipes and members of the all-white Northwest Civic Association, requesting that they "kindly vacate the property." After the McGhees refused, Sipes and the association sued to keep them out, claiming that the covenant required that none of the homes in the neighborhood could be "sold [o]r leased to, [o]r occupied by any person other than one of the Caucasian race." Both the trial court and the Michigan Supreme Court upheld the agreement.

When the cases reached the U.S. Supreme Court, the decisions represented a substantial departure from precedent. The justices did not invalidate the covenants themselves but instead ruled that state enforcement of race-specific restrictive covenants violated the Fourteenth Amendment's Equal Protection Clause. Chief Justice Vinson wrote: "So long as the purposes of those agreements are effectuated by voluntary adherence to their terms, there has been no action by the State and the provisions of the [Fourteenth] Amendment have not been violated." In these two cases, however, Vinson observed that the enforcement of the covenant by the state judiciary "denied petitioners the equal protection of the laws."

The high court's ruling, however, did not mean the end of this practice. Restrictive covenants continued to operate both in the city of Detroit and its suburbs. In fact, the federal government, which aided in the development of suburbs in the 1940s and 1950s, actually advocated that these agreements be honored in the appraisal process for suburban homes. Moreover, once the enforcement of racially based covenants was declared illegal, other types of agreements took their place. New covenants prescribed architectural standards and lot size and barred multifamily occupancy; these regulations limited the home-owning possibilities for many black families, who lacked the resources to purchase or rent an entire house. These restrictions became indirect methods for maintaining Detroit's racial boundaries.

HOLC RATING SYSTEM AND RESIDENTIAL SECURITY MAPS

In addition to recommending the use of restrictive covenants, the federal government instituted other policies that worked hand-in-hand with private sector practices to maintain racially segregated housing in the city and suburbs. During the 1930s, 1940s, and 1950s, the federal government enacted a series of policies designed to spur home ownership and boost the construction industry. The Home Owners' Loan Corporation (HOLC), a program created in 1933 during the Great Depression to provide mortgage assistance to homeowners facing foreclosure, was operated in a racialized way. HOLC established a rating system for determining the risks associated with granting loans to specific urban neighborhoods. The system was based on four categories of neighborhood quality, with letter and number codes as follows:

First Category	A	Green
Second Category	B	Blue
Third Category	C	Yellow
Fourth Category	D	Red

The top two categories received the lion's share of HOLC loans. These were neighborhoods that were considered to be "new, homogeneous, and in demand in good times and bad" (green) and those that "had reached their peak" but were stable and still desirable (blue). The bottom two categories received the fewest loans. Massey and Denton observe that the HOLC system "undervalued older central city neighborhoods that were racially or ethnically mixed." Indeed, every neighborhood with a black population, no matter how small, was coded red. HOLC ratings were assigned to every block in the city, and this information was used to prepare color-coded "Residential Security Maps." This is the origin of the term and practice of "redlining."

The greatest impact of the HOLC mortgage program was in serving as a model for other institutions in the private and public sector. For example, private banks utilized the rating system in making their loan decisions, and the use of the "Residential Security Maps" became widespread throughout the metropolitan area. Most importantly, the HOLC system was institutionalized in the loan programs of the Federal Housing Administration (FHA), established in 1937, and in the Veterans Administration programs, authorized in the Servicemen's Readjustment Act of 1944, popularly known as the G.I. Bill. These two programs are acknowledged as a major force driving suburbanization during the post–World War II period. The FHA and VA housing initiatives guaranteed loans made by private banks, making it less costly for working- and middle-class people to purchase homes. These loans helped to lower the down payment required and extended the length of the repayment period, resulting in lower monthly payments for homeowners. These programs generally favored suburban development and — because they were based on the HOLC rating system — encouraged racial segregation. The FHA generally provided substantial loans for the construction of new homes in the suburbs but not for purchasing or remodeling homes in the central city.

According to Massey and Denton, the key to the FHA's reinforcing segregated housing patterns was that "the agency followed the HOLC's earlier lead in racial matters; it too manifested . . . a concern with the presence of what the 1939 FHA *Underwriting Manual* called 'inharmonious racial or nationality groups.'" According to this manual, "if a neighborhood is to retain stability, it is necessary that properties shall continue to be occupied by the same social and racial classes." And, as noted above, the FHA advocated the use of restrictive covenants to ensure "neighborhood security," even after the Supreme Court in 1948 invalidated their enforcement. Private builders and developers, relying on the availability of FHA and VA loans for prospective home buyers, complied with these racially restrictive practices.

HIGHWAY DEVELOPMENT

Federal policies regarding highway development and urban renewal contributed to the color line in housing, both urban and suburban. Charles M. Lamb discussed the role of federal highway funding on the development of suburbs across the United States and on housing segregation. According to Lamb, the interstate highway system that began during the Eisenhower administration (1953–1961), along with the dramatic expansion of automobile use in the 1960s, made it possible for whites who worked in the city "to escape to surrounding areas to live and raise their families." In addition, some of these federally funded highway projects removed minorities from certain neighborhoods and segregated them elsewhere.

In Detroit, federal and local highway projects in the late 1940s and the 1950s resulted in expressways that had a significant impact on both the city and suburbs. Densely populated black neighborhoods were destroyed to make room for the Chrysler, Lodge, and Ford Freeways, without providing sufficient alternative housing for the displaced residents. At the same time, these new expressways permitted white suburbanites to commute to downtown areas for work or recreation while maintaining racially exclusive communities in the suburbs.

Also devastating to black neighborhoods were urban renewal programs in the 1950s and 1960s, which condemned large areas of Detroit inhabited by poor and working-class blacks to make room for private development of middle-class housing. Like the highway projects, these "slum clearance" programs razed "blighted areas" without providing the residents with alternative places to live.

PUBLIC HOUSING

The primary means for addressing the displacement problem became the construction of public housing developments, but this proved to be a major point of contention. Even before the urban renewal projects of the 1950s and 1960s, there was significant conflict over using public housing developments as a means to deal with housing shortages. President Roosevelt's New Deal programs provided federal assistance for building low-income housing but left program implementation to local officials, who generally sought to maintain racial segregation in the developments. Moreover, the federal initiative for greater investment in public housing clashed with another important New Deal value – the commitment to provide financial subsidies for individuals to construct and purchase single-family homes, as reflected in the FHA and VA programs. Not surprisingly, developers and realtors also were adamantly opposed to public housing initiatives for fear that this would undercut the private housing market. But there also was significant opposition from homeowners.

Sojourner Truth Housing Project

These conflicts over public housing and private development increased racial tensions and, ultimately, resulted in violence. A prime example is the creation of the Sojourner Truth housing project in northeast Detroit in 1941–1942, in the Seven Mile–Fenelon neighborhood. White homeowners mounted fierce opposition to building the project, while civil rights and pro–public housing groups lobbied housing officials to designate the project for black families to alleviate the housing shortage. After initially designating the housing project to be for white families, under pressure, housing officials changed course and decided that it would be open to black occupants. Ironically, the white residents of the Seven Mile–Fenelon neighborhood who opposed the project were joined briefly by middle-class black residents

{ *Chapter 2* }

from a community nearby. What explains this unlikely coalition? Some of Detroit's middle-class blacks, like their white counterparts, were concerned about the potential negative impact of public housing on their property values, and they too strongly supported the New Deal value of private, single-family housing. As a result, these black residents formed community associations to influence the FHA to support the development of single-family homes in their neighborhoods. The conflict over the Sojourner Truth housing project erupted in violence in February of 1942 when the first black families moved in. Forty people were injured and 220 arrested. Following this incident, the local housing authority established a policy requiring that racial segregation in public housing projects be maintained.

Eight Mile–Wyoming

While the Sojourner Truth controversy was a major episode, Sugrue identifies the primary battleground in the 1930s and 1940s for the two competing visions of federal housing policy — public housing versus single-family homes — as the Eight Mile–Wyoming area of northwest Detroit, a modest black settlement. Eight Mile Road remains a strong racial symbol even today, as many residents of the Detroit metropolitan area recognize it as the dividing line between black and white Detroit. The name also became part of the national popular culture in 2002, when white rapper and Detroit native Eminem starred in *8 Mile*, a semi-autobiographical movie that helps to symbolize the racial boundary characterizing the city.

In the late 1930s, black residents of Eight Mile–Wyoming were unsuccessful in their attempts to obtain federal assistance for home improvement and construction, and they formed neighborhood associations to lobby the FHA. By the early 1940s, their goals clashed with those of private developers, city officials, and public housing advocates. Developers wanted to build a white subdivision next to a black neighborhood, but they were not eligible for FHA funding because the location was adjacent to an area classified as "high-risk." The solution was to build a massive wall — a foot thick and six feet high — on the property line separating the two neighborhoods. (Parts of the wall still stand today — a continuing reminder of the physical and psychological racial boundaries in metropolitan Detroit.) City officials initially were interested in building an airport in the area, but they eventually chose another location. Public housing advocates pushed the planning commission to develop public housing in the area. Eventually a compromise was reached: temporary war housing was constructed and FHA subsidies for single-family homes were permitted.

For the most part, Detroit's working- and middle-class whites were successful in pressuring local officials to refrain from building public housing in their neighborhoods. In addition, attempts to persuade all- or nearly all-white suburban communities to accept public housing projects also were soundly defeated. As Sugrue notes, for many whites, the term "public housing" became synonymous with "Negro housing."

Dearborn and Orville Hubbard

In the 1940s, the city of Dearborn and its mayor, Orville Hubbard, became potent symbols of hostility to public housing in suburban Detroit. Dearborn was the location of a major Ford plant that employed a significant number of black workers during World War II. When federal officials proposed a project to house these workers, Dearborn officials vehemently objected. In 1944, the city council passed an anti–public housing resolution, and throughout his thirty-two-year tenure, Hubbard promised to keep Dearborn "lily white." He used inflammatory rhetoric to make his point. Referring to federal public housing officials as "goddam nigger-lover guys," he declared that "Housing the Negroes is Detroit's problem" and "When you remove garbage from your backyard, you don't dump it in your neighbor's." Not surprisingly, federal officials chose another site for the wartime project.

BELLE ISLE RIOT

Between the Sojourner Truth riot in 1942 and the controversy surrounding the Eight Mile–Wyoming community in 1943–1944, racial tensions in the city reached a boiling point. The most serious clash occurred in June 1943 at Belle Isle Park, a large city park located on an island in the Detroit River and frequented by members of both races. The riot began after fights broke out between young blacks and whites inside the park in the afternoon and on the bridge back to Detroit in the evening. Subsequently, blacks and whites engaged in street battles in downtown Detroit and in a black community known as Paradise Valley. Blacks looted white-owned stores, and whites retaliated the next day with attacks on blacks. In three days of disorder, 34 people were killed, 675 were injured, and nearly 1,900 were arrested before federal troops could restore order. The Belle Isle Riot, one of the worst in the United States in the twentieth century, led to the creation of the Mayor's Interracial Committee to reduce racial tensions, but the city initially did little to address the main underlying causes of racial inequality—housing and employment. And neither the riot nor the conditions preceding it dampened black migration to Detroit. (See Table 2.3)

BLOCKBUSTING

Racial clashes in the city intensified in the 1950s and 1960s as blacks continued to move beyond existing racial boundaries. In the mid-to-late 1940s, black elites moved out of the inner city to more exclusive areas within Detroit, and by the early 1950s, middle- and working-class blacks with steady employment also began to move to previously all-white neighborhoods. After the Supreme Court's 1948 decision on restrictive covenants, open housing advocates, including the Mayor's Interracial Committee, fought to abolish discriminatory housing. They sought to end blockbusting, a tactic that changed racial boundaries while simultaneously increasing profits for real estate brokers. After helping a black family move to an all-white neighborhood, brokers would inform white homeowners that their property values would decrease. Having helped create a panic among whites, brokers would persuade them to sell their homes at lower prices and then would resell them to black buyers at higher prices. As more homes changed hands, the racial character of the neighborhood changed as well. Another blockbusting tactic Sugrue mentions involved "paying a black woman to walk her baby through a white neighborhood to fuel suspicion of black residential 'takeover.'" With blockbusting, neighborhoods shifted from all-white, to predominantly black, to all-black within a short period of time. Many of these previously all-white communities were very close to the borders of black neighborhoods, so homeowners there became prime targets for blockbusting agents.

The challenge to Detroit's housing boundaries also illustrated class divisions among its black residents. Some members of the black elite and black middle class also sought to disassociate themselves from lower-class blacks. This is not surprising, given the potential impact of negative racial stereotypes on their opportunities for advancement.

HOMEOWNERS' ASSOCIATIONS

As blacks sought entry into all-white neighborhoods, some white homeowners attempted to defend themselves against what they perceived as a black invasion. The resistance to open housing initiatives in the 1950s and 1960s had its origin in the homeowners' movement, which began in the 1940s. Between 1943 and 1965, white Detroiters created nearly two hundred grassroots organizations, also known as civic associations, protective associations, improvement associations, and homeowners' associations. Although not created initially for the purpose of racial exclusion, by the 1950s, as more working-class whites became homeowners, the issues of race and housing became intertwined in their minds. These groups, therefore, worked to maintain the racial homogeneity of their neighborhoods. They cited concerns about conditions in the ghetto, as well as fears of crime and racial intermingling. Home ownership became synonymous with citizenship, and homeowners' associations, co-opting the language of protest movements, began to emphasize "homeowners' rights."

The 1948 *Shelley* and *Sipes* decisions on restrictive covenants and the 1949 election of Albert Cobo as mayor of Detroit were critical developments for the movement. The homeowners' groups found a great ally in Cobo, who served from 1950 to 1957. He appointed members of the groups to city commissions concerned with issues of housing, race relations, and urban planning and development. He also weakened and renamed the Mayor's Interracial Committee, including appointing a strong neighborhood association advocate as its head. Cobo's election and influence was particularly striking, given that he was a Republican in a Democratic, strongly union city.

The strong influence of the homeowners' groups on local politics is also seen in their ability to get a Homeowners' Rights Ordinance placed on the ballot in 1964. The ballot drive was spearheaded by Thomas Poindexter, a local Democratic Party activist who became known as the "Home Owners' Champion" and who was elected to the Detroit Common Council that same year. The ordinance was meant to preserve white homeowners' perceived right to uphold segregated housing and to discriminate in real estate sales. This effort was a tremendous success, as voters approved the proposal by a margin of 55 to 45 percent. However, a year later, the Wayne County District Court declared the ordinance unconstitutional, and it never was implemented.

Although African American civil rights activists and their white allies organized to resist discrimination in housing and other areas, Sugrue notes that homeowners' groups continued to exert considerable influence on local and state politics. "White Detroit groups pressured local politicians to oppose civil rights legislation. Their votes played a crucial role in the defeat of Michigan's Democratic governor, G. Mennen Williams, in 1966, and in the defeat of local referenda to raise taxes to pay for Detroit's increasingly African American public schools."

VIOLENCE

One of the most potent weapons associated with the homeowners' movement to resist housing integration was violence, directed especially toward "black pioneers," the first newcomers to all-white neighborhoods. Sugrue reports that between World War II and the 1960s, "white Detroiters instigated over two hundred incidents against blacks moving into formerly all-white neighborhoods, including harassment, mass demonstrations, picketing, effigy burning, window breaking, arson, vandalism, and physical attacks." These attacks peaked between 1953 and 1957 and again in the early 1960s. The incidents usually followed association meetings, and the violence was not random but was organized and widespread. Attacks occurred in nearly every racially changing neighborhood, but they were most prevalent in the three white predominantly working-class areas where residents were members of the most powerful homeowners' groups.

SUBURBAN RESISTANCE

White Detroiters were not alone in resisting racially integrated housing; as the earlier example from Dearborn demonstrates, the suburbs were not welcoming to blacks, either. Farley, Danziger, and Holzer observe: "No other Detroit suburb has a history of racial exclusion as thoroughly documented as that of Dearborn, but very few African Americans moved to the suburban ring during or after World War II (see Table 2.2). Those who sold real estate cooperated with the officials of suburban governments and school systems to convey the message that Detroit's suburbs did not welcome black homeowners or renters." Population figures from 1970, the year that *Milliken* began, bear this out. Dearborn, Warren, and Livonia were the three largest Detroit suburbs. Of 400,000 residents in these three communities, only 186 were black — 13 in Dearborn, 41 in Livonia, and 132 in Warren. In addition, for the other twenty-four suburbs with populations of 35,000 or more, in all but two — Inkster and Highland Park — the black population was less than 3 percent; most had less than 1 percent. Again, Mayor Orville Hubbard of Dearborn represented the most prominent face of suburban resistance to integration. In 1948, he opposed even a private housing development project for upper-middle-class residents out of fear that it would include black residents. Before the project was voted on, he dispatched city employees to distribute leaflets that read:

KEEP NEGROES OUT OF DEARBORN
PROTECT YOUR HOME AND MINE!
VOTE NO ON THE ADVISORY VOTE

Voters rejected the proposal. In a 1956 interview with a Montgomery, Alabama, newspaper, Hubbard explained his community's ability to keep blacks out:

A. We say it's against the law to live here. They say, "You know what the Supreme Court says." I tell them we're talking about the law of custom, the law of habit.
Q. Do you mean a city law?
A. The unwritten law.
Q. In other words, all the property owners would have to be in agreement with you?
A. Well, that's why I'm still mayor — 15 years.
Q. They just won't sell to Negroes?
A. That's the way you do it.

Violence was not as prevalent an exclusionary tool in the suburbs as it was in the city of Detroit. Public policies and real estate practices that reinforced segregated housing, municipal boundaries that kept services contained within each suburban community, and the refusal of suburban governments to participate in regional/metropolitan government projects made violent attacks less necessary. Sugrue concludes, "Residents of suburbs lived in communities whose boundaries were firmly established and governmentally protected, unlike their urban counterparts who had to define and defend their own fragile borders."

There were, nevertheless, some incidents of violence connected to black attempts to move to all- or nearly all-white suburbs. For example, when a black family bought a house in Sterling Heights in 1964, it was destroyed by fire even before they moved in. Three years later in Warren, a mob of whites threw stones and broke windows at the home of an interracial couple who recently had moved there. The police dispersed the crowd but did not arrest any of the offenders. There were some attempts at interracial cooperation to achieve integrated housing in the suburbs through the establishment of human relations organizations, particularly in Livonia and Royal Oak. But as the population statistics in Table 2.2 show, those efforts met with extremely limited success.

A Ticking Time Bomb

Although from outward appearances it may not have seemed so, one could argue that by the mid-1960s Detroit was ripe for a major confrontation like the 1943 Belle Isle riot. Sure enough, Detroit had escaped the kind of disorder that swept through Harlem in 1964 and the Watts area of Los Angeles in 1965. And, for a variety of reasons — in spite of its economic, political, social, and racial problems — Detroit was thought to be immune from a major race riot. It was the only city in the nation at the time with more than one African American member of the United States House of Representatives (John Conyers and Charles Diggs). In 1966, *Look* magazine and the National Municipal League named Detroit an All-America City, and Jerome Cavanagh, who was elected mayor in 1962 with strong support from black voters, was successful in bringing in millions of dollars in federal funding for local programs. Under his leadership, the city obtained $200 million in federal grants for jobs, job training, recreational activities, and other projects. Cavanagh also worked to integrate the predominantly white police force, which had been a longstanding source of tension and hostility in the black community. Furthermore, despite the problems of economic decline and workplace discrimination, some black Detroiters managed to obtain relatively secure, good-paying jobs and were able to purchase their own homes, albeit on a segregated basis. In addition, Detroit was a center of civil rights activism in the early 1960s. The Detroit branch of the NAACP, with 20,000 members, was the largest in the country. The Detroit Council for Human Rights organized a successful freedom march in June 1963, two months before the famous March on Washington where Dr. Martin Luther King delivered his "I Have a Dream" speech. King gave an early version of this speech at the Detroit march and, with Mayor Cavanagh, led 125,000 participants from Woodward Street to a rally at Cobo Hall. At the time, it was the largest rally on behalf of civil rights in the nation's history.

On the surface, therefore, Detroit appeared to be in a state of enlightened calm. But this masked reality. As noted earlier, much of the city's federal funding was devoted to urban renewal and highway projects, programs that destroyed black neighborhoods and displaced black residents. Henry Hampton and Steve Fayer describe this. The expressways permitted white Detroiters and suburbanites to "ride over or around the city's black poverty on the way to shop or play or work downtown." As a result, frustration and anger built in the black community. "The talk on the corner was of black workers being kept in the heat of the foundries and off the assembly lines, and, once on the lines, away from the supervisory jobs that could be the ticket out of the ghetto. There were still many jobs, neighborhoods, places of business, where blacks were not welcome. To many, Motown was a hostile place." Added to this mix was an emerging militant black leadership responding to the discontent, competing for attention with mainline civil rights groups like the NAACP. These dynamics created an environment whereby a single spark ignited a raging fire.

The 1967 "riot" began after the Detroit police raided a "blind pig," an illegal after-hours nightclub in one of the city's largest black neighborhoods in the wee hours of a Sunday morning in July. Tempers flared, and before long, fires, looting, and vandalism rocked a six-block area of the city. Over a five-day period, the police arrested over 7,200 people, 43 people (33 blacks and 10 whites) were killed, and property damage was in the millions. The violence caught many Detroit residents off guard; for others, however, the disorder was not only not surprising but in many respects predictable. In an interview for the *Eyes on the Prize* television documentary series, Ron Scott, a black Detroiter, described the situation this way: "Inside of most black people there was a time bomb. There was a pot that was about to overflow, and there was rage that was about to come out. And the rebellion just provided an opportunity for that. I mean, why else would people get upset, cops raiding a blind pig. They'd done that numerous times before. But people just got tired of it. And it just exploded." The Kerner Commission's report on civil disorder in the cities affirmed Scott's observation. "Many grievances in the Negro community result from the discrimination, prejudice and powerlessness which Negroes often experience. They also result from the severely disadvantaged social and economic conditions of many Negroes as compared with those of whites in the same city and, *more particularly, in the predominantly white suburbs*" [emphasis added].

Scholars, politicians, and average citizens continue to disagree about whether the civil unrest and disorder in Detroit and other cities in the 1960s should be viewed as a racial rebellion aimed at bringing about social reform or simply as mass lawlessness and criminal behavior. Whatever the case, the 1967 uprising in Detroit only hardened racial lines between blacks and whites in the city and between Detroit blacks and white suburbanites. The population statistics in Tables 2.2 and 2.3 demonstrate that white flight, which had begun many years earlier, intensified as more and more white residents who had sufficient resources left the city to seek what they perceived to be a safer, more secure life in the suburbs. In 1940, the black population of Detroit was 9.2 percent. Largely as a result of white residents relocating from Detroit to the suburbs, that figure increased dramatically in the next two decades — reaching 44.5 percent in 1970.

It is in this context that *Milliken* arises. In a city battered by economic decline, social distress, racial fears and resentment, and racial violence, calls for integrating the public schools provoked strong reactions. And, given the rigid housing segregation that defined the entire Detroit metropolitan area, school integration clearly was going to be a difficult task. This nexus between housing segregation and school segregation is critical to understanding the dynamics at work in *Milliken*. This link will be explored more extensively in Chapters 3 and 5.

{ *Chapter 2* }

CHAPTER 3

Separate but Unequal,
Northern Style

As Detroit struggled with its own conflicts over racial segregation, the struggle to end segregated schools in the South continued unabated. The South's organized "massive resistance" to desegregation in the decades after the 1954 and 1955 *Brown* decisions led many to question whether the rulings would ever be implemented. It became obvious that the federal courts would not be able to do this alone but would need the assistance and cooperation of Congress and the executive branch in order to end segregated schools in Dixie. In addition, it became increasingly clear that racial segregation also was deeply entrenched in northern public schools.

"Too Much Deliberation and
Not Enough Speed"

As the data in Table 3.1 show, by 1964, the end of the first decade after *Brown*, the proportion of black students attending majority-white schools in the South was only 2.3 percent. That number finally rose to more than 36 percent by the end of the second decade and reached nearly 44 percent fourteen years after that. What accounts for these changes?

The ultimate success of school desegregation in the South is tied to the efforts of the legislative and executive branches in forcing school districts to take action. In 1964, after a decade of civil rights demonstrations and lobbying, Congress passed the Civil Rights Act. The most well known provisions of this landmark legislation deal with public accommodations and equal employment opportunity. Title II prohibits discrimination on the basis of race, color, religion, or national origin, in motels, inns, hotels, restaurants, lunch counters, soda foun-

Table 3.1. Percentage of Black Students in Majority-White Schools in the South, 1954–2000

	Percent Black in Majority White Schools
1954	0
1960	0.1
1964	2.3
1967	13.9
1968	23.4
1970	33.1
1972	36.4
1976	37.6
1980	37.1
1986	42.9
1988	43.5
1991	39.2
1994	36.6
1996	34.7
1998	32.7
2000	31.0

Source: Gary Orfield and Chungmei Lee, "*Brown* at 50: King's Dream or *Plessy*'s Nightmare?" Harvard University: The Civil Rights Project (January 2004), 19.

tains, concert halls, sports arenas, and other public venues. Title II is a response to the numerous direct-action tactics conducted by civil rights protestors, beginning with the Montgomery bus boycott in 1955, and especially the sit-ins carried out by student activists in the early 1960s. Title VII prohibits discrimination in the hiring and classification of employees on the basis of race, color, religion, sex, and national origin, and it authorized the creation of an Equal Employment Opportunity Commission (EEOC) to investigate charges of discriminatory employment practices. The federal courts have decided numerous employment discrimination cases under Title VII since this provision was passed.

Also included in the 1964 Act were two provisions related to education, one directly and the other indirectly. Title IV authorized the

　　　{ *Chapter 3* }

attorney general of the United States to file lawsuits to desegregate public schools upon receiving legitimate written complaints. This was particularly important because at the time, responsibility for carrying out desegregation lawsuits in federal courts was the responsibility of individuals, and black parents generally did not have adequate resources to bring such suits. And, even if they did, they became subject to threats and intimidation. In addition, the NAACP, which had conducted much of the litigation, did not have adequate resources to handle all of the lawsuits necessary to push desegregation throughout the region. Kenneth Vines, quoted in J. W. Peltason's *Fifty-Eight Lonely Men*, describes the impact of the attorney general in school desegregation litigation:

> Attorneys appearing for state and local southern governments were now matched with the Justice Department's attorneys appearing for the national government. Perhaps most important of all was the potential for planning and systematic action that the Justice Department could bring into the desegregation process. Through centralized direction of litigation the Attorney General could bring an orderly scheme to the determination, time, strategy, and location of desegregation suits. The presence of United States attorneys made it possible for the Attorney General to develop simultaneous suits in school districts throughout the South and so avoid the hit-or-miss efforts that had characterized former desegregation litigation.

Title VI provided a potentially more effective tool for desegregating schools by prohibiting racial discrimination in the conduct of any program receiving federal funds: "No person in the United States shall, on the ground of race, color, or national origin, be excluded from participation in, be denied the benefits of, or be subjected to discrimination under any program or activity receiving Federal financial assistance." Most importantly, the act authorized federal agencies to terminate the funding of programs that practiced discrimination and directed those agencies to develop and issue guidelines for doing so. While the act also required those subject to these provisions to have a hearing before funds could be terminated and permitted them to seek judicial review, it nonetheless offered a potentially powerful sanction against those school districts determined to continue to operate segregated schools. Following the passage of the act, President Lyndon Johnson authorized the attorney general to coordinate Title VI activities, resulting in the development of procedural guidelines for agency officials to follow in interpreting and applying the statute.

Subsequently, the Office of Education in the Department of Health, Education, and Welfare (HEW) issued its guidelines. The 1965 guidelines permitted school districts to develop three types of desegregation plans: geographic attendance areas, freedom of choice, and a combination of geographic attendance areas and freedom of choice. The geographic area plans were to abandon racially separate attendance zones, with "each attendance zone to be part of a single, nonracial system of attendance zones." Freedom of choice plans, which supposedly permitted both black and white students to attend their school of choice, had been used in most school districts under orders to desegregate. The 1965 guidelines proved to be very weak, as they incorporated freedom of choice without including any requirements for measuring progress. As such they were largely ineffective because, despite the theoretical and rhetorical simplicity, the political and social dynamics in southern communities prevented desegregation from occurring. White parents did not send their children to all-black schools, and black families who tried to send their children to previously all-white schools became targets of harassment and economic intimidation. Indeed, in his testimony at a congressional hearing on civil rights, a federal education official expressed a "sense of guilt" for helping to perpetuate the use of the term "freedom of choice" given that there was "in no sense really a free choice" in an oppressive political and social environment.

HEW revised the guidelines in 1966 to make them much more detailed and included a test for measuring the effectiveness of freedom of choice plans. They contained a percentage scale for determining expected progress in transferring students from segregated schools. In the absence of such progress, the commissioner of education was authorized to require additional steps by the school system to remedy problems with its freedom of choice plan and ultimately to order a different plan if deemed necessary.

Title VI, litigation by the attorney general's office, and the 1966 HEW guidelines represented a "stick" approach to school desegregation, while passage of the Elementary and Secondary Education Act of 1965 (ESEA) supplied federal officials a "carrot" to be used to entice southern officials to end segregation. The ESEA provided over $1 billion annually to assist schools with large numbers of poor children, many of whom were located in the South. The caveat: funding would not be available to those districts not in compliance with federal court desegregation orders. Although the effects of the ESEA were not immediate, it did contribute to the desegregation efforts of the legislative and executive branches.

By 1967, real progress in school desegregation was beginning, as the percentage of black students attending majority white schools in the South increased from a paltry 2.3 percent three years earlier, to 13.9 percent. [See Table 3.1] The percentage rose to 23.4 percent a year later. The joint efforts of the Justice Department and HEW paid dividends in the years after passage of the 1964 Civil Rights Act and ESEA, with lawsuits filed against more than 500 school districts and more than 600 actions by HEW against them.

Also of critical importance was the Supreme Court's decision in 1968 in *Green v. County School Board*, a case involving a rural Virginia county's freedom of choice plan. In striking down the plan, the Court noted that only 15 percent of black students attended the previously all-white school, and no white students enrolled in an all-black school. Justice Brennan ordered the school board "to come forward with a plan that promises realistically to work, and promises realistically to work *now*" [emphasis in original]. He stressed that *Brown II* gave school boards "the affirmative duty to take whatever steps might be necessary to convert [a dual school system] to a unitary system in which racial discrimination would be eliminated root and branch." Brennan expressed strong skepticism that freedom of choice plans ever could be effective in achieving desegregation, although he did not say that they automatically were invalid. Most importantly, he identified six factors to be considered in determining whether a previously segregated school system has achieved unitary status: student assignments, transportation, physical facilities, extracurricular activities, faculty assignments, and resource allocation. These six *Green* factors became indispensable to district court judges in supervising desegregation plans for many years after.

Actions of the Justice Department and HEW during the Johnson administration demonstrated the importance of the executive branch in implementing desegregation, but the succeeding administration backed away somewhat from vigorous enforcement activities. In his presidential campaign in 1968, Richard Nixon had adopted a "Southern strategy," which entailed opposition to strong enforcement of federal civil rights laws in order to attract electoral support from Southern conservatives. His stance on civil rights soon was reflected in the administration's position on the implementation of Titles IV and VI by the Justice Department and HEW officials. Nixon officials decided to deemphasize Title VI's provision for fund cutoffs to school districts not in compliance with desegregation orders, and they announced in July 1969 that new procedures to achieve full compliance would be pursued. Those new procedures, however, included a loophole which permitted school districts to receive approval for a "limited delay" as long as they had a "bona fide" excuse. That summer, officials in the Nixon Justice Department and HEW petitioned the federal courts to allow a number of Mississippi school districts to postpone desegregation for another year. This action was widely criticized, with nearly two-thirds of the attorneys in the Justice Department's Civil Rights Division signing a petition protesting the decision to support the delay.

When this case (*Alexander v. Holmes County Board of Education*) reached the Supreme Court in 1969, the justices rebuffed this effort at delay. The per curiam opinion called for the end of *Brown*'s "all deliberate speed" standard, emphasizing that "the obligation of every school district is to terminate dual school systems at once and to operate now and hereafter only unitary schools." The Supreme Court's decision did not change Nixon's position. H. R. Haldeman, his chief of staff, described the president's attitude in February 1970, writing in his diary that Nixon "is really concerned about situation in Southern schools and feels we have to take some leadership to try to reverse Court decisions that have forced integration too far, too fast. Has told [Attorney General] Mitchell to file another case, and keep filing until we get a reversal." In addition, the president forced the director of HEW's civil rights office, Leon Panetta, to resign, reportedly because he was in favor of strong enforcement of school desegregation and other civil rights policies.

In spite of the Nixon administration's lackluster efforts, the Supreme Court's 1969 decision in *Alexander* prodded the lower federal courts and school districts to make significant progress in deseg-regation. Again, these changes are reflected in Table 3.1. The per-centage of black students in majority white schools increased from 23.4 in 1968 to 36.4 in 1972 and reached a high of 43.5 in 1988. After 1988, these numbers declined steadily, largely due to a series of Supreme Court decisions (discussed in Chapter 7) that permitted fed-eral courts to withdraw their supervision from school districts that previously had been under desegregation orders.

———

Separate, but Unequal, in the North

As southern school districts became desegregated in the 1960s and 1970s, northern school systems actually became more segregated than those in the South. How did this happen? By the late nineteenth cen-tury, most northern states had not only repealed their laws permitting or requiring segregated schools but actually had adopted laws and con-stitutional provisions forbidding segregation. School board practices, however, that created or maintained segregation, continued. More-over, restrictive covenants, steering, blockbusting, federal housing loan programs, and local zoning policies — as described in Chapter 2 — con-tributed to housing segregation, which, in turn, reinforced patterns of school segregation.

Lamenting the paucity of attention to this subject, Davison Dou-glas offers an exhaustive and richly detailed account of school segre-gation in northern communities. Douglas begins by focusing on the period prior to the Civil War. It is not surprising that there were seg-regated schools in the North during the antebellum period or that black education was ignored altogether in some communities. Although slavery ended earlier in the North, many northerners shared the racial attitudes of those in the South. From the 1820s to the 1850s, white views about the inferiority of blacks, concerns about competi-tion for jobs, and fears of increased black migration led to the passage of "black laws" in Ohio, Indiana, Illinois, and Michigan. Some statutes banned the entry of new black immigrants, while others required blacks to register with local officials and document their free status, prevented them from testifying against whites in court, excluded them from juries and state militias, and denied them the right to vote. Many northern whites called for the colonization of blacks in Africa (a view shared by some blacks), antiblack views were widely disseminated in the popular press, and vigilante violence was commonplace. Similar sentiments existed in the western territories as well, including Kansas, Nebraska, California, and Oregon.

Douglas reports that in the 1820s and 1830s, several communities in the North were somewhat more hospitable to the education of black children, although the public schools were racially segregated. Philadelphia, in 1822, was one of the first to provide for black education, and the New England cities of Boston, Hartford, New Haven, Portland, and Salem established separate schools for black children by 1830. New England, however, was not immune from the antiblack sentiments that characterized other northern communities. Major protests in New Haven in 1831 led educators to abandon a plan to establish a private college for blacks, and in Canterbury, Connecticut, in 1833, Prudence Crandall's efforts to operate a private school for black girls failed. The trouble began when she enrolled one black student in her all-white academy. After white parents removed their children, she tried to run an all-black school, but the harassment from the local community was so great that she was forced to abandon that effort as well.

As the common school movement continued to develop in the 1830s and 1840s, black children either were routinely excluded by law from these schools or they were relegated to separate and inferior schools. During the antebellum period, black leaders and white abolitionists fought heartily for black education and were successful in getting private schooling established for black children in cities like New York, Philadelphia, and Cincinnati, as well in some small communities in Indiana and Ohio. Public schools were open to blacks in New Jersey, Pennsylvania, and New York, albeit on a segregated basis. By and large, however, states in the Midwest (Indiana, Illinois, Iowa, and Ohio) limited their public schools to white children during the period before the Civil War.

Even when public schools for black students were established, they were inferior to those for whites in physical facilities, teachers, and curriculum. The buildings typically were old, dilapidated, dark, and damp, with broken furniture and equipment. Teachers in black schools, most of whom were white, were given smaller salaries than their counterparts in white schools, and the curriculum was more

{ *Chapter 3* }

rudimentary. Most black schools did not teach academic subjects such as history and geography, and black schools generally were ungraded. Despite these problems, there were disagreements in the black community over the propriety of fighting for integrated schools. Some, like abolitionist Frederick Douglass, argued that segregated schools perpetuated beliefs about black inferiority and white superiority. Other blacks were concerned that if the schools were integrated, their children would be harassed by white classmates and teachers, and those teachers would not provide a nurturing environment for learning. These fears were not misplaced, as Douglas cites accounts of black children being taunted in integrated schools and of teachers requiring segregated seating in their classrooms. In fact, a disciplinary tactic used by some teachers to handle behavior problems was to threaten white students with integrated seating. In Boston, for example, this punishment was described as assignment to the "nigger seat."

Ambivalence aside, some in the black community did challenge segregation through petitioning state legislatures and school boards, conducting school boycotts, and filing court cases. Perhaps the most significant challenge began in Boston in the 1840s and led to a landmark decision by the Massachusetts Supreme Court in 1849. The Boston School Committee rejected demands to integrate its schools, and a black printer named Benjamin Roberts filed a suit after failing repeatedly to have his daughter admitted to a white school. Roberts was represented by Charles Sumner, a prominent abolitionist (and later U.S. senator), who argued that school segregation violated the state's constitution, which guaranteed that "All men are born free and equal."

The state supreme court disagreed unanimously in *Roberts v. City of Boston* (1849), holding that the school board was acting within its authority in providing separate schools for black and white children. Chief Justice Lemuel Shaw declared that although individuals were guaranteed equal rights under the Massachusetts constitution, "what those rights are, to which individuals . . . are entitled, must depend on laws adapted to their respective relations and conditions." According to Shaw, the heart of the problem was social prejudice, not legal action. "It is urged, that this maintenance of separate schools tends to deepen and perpetuate the odious distinction of caste, founded in a deep-rooted prejudice in public opinion. This prejudice, if it exists, is not created by law, and probably cannot be changed by law."

Five years later, however, the Massachusetts legislature became the first in the nation to pass a law prohibiting segregation in public schools and authorizing damages for violations of the statute. The new law notwithstanding, the *Roberts* ruling continued to be legally significant, as it was used nearly half a century later as precedent by the U.S. Supreme Court in *Plessy v. Ferguson* (1896) to justify the "separate but equal doctrine," as well as by other state courts to uphold their school segregation laws.

The Civil War did not end antiblack sentiment in the North, as the migration of some freed slaves actually increased hostilities. Challenges to segregation in public schools continued, nonetheless, through the efforts of African Americans and their white allies, many of them former abolitionists. They petitioned local school boards and engaged in school boycotts, litigation, and lobbying at state legislatures, and in the 1870s and 1880s they achieved some success in small communities in New Jersey, Illinois, and Ohio, primarily because it was too expensive to operate dual schools.

Litigation challenging school segregation generally was ineffective unless there was a state law prohibiting it, and state courts rejected attempts to use the Fourteenth Amendment's Equal Protection Clause or Privileges or Immunities Clause to end segregation. For example, an 1874 decision by the Indiana Supreme Court used language similar to that in Chief Justice Roger Taney's opinion in the infamous *Dred Scott v. Sanford* case from 1857. Taney wrote that blacks, "whether slave or free, were not included, and were not intended to be included, under the word 'citizens' in the Constitution, and can therefore claim none of the rights and privileges [of] . . . citizens of the United States." Similarly, the Indiana high court concluded that the "privileges and immunities . . . [of the 1851 Indiana Constitution] were not intended for persons of the African race; for the section expressly limits the enjoyment of such privileges and immunities to citizens, and at that time negroes were neither citizens of the United States nor of this State."

Although litigation efforts were largely unsuccessful, in some instances they did help to stimulate passage of antisegregation laws by state legislatures. According to Douglas, "Between 1866 and 1887, *every* [emphasis in original] northern state except Indiana that had previously required or permitted school segregation by law enacted legislation that either explicitly or implicitly prohibited the continued operation of segregated schools." Passage of these laws, however, did not mean the end of segregation. Many local communities simply refused to comply with state law, and those laws contained few, if any, enforcement provisions. Success in achieving racially mixed schools tended to be in areas with small black populations, including upstate New York, and the upper Midwest states of Wisconsin and Minnesota. Once these new laws were passed, however, attempts to use litigation to enforce them were limited. It was expensive to take cases to appellate courts, there were no organizations like the NAACP that could handle litigation on behalf of black plaintiffs, and there were few black lawyers to take on these lawsuits. Also, even when state appellate courts issued favorable rulings, not much changed because the remedy usually was limited to the plaintiff named in the suit.

Ambivalence in the black community towards school integration was another important factor limiting the possibility of using litigation to enforce the laws. As in the antebellum period, some blacks were concerned about the mistreatment of their children by white teachers and classmates, and they believed that black students would fare better if taught by black teachers. Moreover, some black teachers, especially those in Ohio and Indiana, vigorously opposed the push for racially mixed schools because of fears that their own jobs would be lost in the process. At that time, black teachers generally were not permitted to teach in white schools, so integrated schools could destroy their careers. These fears were not misplaced; for example, teachers in parts of Ohio, as well as in Pittsburgh, Philadelphia, and New York City, were fired after the passage of antisegregation laws.

School segregation in the North expanded in the last decade of the nineteenth century and into the first few decades of the twentieth in conjunction with the first phase of the Great Migration (described in Chapter 2). As tens of thousands of southern blacks migrated to northern communities in the period around World War I, antiblack hostilities increased, and residential segregation also took hold. With fears of a larger black presence, racial violence in the form of vandalism, riots, and lynchings rocked northern communities.

Racial hostility also led to the creation of what became known as "sundown towns" throughout the North. James Loewen's *Sundown Towns: A Hidden Dimension of American Racism*, describes this phenomenon. "Beginning in about 1890 and continuing until 1968, white Americans established thousands of towns for whites only. Many towns drove out their black populations, then posted sundown signs. . . . Other towns passed ordinances barring African Americans after dark or prohibiting them from owning or renting property; still others established such policies by informal means, harassing and even killing those who violated the rule." The signs usually read "NIGGER, DON'T LET THE SUN GO DOWN ON YOU IN _____." The most well known of these sundown towns were in Illinois, a state that was at the center of numerous conflicts over black education in general and school segregation in particular.

During the early twentieth century, northern school officials took numerous actions to maintain segregation, including: (1) creating separate schools, (2) racially gerrymandering school district lines while providing liberal transfer policies for white students who might fall into the "wrong" attendance zones, (3) placing new schools in racially segregated areas, and (4) closing schools in ways that perpetuated segregation. In some areas that had eliminated separate black schools, school authorities reestablished them. Economic retaliation, a tactic used in the Jim Crow South, contributed to the maintenance of school segregation, as blacks were threatened with termination of their jobs and housing leases if they pushed too hard for integration. Prior to 1940, efforts by the NAACP and civil rights groups to end segregated schools were largely unsuccessful because of opposition not only from whites but also from some in the black community, for reasons described earlier.

Increased civil rights activism in the 1940s finally led to the demise of explicit school segregation statutes in the North, with Indiana in 1949 becoming the final state to ban school segregation statewide. These changes came about for several reasons. The second phase of the Great Migration, beginning with World War II, brought several million more southern blacks to northern states to take advantage of employment opportunities, resulting in a substantial increase in political power. White public officials realized that potential electoral success was connected with gaining black votes. The NAACP also benefitted from the increasing black population, as its membership climbed dramatically during and after the war. This, in turn, helped the organization step up its attacks on segregation policies, even though some blacks continued to resist school desegregation. More-over, the black community became more committed to ending segregation in all its forms, particularly as black involvement in World War II demonstrated the disconnect between the American rhetoric about democracy abroad and its racial practices at home. As one person quoted by Douglas put it, "why do Americans go 1,000 miles across the ocean to defend Democracy against the same evils as they are tolerating here upon our race?" Some in the white community began to see the contradiction as well, and concerns about the damage to the American image abroad decreased their resistance to changing school segregation laws.

In spite of the successes in changing explicit segregation policies in the 1940s and early 1950s, racially segregated schools remained. Local school officials continued to racially gerrymander attendance lines and enact policies to permit white children residing in black districts to transfer to white schools. More importantly, however, rigid residential segregation ensured that school segregation would continue, even in the absence of official state laws or school policies. And this residential segregation did not occur naturally but, as Chapter 2 described, resulted from the decisions and policies of many actors in both the private and public sector, especially the federal government.

––––––

Michigan: "Beacon of Liberty"?

Michigan's history on race, civil rights, and public education differs to some degree from its midwestern counterparts. This is due in part to the fact that Michigan's early settlers came from the New England states and New York, states that had been somewhat more tolerant of blacks, while early immigrants to the southern regions of Ohio, Indiana, and Illinois arrived from southern and border states. In the antebellum period, both before and after gaining statehood in 1837, Michigan gained a reputation as "a beacon of liberty on the Great Lakes," based largely on its antislavery activism. During the 1830s–1850s, Michigan abolitionists were very active participants in the Underground Railroad, especially across the southern portion of the territory/state. In addition to providing shelter and support to those escaping bondage, Michigan abolitionists gained notoriety for several high-profile incidents of helping to escort fugitive slaves to freedom in Canada. Furthermore, these activists formed many local antislavery societies, which later combined into an impressive statewide organization, the Michigan Anti-Slavery Society. Michigan abolitionists not only fought against the federal fugitive slave acts of 1793 and 1850, but they also worked through the political process to bring about reform. Some of their work led to the formation of anti-slavery political parties, which enjoyed some success in local and state elections.

Despite this record of antislavery activism, Michigan's reputation as "a beacon of liberty" is not entirely warranted, as it too passed "black laws" that restricted the lives of its black residents both before and after statehood. In 1827, for example, the territorial government passed a law that provided some protection for free blacks as well as fugitive slaves. This law protected free blacks from kidnapping and required court proceedings before fugitives could be returned to slavery. This law, nonetheless, required blacks to register with the clerk of their county of residence and to obtain a certificate indicating their status as free people. Other laws prohibited blacks from voting, excluded them from militia service, banned interracial marriage, and allowed for local governments to provide education on a racially segregated basis. Black residents also were restricted in their daily lives through de facto segregation of public facilities and common carriers.

These black laws and de facto segregation, as in other northern states, reflected white ambivalence about the growing presence of African Americans in Michigan. Black migration grew steadily in the antebellum period, as did the population of white residents. While the black population increased from 293 in 1830 to 2,583 in 1850 to nearly 7,000 in 1860, blacks nevertheless accounted for less than 1 percent of the total population. The initial increase after 1830 was due in part to the fact that the 1827 registration law was not really enforced, so blacks felt encouraged to come. Initially, black residents lived primarily in rural areas, particularly in the southwestern part of the territory/state. As migration accelerated, they increasingly took up residence in Detroit and in smaller cities such as Kalamazoo, Battle Creek, Marshall, Jackson, and Ann Arbor. Even so, about 80 percent lived in the southernmost counties, close to the Indiana and Ohio borders.

As the black population increased, so did white ambivalence and fear of the larger black presence. This ambivalence and, in some cases, outright hostility can be seen in the debates over black suffrage at the 1835 constitutional convention, in newspaper editorials of the time, and in the black laws. Even after statehood in 1837, white ambivalence continued, although many whites worked to ensure the rights of black residents. As one scholar quoted by Roy Finkenbine noted, despite the passage of black laws, "the state also had churches, politicians, newspapers, abolition societies, and black and white activists battling to improve the lot of black people in Michigan, none of which would have been tolerated further south."

Detroit: From Segregation to Integration and Back Again

Education is one important area that illustrates white ambivalence. In 1835, in preparation for statehood, the new constitution provided for a system of common schools, but black children appear to have been excluded at first. The Public Primary Schools Act, passed in 1846 following statehood, provided partial public funding for common schools, but it also permitted local communities to segregate their schools. As a result, schools in the rural southwest, Cass County, and Ann Arbor were integrated, while schools in Detroit, Kalamazoo, and other small cities were segregated until after the Civil War.

Education was especially difficult for black children in Detroit. Although public education had been established for white children, initially the only option for blacks was a private school that opened in 1836 in a local church, with funding provided by the black community and white benefactors. The black community faced a double burden. While they paid taxes to support public education, their children could not attend those schools, and they also had to assume funding of the private school. After Michigan became a state, Detroit's black residents and their white allies pressed the legislature to provide public schooling for black children. In 1842, the legislature passed a law establishing free public schools, but the schools were to be operated on a segregated basis. The Detroit school board created seven schools for whites, representing each of the political wards, and one citywide school for blacks (Colored School Number One). The provision of only one school for blacks was made possible largely because the black population in the 1840s and 1850s resided primarily in the third and fourth wards. Colored School Number One actually replaced the private school that previously had existed, but after conflicts over the board's replacement of the black teacher with a white one, the black community eventually reestablished a private school as well.

For two decades, public education for black children was held in local churches and in leased buildings. In 1860, the Detroit school board finally found a permanent location for the school and, five years later, also established a second public school. The black private schools continued to operate alongside the public schools, which the school board would admit years later were "poorly calculated for school purposes." David M. Katzman writes about a particularly troubling aspect of the serious inequities in the school system: the provision of twelve years of schooling for white students but only six for black pupils. Another major grievance was that when the black population migrated to areas beyond the third and fourth wards, the schools for black children became quite distant from where they lived. Katzman reports, "Colored School One in the fourth ward, and Colored School Two in the seventh ward left more than 40 percent of Detroit's black children in wards without public schools."

Following the Civil War, in 1867, the state legislature amended the Public Primary Schools Act to end segregated schools. The Detroit school board, however, resisted the legislature's command, claiming that the law did not apply there because Detroit's schools had been created by a special legislative act rather than by the general school act. After agitation by the black community and its allies, the legislature responded in 1869 by repealing part of the original Detroit school charter so that the new law would cover those schools. The board still resisted, but the Michigan Supreme Court upheld the applicability of the law in general, and to Detroit's schools, in particular. The case began when Joseph Workman, a black Detroiter, sued the school board in order to have his son admitted to a white school in the tenth ward. In *People ex rel. Workman v. Board of Education of Detroit* (1869), Chief Justice Thomas M. Cooley wrote: "It cannot be seriously urged that with this provision in force, the school board may make regulations which would exclude any resident of the district from any of its schools, because of race or color, or religious belief or personal peculiarities. It is too plain for argument that an equal right to all the schools, irrespective of such distinctions, was meant to be established."

Cassius Workman was admitted to the white neighborhood school, but for nearly two years after the *Workman* case, the Detroit school board continued its general segregation policies. The board finally acquiesced somewhat in February of 1871 when it moved to integrate the schools while at the same time segregating the students in separate classrooms. The board explained its actions this way:

> A Colored man who has a prejudice against sending a child to a colored school ought not to complain because some white men feel in the same way. When the Fourth Ward school opened the first of this term, there were pupils enough enrolled to fill it and a surplus besides. A full corps of excellent teachers were placed in charge of the schools, but the white children withdrew almost in a body, parents refusing to send them because there were to be so many colored children in the building. As a temporary measure and one dictated by economy, and one with which we thought little fault would be found, we placed the colored children in rooms by themselves, to induce the whites to return to school.

Finally, when the board initiated its new integration policy that summer, it utilized scarce resources to replace double desks with single ones to allay the concerns of white parents and teachers who could not abide black and white children sharing the same desks.

For the last three decades of the nineteenth century, after years of struggle by the black community and its white allies, Detroit's public schools remained integrated. (Despite state passage in 1871 of a law strongly prohibiting segregation in public education, school systems in some areas of Michigan continued segregative practices into the twentieth century.) Jeffrey Mirel analyzes public education in Detroit during the twentieth century in remarkable detail, including the struggles over racial integration. According to Mirel, black children made up about 5 percent of the total public school enrollment, and the city's schools were still integrated as late as 1922.

Black children were among the top four racial or ethnic groups in 33 of the 141 elementary schools in the city. Only two of these schools were majority black, and both of these schools were still over 40 percent white. In addition, black youths were the fourth largest racial or ethnic group, over 15 percent, in the Sidney D. Miller Intermediate School and they comprised almost 4 percent of the total enrollment in the elite, magnet high school, Cass Tech.

In spite of these positive integration trends, Detroit blacks raised other issues of racial inequality, specifically the small number of African American teachers in the schools and practices that largely limited those teachers to assignments in elementary schools and to schools with large black populations. They enjoyed some success from their lobbying efforts, as the school board did hire more black teachers and began to assign them to high schools.

Improvements in teacher hiring and assignment aside, by the mid-1930s, the school system was becoming resegregated, as schools that previously had been integrated became almost completely black, resembling the pattern in the nineteenth century. Much of this resegregation was the result of changing housing patterns, largely because of restrictive covenants and real estate practices. In addition, however, the school board itself took specific actions to resegregate the schools. First and foremost, in 1933 the board transformed Sidney D. Miller Intermediate School into a high school, changing its role as a feeder school for Eastern High. Eastern was integrated and, like other high schools in the city, was experiencing severe overcrowding. In addition to changing Miller to a high school, the board adopted a policy permitting students in the Miller attendance area to transfer to other schools. The Miller attendance zone was overwhelmingly black, so this resulted in the few white students that remained in the area transferring to other schools. Mirel emphasizes the significance of race in the board decisions noting that "despite the severe overcrowding of all the high schools in the city in the 1930s, no other intermediate schools were elevated to senior high status and, with the exception of Western High School (which was rebuilt after a fire in 1936), no new high schools were constructed during this period. In short, the creation of Miller High School was a clear case of deliberate school segregation."

Not only was the creation of Miller High a deliberately segregative act, but board conflicts with the black community continued

{ *Chapter 3* }

because the school was severely underfunded as compared to its counterparts. Interestingly, in spite of resource inequalities, Miller became known widely for its quality programs in academics, athletics, and music. Many of its graduates became teachers, school administrators, lawyers, police officers, doctors, dentists, political and civic leaders, Olympic gold medalists, college All-Americans, professional athletes, and prominent jazz musicians. Miller eventually became a middle school in 1967 and was closed forty years later.

From the 1930s through the 1950s, black parents and civil rights groups continued to press for reforms in the school system, including calls for hiring more black teachers and counselors. The curriculum also became an especially sore spot, as black students were overrepresented in special education classes and the general track, rather than in the college preparatory track, a trend that many attributed to the small number of black counselors. They gained some support from liberal and labor organizations, most notably the Detroit Federation of Teachers (DFT) and the United Auto Workers (UAW).

By the mid-1940s, a liberal-labor-black coalition began to emerge. But this coalition was fragile. Black parents and the DFT often clashed over priorities. Part of the problem was that during the Great Depression and World War II, school enrollment had declined, and there was a moratorium on school construction. This was not much of a problem at that time, but after the war ended and the baby boom began, the results of building neglect became apparent. Demands for new schools increased as the population moved to new areas of the city, and severe overcrowding in existing schools led to very large class sizes. At the same time, the school board had difficulty keeping teachers' salaries on pace with inflation. The upshot of all this was that the board thought it should spend the new resources on school construction, while teachers called for salary increases. The black community agreed with the board because the schools in black areas were the ones hardest hit by the moratorium on construction. At the same time, African Americans were angry with the school board because they saw the concern with overcrowded schools as an excuse to resegregate black students in the system, as the board had done with Miller in 1933.

In 1947, black parents protested what Mirel terms an "even more brazen attempt to transfer black students from a racially mixed school [Post Intermediate] into two other schools that would be predomi-

nantly black [Higgenbotham Elementary and Birdhurst School]."
What was particularly galling to them was that the "board reopened
Birdhurst School, which had been closed in 1931 due to its age and
poor physical condition, to take in the overflow from Higgenbotham."
The parents refused to send their children to either Higgenbotham
or Birdhurst schools, and after a week of negotiations with the superintendent, the protest ended. The superintendent agreed to keep Birdhurst closed, to speed up renovations of Higginbotham school, and to
establish a committee to study the issue of segregation in the school
system.

Despite their disagreements on some issues, during the 1940s and
1950s, the black community, civil rights organizations, the DFT, and
other labor groups collaborated to influence board personnel decisions, school board elections, millage proposals, and other school
funding issues. In 1949 the alliance was successful in getting two of
its favored candidates elected to the seven-member school board. Six
years later, more candidates backed by the liberal-labor-black coalition won seats on the board, including Dr. Remus Robinson, a prominent black surgeon who became the first black elected official in the
city of Detroit. Three weeks after the election, Superintendent Arthur
Dondineau, who had clashed with the coalition because he was unwill-
ing to admit that discrimination and segregation existed in the school
system, informed the board that he would resign the next year. Samuel
Brownell, the U.S. Commissioner of Education, was appointed to succeed him in 1956. The liberal members of the board were impressed
with Brownell's background as an educational progressive who under-
stood the problems of segregated schools, who was committed to programs designed to address the needs of inner city children, and who
advocated citizen participation in discussions about educational policies.

One of Brownell's early decisions as superintendent was the creation of the Citizens Advisory Committee on School Needs (CAC),
which he charged with "investigating five aspects of the district as a
whole: the school program (curriculum), personnel, the physical plant
(buildings), school-community relations, and finance." Established in
February 1957, the CAC was chaired by future governor George Rom-
ney, who was the president of a major automobile company and a
prominent state Republican Party leader. The CAC's membership

included citizens representing all of the districts in the school system.

As the CAC conducted its survey, the school system faced continuing financial challenges. The 1957 school millage increase was defeated, resulting in budget cuts affecting building construction projects and renewing the conflict about buildings versus teacher salaries. This crisis also brought on a teacher shortage in Detroit schools, as many of the educators were lured to higher-paying jobs in suburban districts. At the same time, there was unbridled criticism of the quality of education in the public schools. In March 1958, the *Free Press* published a series attacking the declining standards in the high school program. In one article, the newspaper reported local employers' complaints that recent high school graduates were "unable to perform jobs requiring basic reading, language, and math skills," because the " 'cafeteria-style education' . . . enabled students to choose 'snap' courses over rigorous academic ones." Another article focused on the decline in the number of academic courses required of students and the increase in what it termed "sandbox and custard" courses, e.g., stage crew, dance band, photography, and family living. The *Detroit News* published a similar series, decrying this dilution of the curriculum and placing the blame for the decline in standards on counselors and teachers. Mirel notes the irony of the business community's criticism of the school system for having made the very reforms that it originally had encouraged during World War II — an "emphasis on 'practical' rather than academic education."

Eight months after the *Free Press* and *Detroit News* series, the CAC issued its report. The report highlighted severe problems of overcrowded schools, decaying buildings, teacher shortages, school organization, and inadequate curricular offerings; it then called for increased funding to the school system and a significant transformation of the curriculum. In January 1959, the school board adopted the CAC's curricular recommendations and called for passage of both a millage increase and a school bond proposal. Both passed with widespread support. Unfortunately for the board, the millage increase and bond victories were accompanied by two setbacks: a significant cut in the school allocation from the County Tax Allocation Board and substantial decreases in revenue from property assessments, which had been declining as businesses and white families left Detroit for the suburbs.

In the midst of all of these developments in the 1950s, the black community continued its protests against segregation in the public schools, which, in addition to school board policies, had been perpetuated by segregated neighborhoods in the city and white flight to the suburbs. Beginning in 1956, Mirel notes that besides seeking the ouster of Superintendent Dondineau, black Detroiters and their allies from liberal and labor groups targeted five areas of concern: "adding and physically improving schools in black neighborhoods; increasing the number of black teachers, counselors, and administrators; ending the policy of segregating black educators in majority black schools; upgrading the instructional and curricular quality in black schools; and stopping the administrative practice of gerrymandering attendance boundaries to segregate schools." By 1960, the alliance made progress in all of these areas, except for the problem of gerrymandered attendance boundaries. This progress was due at least partly to the leadership of Superintendent Brownell, who was much more receptive to their concerns than was his predecessor. From the mid-1950s to the early 1960s, the Detroit schools saw a substantial increase in the number of African American teachers and, to a lesser extent, counselors and administrators. Fair employment policies and practices followed by Brownell and the school board contributed significantly to these gains.

In the early 1960s, the black community stepped up its attack on the gerrymandering of attendance boundaries, but white parents fought back against attempts to desegregate schools in their communities. For example, when the school administration announced in October 1960 that it was going to bus 300 black students from overcrowded black schools in the central district to three white schools in the overwhelmingly white northwestern district, white parents threatened to boycott the schools. They also formed a group – the Northwest Detroit Parents Committee – to fight this busing plan and to recall the school board members. Superintendent Brownell attempted to explain the reasons for the busing plan to both sides, but parents in the three northwestern schools went ahead with the boycott. Brownell, however, would not back down, and the busing plan was implemented. Within a month, opposition to the busing program waned, but school administrators also angered the black community when they decided to keep black students segregated *within* the three schools.

This incident and other skirmishes over attendance boundaries foreshadowed the battle to come in the 1970s over school integration. A particularly significant conflict was the Sherrill school controversy in 1962, which had its roots in an attendance boundary plan drawn three years earlier. That plan, which assigned black students from Sherrill to two largely black high schools — Central and Chadsey — rather than to the predominantly white Mackenzie High, was opposed as blatantly discriminatory by the NAACP, black parents from Sherrill, and an interracial parents' group. Although Brownell initially agreed to delay implementation, in 1961 the administration went ahead with a modified version of the plan that assigned all of the Sherrill eighth graders to a predominantly black district, which guaranteed that they would not attend Mackenzie. A group of parents from the Sherrill area organized and filed a lawsuit charging the school administration with "operating a separate and unequal school system."

The school board responded to these charges by pointing to the improvements made in school construction in black neighborhoods and the increased hiring of black teachers and by denying that it was responsible for creating or maintaining segregated schools. The CAC, which had continued its studies of the system after its initial report in 1958, issued findings in support of the parents' claims. The CAC report concluded that "school boundaries have been used to further racial and class segregation," and it confirmed a "clear-cut pattern of racial discrimination in the assignment of teachers and principals to schools throughout the city."

One of the most damaging findings was widespread discrimination against black students in the apprenticeship programs operated by the school system, unions, and employers. "Since students could not enter these programs without first having a job in the area in which they sought apprenticeships, and unions and employers frequently barred blacks from these jobs (see Chapter 2), black youths could not take advantage of the programs." The culpability of unions in these discriminatory practices contributed to strained relations in the liberal-labor-black coalition as many began to question their commitment to real equality.

The Sherrill suit languished for two years and was withdrawn in 1964 after the school board membership changed. While the Sherrill case demonstrated the black community's continuing resistance to segregation and discrimination in the public school system, it also revealed internal conflicts between traditional civil rights organizations and newer, more militant groups over strategy and tactics. More specifically, the Sherrill lawsuit was not brought by the NAACP (although it eventually joined) but by a parents' committee led by Reverend Albert Cleage, who played a central role in promoting black nationalism in Detroit in the early 1960s. Cleage criticized NAACP officers and other black civil rights leaders, along with white liberals, for moving too slowly and timidly in pushing for change in the school system.

The attendance boundary controversies in northwestern Detroit in 1960 and the 1962 Sherrill incident also had important implications for school finance issues in the mid-1960s. Both working-class whites and the black groups aligned with Reverend Cleage opposed millage and bond increases in 1963 and 1964, albeit for different reasons. Working-class whites opposed additional funding, whether for black schools or for integration. A *Detroit News* editorial summarized the sentiment from many letters it received: "I'm not going to vote money for Negro schools." And a letter in the *Michigan Chronicle* noted, "If you think we're going to vote the Board of Education more money to ship a lot more niggers into white schools, you're nuts." By contrast, the black nationalists argued that their past support for tax increases had not benefitted black schools much and had just helped to maintain segregation. Cleage asserted, "Selling millage to the Negro community will be as hard as selling bleaching cream to Malcolm X."

In the midst of a looming financial crisis, in April 1963 voters overwhelmingly rejected the proposed millage and bond increases. Although Cleage had encouraged blacks to vote against them, the proposals, nevertheless, were supported in predominantly black areas. A subsequent millage *renewal* was approved in November, however, as voters were persuaded that the school system would collapse without it. But racial divisions in this vote, as in April, were apparent. In September 1964, voters again rejected a bond issue for school construction. This was the first election in which the majority of Detroit public school students were black, but the majority of voters were white. The racial composition of the schools had undergone major changes over the years, as whites who could afford it either fled to the suburbs or enrolled their children in private schools. The following data from the Detroit public schools' Bureau of Statistics and Reference illustrate the change in enrollment patterns:

Year	Black Students	White Students	Total Enrollment
1921	5,680 (4.4%)	123,302 (95.6%)	128,982
1946	38,529 (17.3%)	183,862 (82.7%)	222,391
1961	130,765 (45.8%)	153,046 (53.6%)	285,512
1963	150,565 (51.3%)	141,240 (48.1%)	293,745
1964	155,852 (53.0%)	136,077 (46.3%)	293,966

According to Mirel, the 1963 and 1964 school tax and bond elections showed that many "white, working-class voters, particularly Catholics, were abandoning the liberal-labor-black educational coalition and were the first glimmer of what would come to be known as white 'backlash' against school integration, against the Democratic party, and against such liberal union leaders as Walter Reuther." Moreover, the school tax and bond proposal defeats, along with the shrinking revenue from property taxes and state aid, left the system in dire financial straits. Thus, the increased efforts to integrate the Detroit public schools occurred precisely at a time when the school system was in major economic decline.

As the school system's struggle against this major financial crisis persisted, the board continued to endure protests from civil rights groups over segregation and discrimination, as well as from the DFT over collective bargaining matters. Board members also clashed with Superintendent Brownell over policy issues. The board president subsequently resigned, and two members decided not to seek reelection early in 1964. Consequently, the liberal-labor-black coalition ran a slate to replace these three members; all three were elected. When the three took office on July 1, 1965, the liberal-labor-black alliance finally had gained control of the school board. Within a few years, this coalition initiated a modest school desegregation plan, one that embroiled it in controversy and resulted in a landmark Supreme Court decision that would have major repercussions both within and beyond the city of Detroit, for years to come.

Act 48
Decentralization Trumps Desegregation

Amid the ongoing fiscal crisis, protracted conflicts with the black community over the conditions in predominantly black schools, and labor disputes with the Detroit Federation of Teachers (DFT), the liberal-labor-black coalition on the Detroit Board of Education began working to improve education in the public school system. A key actor was Abraham L. Zwerdling, associate general counsel of the United Auto Workers (UAW), who was elected president of the board. Zwerdling was strongly committed to integration, and under his leadership the board worked closely with school administrators to initiate major reforms. From 1965 to 1967, the coalition was successful in increasing the number of African American school administrators and teachers and in transforming the curriculum through the use of multicultural materials. These were significant changes, but they were not sufficient to quell the controversy over education in the public schools because the pattern of segregation continued. Furthermore, just as the board embarked on these changes, a major crisis erupted that challenged the coalition and illustrated the underlying tensions in the Detroit community over the state of public education in the city.

Testing the Liberal-Labor-Black Coalition

In April 1966, black students at Northern High initiated a walkout to protest the deteriorated academic quality of the school, which had been rated as an outstanding school in the 1920s–1940s when it was all-white. The walkout was precipitated by the principal's refusal to publish an editorial in the school newspaper claiming that Northern students were receiving an inferior education. The editorial, written by an honors student, took aim at the social promotion policy, the inadequate number of college preparatory classes offered, and the generally low academic standards. The student also compared Northern's educational offerings to those at Redford High, a predominantly white school in northwestern Detroit, and concluded that Northern's program was significantly below that of Redford in quality. As the students prepared to walk out on Thursday, April 7, Superintendent Samuel Brownell released them from classes and began working on a possible solution to resolve the conflict. The students were supported in the walkout by parents as well as by some members of the DFT. With Easter vacation approaching that weekend, Brownell ordered publication of the editorial in question and agreed to meet with the students and their adult leaders to address the grievances. He engaged them in extensive negotiations to resolve the issues.

The Northern school controversy became front-page news in the Detroit newspapers, and it divided the community into two groups along racial and political lines. One group was sympathetic to the students, including their demands to fire the principal; this group was composed of civil rights organizations, many DFT members, and other liberals. The other group consisted primarily of white Detroiters, the Organization of School Administrators and Supervisors, conservatives, and the Detroit Education Association (DEA), a rival teachers' union. This group supported the principal and argued that acquiescing to the students' demands to fire him would lead to future attempts to get rid of any teachers or administrators who made decisions they found objectionable.

The liberal-labor-black coalition found itself stuck in the middle of this conflict, as they wanted to support the students but at the same time did not want to lose power or contribute to future conflicts that could result in principals or teachers being removed due to outside pressure. In addition, the Northern school boycott occurred a month before the May 9 millage vote, and school leaders feared it would lead voters to reject the call for a school tax increase. Faced with this situation, Brownell and members of the coalition met with the student leaders and parents and agreed to reassign the principal to another position for the remainder of the school term, to establish a committee to study conditions at Northern, and to create a group to study the other high schools. With these agreements, the students returned to school. Attention then turned to the millage proposal and, as some had predicted, voters rejected the tax increase. The vote was split largely along racial lines, with voters in high school districts with a majority of white students voting against it and those in predominantly black wards and black high school districts voting in favor.

In the wake of the Northern boycott and the May millage defeat, a major personnel change occurred—Norman Drachler succeeded Samuel Brownell as superintendent. Zwerdling apparently had been looking to remove Brownell earlier in the school year on the grounds that he was not pushing hard enough on integration, but the rest of the board would not agree. Subsequently, Brownell decided not to seek a renewal of his contract, and in July 1966 the board unanimously selected Drachler, who was then serving as the assistant superintendent for community relations. Drachler was well respected by civil rights leaders and the DFT. He was committed to integration and had come up through the ranks, beginning as a teacher in the Detroit public schools thirty years earlier. During the next several years, Drachler worked closely with African American groups to reform the school system and was successful in several areas. The proportion of black teachers and black administrators increased significantly from 1966 to 1970—from 31 percent to 42 percent for teachers and from 11 percent to 37 percent for administrators. He hired the school system's first black deputy superintendents, and under his leadership the system challenged textbook publishers to improve their presentation of blacks. When commercial publishers failed to do so, Drachler had the school system publish its own textbooks. He also implemented affirmative action in contracts with the school system, requiring contractors to demonstrate that they employed a reasonable number of blacks. Finally, he modified the transfer enrollment policy to require that transfers be granted only if they helped to achieve integration.

Community Control versus Integration

Superintendent Drachler's leadership on school reform in general and integration in particular did little to stem the tide of criticism from some members of the community who were impatient with the pace of change in the mid-to-late-1960s. Furthermore, his push toward integration was rebuffed by anti-integration forces in the black community who began to call for "community control" of black schools as the only way to improve them. Reverend Albert Cleage, leader of an anti-integration group, charged the school system with deliberately miseducating black children and declared that the only way to solve the problem was to have black schools run by black teachers and administrators.

Cleage's call for community control reflected the changing environment in the larger civil rights community in the mid-1960s, both North and South. While most of the publicity about civil rights activities focused on the work to end Jim Crow segregation and disenfranchisement in the South, activists in the North also had been engaged in efforts to deal with their own problems of segregation and inequality. In the South, after passage of the 1964 Civil Rights Act and the 1965 Voting Rights Act, disagreements between the older, traditional civil rights leaders and younger, more militant activists over the tone and tactics of the movement rose to the surface. The new militancy of young activists can be traced in part to the influence of Malcolm X, who met with several members of the Student Nonviolent Coordinating Committee (SNCC) in 1964 and 1965. Northern activists already had been influenced by Malcolm X's teachings. This included Cleage, who helped to organize a rally in Detroit in 1963 with Malcolm as one of the keynote speakers.

By 1966, some SNCC leaders had moved away from integration toward a more black nationalist position, as Cleage had done earlier. During the last major march of the southern phase of the movement, in mid-June 1966 in Greenwood, Mississippi, Stokely Carmichael and members of SNCC transformed the movement's slogan from "freedom now" to "black power." This "March against Fear" was inspired by James Meredith, who in 1962 had become the first black student to attend the University of Mississippi. On June 5, 1966, Meredith set out on a 220-mile journey from Memphis, Tennessee, to Jackson, Mississippi, with the stated purpose of encouraging black voter registration in his home state. After he was shot on the second day, the march was continued by Dr. Martin Luther King, Jr., and other members of the Southern Christian Leadership Conference (SCLC), Carmichael and other SNCC members, leaders of the Congress of Racial Equality (CORE), and some white activists, including students from northern universities.

SNCC's shift to black power became the subject of nationwide criticism from both whites and blacks, and Carmichael tried to address the issue in an essay later that year:

Where Negroes lack a majority, black power means proper representation and sharing of control. It means the creation of power bases from which black people can work to change statewide or nationwide patterns of oppression through pressure from strength instead of weakness. Politically, black power means what it has always meant to SNCC: the coming together of black people to elect representatives and *to force those representatives to speak to their needs.* [emphasis in original] . . . The power must be that of a community, and emanate from there.

Carmichael's explanation notwithstanding, the new focus on black power was threatening to many whites, including some who had participated in civil rights demonstrations in the South. It resonated, however, among many blacks, especially those impatient with the slow pace of change in the South and North, including residents of the Ocean Hill–Brownsville section of New York City. Local activists there initially had pushed for desegregation of the city's schools, but they had become frustrated with the lack of progress. Tensions erupted in 1964 when a new school in Harlem was built to ease overcrowding. Despite the board of education's assurances to parents that the school would be integrated, the parents soon learned that it would be 50/50 black and Puerto Rican, with a Jewish principal rather than a black or Puerto Rican one. This event helped precipitate the call for parental and community involvement in the operation of neighborhood schools. Henry Hampton and Steve Fayer's *Voices of Freedom* quotes one parent: "Either they bring white children in to integrate [Intermediate School] 201 or they let the community run the school — let us pick the principal and the teachers, let us set the educational standards and make sure they are met."

Similarly, in Detroit in June 1967, Albert Cleage and his Inner City Parents Council presented the school board with a demand for black control of black schools, after issuing a scathing report on the condition of black education. The report contended that low test scores and high dropout rates among black students "reflect a deliberate policy of racial discrimination which makes it impossible for the Detroit school system to educate inner city children until basic changes are made in its structure and orientation." The board, especially members of the liberal-labor-black coalition, was appalled by the charge of deliberate discrimination, but it did not initiate any new policies in response to the report and presentation.

By contrast, the board of education in New York City decided to support an experiment in community control, setting up three small experimental school districts, including one in Ocean Hill–Brownsville. This experiment in school decentralization, which began in August 1967, threatened to tear the community apart, as it led to a bitter teachers' strike and racial polarization of the city. Consequently, near the end of the 1968–1969 school year, the state legislature passed a law abolishing the three demonstration districts altogether, including the one in Ocean Hill–Brownsville.

In Detroit, opponents of community control pointed to the events in Ocean Hill–Brownsville as justification for not pursuing a similar experiment. The fact that Detroit had erupted in violence a month after Cleage approached the school board with the demand for community control only added to these fears. The July 1967 disturbance widened racial divisions within the city, and a survey of blacks in the area indicated that nearly a quarter of them cited the poor quality of education in black schools as a reason for the disorder. Consequently, school officials proposed a major increase in funding to improve the schools. Superintendent Drachler suggested that the money go toward decreasing class sizes, upgrading textbooks, and renovating classrooms and buildings, many of which had been built nearly a century earlier. Cleage and his allies ridiculed this approach as insufficient to solve the problems, and they continued to push for community control. Events in 1968 added to the precarious climate in the city, including clashes related to plans to transfer black students from overcrowded black schools to white ones, black anger over the assassination of Dr. Martin Luther King, Jr., mixed with insensitivity on the part of some whites, and the overwhelming defeat of yet another millage proposal.

The growing crisis in the schools prompted black leaders to call a citywide conference in February 1968, with participation from a broad spectrum of folks, all of whom called for a major reform in school governance, though not necessarily complete community control as conceived by Cleage and others. This call for reform was buoyed by a report issued in June by the High School Study Commission (HSSC), which had been established after the Northern High boycott in 1966. HSSC was an interracial body composed of liberals, labor activists, and civil rights leaders and was led by white and black co-chairs, Edward Cushman, head of the Detroit Commission on Community Relations, and Damon J. Keith, a federal district court judge. After eighteen months of studying every aspect of school operations, HSSC concluded that "the public schools are becoming symbols of society's neglect and indifference, rather than institutions that serve the needs of society by providing upward social and economic mobility," and this was especially true for the majority black high schools. HSSC pointed to the educational bureaucracy and lack of teacher accountability as the primary culprits for these problems and recommended "the decentralization of administrative authority in the system and increased accountability for teachers."

The Legislature Gets Involved

The HSSC recommendations were not nearly as radical as Cleage and other advocates of community control desired, but the report did encourage support across the city for some type of reform of school governance. By 1968, community control advocates also had gained two allies from Detroit in the Michigan House of Representatives. James Del Rio, a black Democrat, and Jack Faxon, a white Democrat, each introduced a bill on the subject, although neither bill gained much support.

The Detroit school board was not absolutely opposed to decentralization. Board members were persuaded by the HSSC report and other events that some form of administrative decentralization and community involvement was appropriate, but not the complete community control that Cleage and others were advocating. Cleage and his allies were advocating for community control over every aspect of school operations — hiring, curriculum, and administration. Another important development occurred with the November 1968 school board election when one community control advocate who had the support of the Cleage coalition was elected along with four pro-integration liberals and two anti-integration conservatives.

Following the school board election, the Del Rio and Saxon bills were reintroduced early in the legislature's 1969 session, but once more neither bill attracted sufficient legislative support to move forward.

The issue, however, was far from dead. On April 8, 1969, the Detroit branch of the pro-integration NAACP introduced to the school board a decentralization plan for a "community centered school." Under this plan, an elected board would "oversee each of the city's 330 schools," and these boards then would select representatives to serve "on a board for the entire high school area." A few days after the NAACP proposal was presented, Coleman Young, a Detroit Democrat who later became the city's first black mayor, introduced into the state senate a revised version of Representative Faxon's bill.

The school board carefully studied both the NAACP plan and Young's bill. Four board members indicated cautious support for the NAACP plan. At the same time, the board did not overtly oppose either Young's bill or decentralization; its members had come to believe that some form of decentralization was inevitable. The board's legislative lobbyist was directed to take a neutral position on the bill, but Young agreed to a modification that would preserve the board's authority. Although Young's bill would divide Detroit into several regions, each with its own governing board, there would continue to be a central city board that would adopt guidelines for the regional boards to follow. To obtain DFT acceptance of his bill, Young, a former unionist himself, added language to protect teachers from potential problems: "the rights of retirement, tenure, seniority, and other benefits of any employee transferred to a regional school district or between regional school districts . . . shall not be abnegated, diminished or impaired."

As Young's bill made its way through the state legislature, the board continued to wrestle with the issue of decentralization versus integration. Given the existence of housing segregation in the city, the two concepts appeared to be incompatible. Simply allowing each community to control the operation of its schools likely would maintain the pattern of segregated education. That pattern of segregation only could be abated through a deliberate plan of integration. On the school board, Andrew Perdue and Abraham Zwerdling embodied these two approaches most clearly. For Perdue, community control was the key to improving the educational system. "The schools must be responsive to the needs of the children and the only way this is going to happen is that the administrators be directly accountable to the community. Power is the name of this game. Power vested in the people whereby they have a voice in the operation of their schools, this is the burning issue of the times." Zwerdling, by contrast, acknowledged a need for more community input into school decisions, but he remained firmly committed to integration. "If I have to vote between a step involving decentralization and integration, I would vote against decentralization if it were at the expense of integration." The disagreement between Perdue and Zwerdling may have seemed irreconcilable, but the board found a way to move forward. In May 1969, the members unanimously adopted a resolution written by Perdue that called for "developing a viable plan for the transference of meaningful power to the community."

The next month, Young's bill made it through the education committee and passed the full senate by a lopsided vote of 25-5. The bill then moved to the state house, where it also passed by a significant margin: 83-18. The final bill, Public Act 244, was signed into law by Governor William Milliken on August 11, 1969. William Grant, education reporter for the *Detroit Free Press* at the time, reported that "in Detroit, nobody was particularly happy with the new law. Blacks thought it did not go far enough in securing community control. Many whites believed that decentralization was unnecessary and a waste of money, although some conservatives were quick to recognize that community control would be a boon to them."

The deadline set by the legislature for implementing Public Act 244 was to be January 1971, so with or without public support, the Detroit school board had to come up with a plan to do so. And it would have to undertake this task amid its continuing fiscal woes, because the law did not provide any funding to assist in implementation. The board already found it difficult to operate the schools, given the city's deteriorating tax base, limited funding from the state, salary increases for teachers, and the inability to raise sufficient additional revenue through millage and bond proposals. Declining property values decreased the amount of revenue that could be raised from property taxes, and, despite some increases in state aid in the mid-1960s, the per-pupil allocation for Detroit schools was still well below the state's average. Moreover, in November 1968, 62 percent of the voters had rejected yet another millage increase.

Decentralization or Integration or Both?

In this context then, the board moved ahead to develop a plan. The first step was to determine the regional boundaries. To assist it in this process, the board held a series of public hearings in the fall of 1969. Not surprisingly, the hearings revealed major differences between various segments of the community in the approach to be taken. Coleman Young and other community control advocates argued against creating integrated regions, in favor of regional boundaries that would ensure black control of black schools. William Grant observes that this position was due largely to simple demographics—a majority black student population but a majority white electorate. "If the regions were fully integrated—with each region's racial mix duplicating the mix of the city as a whole—they all would have black student majorities and black voter minorities." At the other end of the spectrum were many white Detroiters who preferred to draw the boundaries along existing administrative lines which, along with neighborhood schools, would preserve the prevailing system of racial segregation.

Each side forcefully presented its arguments to the school board during the public hearings, but after the hearings ended, early in 1970, Zwerdling advanced a different idea. His hope was to use decentralization to create integrated regions that would promote racially integrated schools in the future. Zwerdling acknowledged that his proposal "will not change where anyone goes to school," but he steadfastly argued for this approach:

> It is not going to end racial isolation. But if we drew boundaries that put blacks into one region and whites into another region there could never be any integration. We would have frozen things. But . . . we seek to achieve integration, and so what we can do is create a situation where blacks and whites working together on region boards can move to end the segregation within their own region.

Zwerdling's plan for integrated regions was supported by the other three liberals. That would have constituted a majority for approval, but one of them, Remus Robinson, was hospitalized with terminal cancer early in 1970 and thus was unable to participate in a formal vote

{ *Act 48* }   77

on the proposal. According to Grant, Zwerdling delayed the vote for several weeks in hopes that Robinson might recover long enough to attend a board meeting and cast the deciding vote. Although the two conservatives opposed Zwerdling's plan and Robinson was unavailable, a majority vote still could be reached if Perdue, who previously had advocated for community control, could be persuaded to support the plan. Zwerdling succeeded in obtaining Perdue's vote, but at a big price. Perdue contended that if the board were truly committed to integration, it would change not only regional boundaries, but student attendance boundaries as well.

Once it became clear that Robinson's illness would prevent him from participating in another board meeting, Zwerdling directed Superintendent Drachler to devise an integration plan in order to secure Perdue's vote. In mid-March, Drachler's aides did so, using the regional boundaries in Zwerdling's plan but redrawing the boundaries of high school districts within five of the seven regions that had been established. This modest new plan would significantly alter the racial composition of eleven of the city's twenty-two high schools, and the three remaining schools that were overwhelmingly white would gain a substantial number of black students (see Table 4.1). Cody, at 2.1 percent black, would become 31.3 percent black; Redford and Denby would go from 2.2 percent and 3.1 percent black to 29.2 percent and 53 percent, respectively. Subject to less attention in this controversy was the change in some of the high schools that were nearly all-black. Mackenzie, Kettering, and Southwestern were to shift from 91.6 percent, 89.3 percent, and 87.7 percent black, to 69.9, 65.1, and 53.0 percent black, respectively. These changes were to occur over a three-year period beginning in the fall of 1970, and about 9,000 students — half of them white — would be affected. The changes were to apply only to students graduating from junior high in June 1970 or later, not students already in high school. Also, under the new plan, no elementary school attendance areas were changed. This would, nonetheless, be the first time in the district's history that the board required two-way integration.

Zwerdling and Robinson supported the proposal. On Tuesday, March 31, 1970, Drachler shared it with the full board at a secret dinner meeting. Perdue confirmed his support, one of the conservatives affirmed his opposition, and the board agreed to present the plan for

Table 4.1. Percentage of Blacks in Each High School under April 7, 1970, Integration Plan

School	April 1970	Fall 1970	Fall 1971	Fall 1972
Western	38.6	39.2	44.6	51.0
Southwestern	87.7	71.3	60.8	53.0
Cody	2.1	9.7	20.9	31.3
Mackenzie	91.6	83.8	78.9	69.9
Redford	2.2	11.4	20.5	29.2
Cooley	57.5	53.0	49.7	42.6
Ford	12.4	16.3	26.5	31.3
Mumford	94.6	94.9	94.4	93.8
Pershing	57.5	50.9	46.5	41.8
Osborn	14.1	22.6	32.7	45.8
Kettering	89.3	81.3	73.9	65.1
Denby	3.1	19.3	36.2	53.9

Source: Pages Ia40–42 of Joint Appendix, vol. IA – Pleadings, Exhibit D.

adoption at its next official meeting, scheduled for Tuesday, April 7. On Friday, April 3, each board member received a full copy of the plan, which was leaked to a local news reporter. Subsequently, that Sunday (April 5), the *Detroit News* and the *Free Press* published front-page stories announcing the board's plan to adopt "a sweeping integration plan."

The plan provoked angry reactions from many Detroiters, especially residents of the white northwest and northeast areas of the city. The day before the pending vote, parents from four of the junior high schools included in the plan refused to send their children to school. In addition, at a meeting later that evening, a group of white parents established a citywide organization to protest the plan – the Citizens' Committee for Better Education (CCBE). Twenty-four representatives were elected: twelve each from the east and west sides. Edward Zaleski, a Detroit police officer, was elected to serve as temporary chairman. Alexander Ritchie, a local attorney, agreed to serve as CCBE's legal advisor. The school boycott continued into the next day as well.

The scene at school district headquarters where the board held its meeting was chaotic. All 250 seats in the meeting room were filled, and hundreds of others demonstrated in the hallways and outside the building. At one point during the five-hour meeting, some of the parents, chanting "Hell no, we won't go," tried to break down the glass doors leading to the meeting room. In this chaotic atmosphere, for three and one-half hours, board members listened to statements from over thirty speakers. The Wayne County auditor and leaders from the NAACP, Urban League, and American Civil Liberties Union (ACLU) expressed support for the plan, as well as appreciation to the board for courageously promoting integration of the schools. The majority of speakers, however, strongly disapproved of the plan and criticized the board for creating it; most of them were white residents from the northeast and northwest areas of town. One speaker declared, "My kid won't go to Mackenzie. I will move out in the suburbs, which I can't afford to live in and I don't want to live in, but I will go there and I will go to work so I can live there because my kids are going to go to the best high school available for them." Reverend Cleage spoke on behalf of the Inner City Parents Council, the Black Teachers Caucus, and the Action Committee of the Shrine of the Black Madonna. Cleage told the board that these black groups "are unalterably opposed to the plan presented here today. . . . So-called integration is not only destructive to the best interests of black people, in fact, it is a form of genocide from our point of view."

After hearing from the audience, board members made statements before taking the final vote. Zwerdling tried to appear empathetic to those opposing the plan, but, predictably, he emphasized the necessity of integration. Conceding that the plan did "not give the black and the poor the maximum amount of control," Perdue exhorted community members to give the plan a chance because "maximum integration for our schools is important." After statements from other members, the board adopted what became known as the April 7 plan by the predicted 4-2 vote.

The heated board meeting was only the beginning of the turmoil that rocked the city for many months afterwards. There were bomb scares, racial conflicts, and walkouts in some junior and senior high schools, and Zwerdling received death threats. On the political front, CCBE continued to organize and elected a permanent chairman, Aubrey Short, an engineer at General Motors. On May 4, CCBE initiated a campaign to recall the four liberal board members who had supported the April 7 plan.

———

The Legislature Weighs In: Round Two

The school board's adoption of the "decentralization with integration" plan was also met with anger from state legislators. On April 8, 1970, just one day after the board meeting, James Del Rio, the black Democrat who earlier had introduced a community control bill, joined with a conservative white representative from Detroit to try to kill the plan. They pulled from committee a bill authorizing a voter referendum on decentralization, and they included an amendment to mandate neighborhood schools, a move that—given the existing residential segregation—would ensure the maintenance of segregated schools. The amended bill passed by a vote of 68-31 the next day. The majority voting in favor of the bill consisted of white Detroit conservatives and representatives from suburban and rural areas. None of Detroit's black representatives supported it (Del Rio was absent from the vote). Representative Jackie Vaughn, one of the black legislators, summed up the feelings of his colleagues:

> I think this is perhaps the saddest day—April 9 will go down in history—in Michigan history. It is the day the House of Representatives, at the State Capitol, Michigan voted officially to nullify the Bill of Rights and the Constitution and violate the basic laws of the United States Supreme Court. . . . And what did the State House today say: We *must* segregate. . . . This is what Southern senators do—plot on how to circumvent a basic rule, a basic rule that would bring the schools together.

The state senate took a different, though equally radical, approach. By a vote of 22-9, the senate voted to repeal the decentralization law altogether.

Once again, Senator Coleman Young intervened to find a solution more acceptable to a majority of legislators in both houses. He recognized that some legislators were interested not only in prohibiting decentralization in any form, they also wanted to pass an anti-integration law. In addition, Young was upset with the Detroit school board for adopting what he termed a "chicken shit integration plan." To make the best of a difficult situation, he worked with the house leadership and conservative legislators to develop a bill that authorized decentralization but that also repealed the April 7 plan. From April to June, the group worked on a compromise, but the sticking point was where to draw the boundary lines for the new regions to be created by decentralization. The conservatives wanted them to be drawn along existing legislative district lines, which clearly would maintain segregation. Liberals, on the other hand, thought the regional boundaries should be based on school attendance boundaries. Moreover, Governor Milliken said he would sign a bill only if all of Detroit's legislators—black and white—approved it.

The working group reached a compromise in June. Under the provisions dealing with decentralization, the integrated regions were voided, and eight regional districts were to be established, each of them to be governed by a five-member board. The chairpersons of the regional boards would be the candidate receiving the most votes in that region, and these regional chairs would serve on a thirteen-member central board. The other five members of the central board would be elected at large, so region chairs would be in the majority. Responsibilities for operating the schools would be divided between the central and regional boards. Labor negotiations, the distribution of lump-sum budgets to each region, and the construction of new schools would fall under the auspices of the central board, while the regional boards would carry out the other administrative functions. Having deadlocked on how to draw the regional boundaries, the negotiators provided a mechanism to achieve this. If the legislators could not agree on the boundaries within seven days of the bill's passage, the governor would appoint a three-member boundary commission to complete this task.

Section 12 of the bill specifically repealed the April 7 plan, and the bill mandated neighborhood schools but included an "open enrollment" policy by which white students left in neighborhoods that were transitioning from white to black could transfer out of black schools. The bill also attempted to head off the recall campaign by shortening the terms of the pro-integration board members by one year. (Remus Robinson died on June 14, so the bill also limited the board's authority to fill his seat.) These provisions were written with the understanding that CCBE would end the recall campaign.

With the compromises reached and a complete bill in place, the state house approved it by a vote of 93-1, while the senate approved it unanimously, 30-0. Young had persuaded black legislators to support it, using the argument that the anti-integration provision was sure to be invalidated in court. Governor Milliken signed the bill, known as Act 48, into law on July 7, 1970. On the boundary issue, predictably, no agreement was reached, so Governor Milliken appointed the three-member commission: a prominent black liberal minister, a conservative white member of the city council, and a Wayne State University law professor.

The only legislator to vote against the bill, Representative Nelis Saunders, made an impassioned statement on the house floor:

I voted no . . . because I believe it can only have the result of furthering and intensifying segregation in education, a segregation which has been contrary to the law of the land since 1954. Many of you sat smugly in Michigan while the Southern states protested the *Brown v. Topeka Board of Education* landmark decision. You thought you were so much more virtuous in this basic humanitarian tenet of considering all men as equal. . . . I am disappointed—I'm deeply disappointed—I'm ashamed of your action and response to racist fears. You have helped to both divide and move our society in a backward direction.

William Grant, the *Free Press* reporter and a Kentucky native, also remembers thinking of the irony at the time. "It astonished me that at the moment the legislature passed the law, and the governor signed the law, Michigan had become a state with legalized segregation. Did nobody know what had happened in the South after Reconstruction? Did nobody know they were crossing a line that practically begged for the federal courts to come in?"

Despite the provisions shortening the terms of the integrationists on the Detroit school board, CCBE went back on its word. Shortly after Act 48 became law, CCBE chairman Aubrey Short announced that the recall campaign would continue. "A lot of people have decided they don't like the board of education. If they have changed their minds, then they can vote against the recall on election day." William Grant later described this recall campaign as "one of the amazing success stories of modern Detroit politics." Within two weeks after the campaign began, CCBE had obtained more than half of the 114,000 signatures necessary to place the issue on the ballot. By the time the group filed the petitions, it had obtained 130,000 names. This success was due in part to the group's ability to utilize the network of homeowners' associations that had fought hard against integrated housing (discussed in Chapter 2). In fact, leaders of some of the homeowners' groups served on CCBE's governing board.

The recall vote was set for August 4, the same day as a primary election. Several suits to exclude the recall issue from the ballot were filed in state and federal courts, and opponents were able to get a lower court to remove it. On July 31, however, the Michigan Court of Appeals overturned that decision and ordered the issue to be reinstated on the ballot. The litigation efforts did not leave much time for the recall opponents to organize against it. On election day, the overall voter turnout was light (23 percent of eligible voters), but it was heavy in white neighborhoods. In some areas where the April 7 plan required white students to attend black schools, 90 percent voted for the recall. Voters in black neighborhoods opposed the recall as strongly as their white counterparts supported it, but turnout in the black community was much lighter. In the end, 60 percent of voters voted to recall the board members. This was the first time in the 128-year history of the Detroit school system that a recall effort was successful.

For two weeks before the recall vote, the boundary commission worked to draw the regional boundaries in order to move the decentralization process forward. Early on, the members agreed that integration was not to be a condition of any plan and that political power should be divided equally between blacks and whites. On election day, the group announced the creation of four white-controlled and four black-controlled regions, based largely on adhering closely to existing school boundaries and to the one-person, one-vote principle established by the U.S. Supreme Court in *Reynolds v. Sims* (1964).

Following the passage of Act 48, local and national NAACP officials strategized about how to respond to the legislature's action. Nathaniel Jones, lead counsel for the national group, weighed the options very carefully. Paul Dimond, one of the attorneys who worked with him on this case, later described the dilemma facing Jones and his staff:

> The legal basis for challenging Act 48 was not sure. The Supreme Court had not yet ruled that *Green v. School Board of New Kent County*, its ruling throwing out "free choice" plans that perpetuated dual school systems in sparsely populated rural areas, even applied to urban districts in the South. The Sixth Circuit [the federal circuit that includes Michigan] had not yet enforced *Green* in rural schools in Tennessee and Kentucky, much less reconsidered its own decision in *Deal [v. Cincinnati Board of Education]*, which made judicial review of school segregation in the North difficult. In sum, Detroit was hardly the place to begin a grand strategy to win legal support for desegregation of Northern urban schools.

According to Dimond, these concerns aside, Jones believed that "he had no choice" but to challenge the law because "the fate of segregation in urban America and the direction of the civil rights movement hung in the balance."

Before the recall vote, NAACP officials worked behind the scenes with school officials to develop a coordinated response. Local NAACP leaders, the school board's attorney George Bushnell, and staff members representing Superintendent Drachler traveled to New York to meet secretly with NAACP officials at their national office. (Ironically, Bushnell was a member of the NAACP board of directors at the time.) At this meeting, school officials said they would move further to integrate the schools if the NAACP were successful in getting the courts to declare Act 48 unconstitutional. But Louis Lucas, Jones's associate, was cautious. He indicated that to win the case, it might be necessary to provide evidence of "preexisting illegal school segregation," and he contended that "a broader case could and should be made against the Detroit school board to insure actual desegregation." Lucas's concerns reflected the fact that the federal courts had made a distinction between de jure and de facto segregation in deciding whether legal violations occurred and whether judges could order remedies in de facto cases.

As national NAACP officials continued to map out a strategy, the local branch held meetings with parents and children who were interested in a lawsuit. Officials there had determined that they would challenge Section 12 of Act 48, the specific provision that overturned the April 7 plan, but the outcome of the recall necessitated a change in strategy. Because all of the supporters of the April 7 plan were recalled and no pro-integration candidates were elected to succeed them, even if a challenge to Section 12 proved successful, there would be no one on the board to push integration. Consequently, the NAACP's national legal staff proposed a comprehensive suit challenging school segregation citywide, not just in the areas covered by the April 7 plan.

Going to Court

On August 18, 1970, Jones and Lucas filed a suit in federal district court for the Eastern District of Michigan against the governor (William Milliken), the attorney general (Frank Kelley), the state superintendent of public instruction (John W. Porter), the Michigan Board of Education, the Detroit Board of Education, and the Detroit school superintendent (Norman Drachler). The suit was filed on behalf of specific students and parents, along with "all parents of minor children . . . attending schools in the Detroit, Michigan public school system," who brought the action "in their own behalf and on behalf of their minor children." The Detroit Branch of the NAACP also was listed as a plaintiff. The complaint challenged the repeal of the April 7 plan and the provisions requiring segregated student assignments and racially identifiable regions. It also requested an injunction, pending the trial, to cover three matters: (1) to require implementation of the April 7 plan, (2) to stop all school construction temporarily, and (3) to halt implementation of the entire law. The complaint charged that racially discriminatory policies and practices had created segregation in the Detroit public schools, and it requested the board to submit a plan for the next school year to eliminate racially identifiable schools. Ronald Bradley, one of the students, was the first person listed in the complaint; thus the name of the case at the trial stage became *Bradley v. Milliken*. (In proceedings in the Supreme Court, the case became known as *Milliken v. Bradley*. For clarity and consistency, *Milliken v. Bradley* or simply *Milliken* will be used through the remainder of the text.)

Nathaniel Jones and Lou Lucas served as the lead attorneys for the plaintiffs. Jones had been appointed general counsel of the national NAACP in November 1969 at a time of great struggle for the organization. His predecessor, Robert Carter, had suffered a series of defeats in northern school segregation cases. In those cases, the federal courts held that although neighborhood schools were segregated, black families had the choice to move to white neighborhoods to seek a better education for their children, so there were no constitutional violations. The lower courts refused, however, to admit evidence of housing discrimination in deciding these cases, and the Supreme Court declined to review them. In addition, the NAACP Legal Defense Fund (LDF), which had been the "primary litigating arm of the NAACP," split from the organization and shifted its attention from northern school cases to focus more intensively on southern school systems which, fifteen years after *Brown*, remained deeply segregated.

Jones, a native of Youngstown, Ohio, began his legal career in solo private practice in 1959, then served as an assistant U.S. attorney for northern Ohio for six years, beginning in 1961. During this time, he was active in the local NAACP branch, and he headed another community group that worked on issues related to school segregation, fair employment, and other matters. In 1967, Jones accepted an offer to serve as deputy general counsel to the National Advisory Committee on Civil Disorders (Kerner Commission), which studied the causes of the unrest that rocked urban communities in the 1960s (see Chapter 2). Following his work with the Kerner Commission, Jones returned to private practice in Youngstown, where, eighteen months later, he was offered the position of NAACP general counsel.

Lou Lucas, a Tennessee native, had extensive experience as a litigator in segregation cases, having served in the civil rights division of the U.S. Justice Department. In this capacity, he worked on cases challenging Jim Crow laws in Tennessee, Mississippi, and Louisiana. Lucas also was a founding member of the first integrated law firm in Memphis, Tennessee. Early in his tenure as NAACP general counsel, Jones had called on Lucas for assistance in a school desegregation case in Benton Harbor, Michigan. J. Harold (Nick) Flannery, Lucas's former colleague in the Justice Department, also would come to play a particularly key role. The Detroit school board was represented by its attorney, George Bushnell, and two assistant attorneys general handled the litigation for the state defendants.

After Jones and Lucas filed the legal complaint against Act 48, under federal district court procedures, the case was randomly assigned to Judge Stephen Roth, a Hungarian immigrant who grew up in Flint, Michigan. Prior to being appointed to the federal bench by President John F. Kennedy in 1962, Roth had served as attorney general of Michigan for two years and as a circuit judge in Genesee County for ten years. He also had been active in the conservative, blue-collar wing of the Democratic Party before becoming a judge, and his record on the bench generally reflected that conservatism.

In the NAACP counsel's first appearance before Judge Roth after filing the suit, he was not very sympathetic to their arguments. Lucas requested immediate implementation of the April 7 plan and a suspension of all school construction until a hearing could be held on the plaintiffs' claim of systemwide discrimination in Detroit's public schools. After being reassured by Bushnell that no such construction was underway, Roth rejected both requests and scheduled a hearing to begin on August 27. A day before the hearing, George Bushnell answered the plaintiffs' complaint, requesting summary judgment. At the hearing, Lucas made another attempt to get the April 7 plan implemented, pending a full hearing on the merits of the case. Roth demonstrated his impatience with the NAACP legal team, telling them "I am not computerized. I am not automated, so you can't expect push-button relief. I am not going to move hastily." A week later, on September 3, he denied Lucas's motion, dismissed the governor and attorney general as defendants, and expressed his skepticism about the plaintiffs' claim of systemwide discrimination. "The proofs are not convincing that there has been a course of action which can be characterized as directed toward the maintenance of a dual system of schools, either *de jure* or *de facto*. To the contrary, the evidence before the court indicates that there has been a conscious, deliberate, progressive and continuous attempt to promote and advance the integration of both pupils and faculty." Roth scheduled the trial to begin on November 12.

Lucas, however, shifted strategy, deciding to file a notice of appeal to the Sixth Circuit Court of Appeals, again seeking an order to implement the April 7 plan. This emergency petition was heard by Chief Judge Harry Phillips. While Lucas argued for the plaintiffs, Eugene Krasicky, Michigan assistant attorney general, represented the state.

After hearing from counsel, Phillips decided to expedite the ap
procedure, requiring both parties to submit full briefs in prepar:
for oral argument before a special three-judge panel to be hel
October 2. Issuing its decision on October 13, the panel declared
Act 48 violated the Fourteenth Amendment. The panel also reinst:
the governor and attorney general as defendants and remanded
case to the district court for further proceedings. It refused, howe\
to overturn Roth's denial of a preliminary injunction that would h:
required the April 7 plan to be implemented.

The NAACP attorneys now recognized they would not be able
prepare adequately for a hearing on the merits that was scheduled 1
begin on November 12, so they developed an alternative strategy. Firs
they again requested implementation of the April 7 plan, to begin a
the start of the second semester. Second, they sought a delay of th(
trial date, with the argument that the claim of systemwide desegregation required much more preparation than could be achieved in one
month. Roth agreed to hear the motion on these two matters on
November 4 and decided to postpone the trial for one month. He also
accepted the DFT's motion to intervene as an additional defendant.
The DFT and other local labor leaders had pledged to support the
plaintiffs if they agreed not to focus on segregation in teacher assignments, but Jones said he "could not absolve faculty segregation while
challenging school segregation." The union's counsel was Theodore
(Ted) Sachs, a noted labor attorney. Two days after the November 4
hearing, Roth ordered the school board to submit an integration plan
to be implemented at the beginning of the second semester. This plan,
to be submitted by November 16, could be, Roth said, the April 7 plan
or an alternative that would achieve "no less pupil integration." As
preparations for the trial continued, the judge permitted another
group of defendants to intervene — a group of white parents in Detroit
who wanted to defend the system against charges of segregation.
Many of them were associated with CCBE, and they were represented
by Alexander Ritchie, the group's legal advisor.

The order to the school board for an integration plan created a
dilemma. The school board members currently serving were lame
ducks who would be replaced by the new thirteen-member board in
January 1971, and none of them supported the April 7 plan. They
scheduled a public session to discuss alternatives to comply with Roth's

order; about 600 white residents showed up to protest any integration scheme. The board then met behind closed doors for six hours and decided on three alternatives for the judge to consider: (1) the April 7 plan, (2) a plan to create several special "magnet" schools at the junior and senior high levels that would be voluntarily attended by black and white students, and (3) a plan for high school students to take part of their course work at a second school, with black and white students enrolled together for part of the school day.

The parties submitted their pretrial statements of the issues in the case to Judge Roth on November 9. At a hearing on the board's three desegregation alternatives, George Bushnell, attorney for the board, pressed the judge to choose the magnet school plan, to be implemented at the start of the next school year (September 1971) rather than the upcoming second semester. The plaintiffs' attorneys countered that previous magnet plans in Detroit had not resulted in desegregated schools, so, once again, they argued for the April 7 plan to be implemented at the beginning of the second semester. When Roth issued his ruling on December 3, he once more rejected implementation of the April 7 plan and ordered the board to implement its magnet plan in the fall of 1971. His rationale was that the April 7 plan was aimed simply at "integration by the numbers," and it did not "offer incentive to or provide motivation for the student himself." By contrast, he said that the magnet school plan "offers the student an opportunity to advance in his search for identity, provides stimulation through choice of direction, and tends to establish security." This plan, according to Roth, held out the best promise for meaningful, long-term integration, based on free choice rather than coercion. In addition, he postponed indefinitely the trial on the merits and expressed skepticism that the plaintiffs could prove a case of unconstitutional, systemwide school segregation. Subsequently, in a press conference held in his chambers, he publicly criticized the NAACP attorneys for pressing the case, referring to them as "outsiders [who] should go away and let Detroit solve its own problems."

While continuing to prepare for a trial on the merits, the plaintiffs appealed Roth's decision to the Sixth Circuit. On February 22, 1971, a three-judge panel refused to reconsider the plaintiffs' claim to implement the April 7 plan and upheld Roth's acceptance of the magnet school plan. Most importantly, however, the panel rejected Roth's

indefinite postponement of the trial and ordered him to hear the issue of systemwide segregation in the Detroit public schools "fully and forthwith." Roth then set the date of trial for April 6, 1971. With that action, the stage was set, and the key players prepared to do battle in a legal contest that ultimately would help shape the state of American public education for many years to come.

Cross-District Integration

Remedying Segregation or
Penalizing the Suburbs?

Roughly six weeks after the Sixth Circuit decision ordering Judge Roth to hear the case on the merits, the trial finally began on April 6, 1971, nearly a year after the plaintiffs filed suit. During that six-week period, counsel for the plaintiffs and defendants worked diligently to prepare, poring over documents related to housing segregation and school segregation, selecting and preparing witnesses for testimony at trial, and conducting depositions of expert witnesses. A joint pretrial statement by the parties affirmed consensus on the issues presented, stipulated the court's jurisdiction and the authenticity of records provided by the Detroit School Board, and included an initial list of witnesses to be called. The trial took forty-one days, spread over nearly four months, and lasted until July 22, 1971.

Curiously, the trial proceedings attracted little attention from media in the Detroit area. Given the near hysteria that marked the school board's adoption of the April 7 desegregation plan, the controversial school board recall election, and the bold action of the state legislature, one might have expected a substantial media presence, but this was not the case. The only reporter to cover the trial on a regular basis was William Grant, education editor for the *Detroit Free Press*. Grant subsequently wrote journal articles about the events leading up to the case, as well as the trial and appellate court proceedings. In an interview, he speculated about why his newspaper provided extensive coverage while the other major city paper, the *Detroit News*, did not. He noted that people who make decisions about news coverage often are influenced by their personal connections to an issue or story. Grant observed that the editors and reporters at the *News* generally were conservative residents of Detroit-area suburbs, so perhaps the case did not mean much to them until it was obvious that the suburbs would be brought in. Many of his colleagues at the *Free Press*, however, were transplanted southerners who had experienced the battles over desegregation in the South; furthermore, many of them actually lived in the city of Detroit. For whatever reason, one of the most important cases in the history of Detroit went largely uncovered in its initial stages. This is surprising, because as Paul Dimond, an attorney for the plaintiffs, describes it, the trial made for "great political theater," with strong advocacy by counsel for both plaintiffs and defendants, compelling witnesses, and dramatic testimony.

Plaintiffs' Two-Pronged Strategy

On the first day of the trial, Lou Lucas, a veteran of school desegregation litigation in the South, began the plaintiffs' case. Lucas asserted that they would provide evidence of "purposeful segregation of the schools" at all levels, including among faculty, and would show that other decisions made and actions taken — some directly and intentionally — resulted in a segregated public school system. The plaintiffs presented two cases. The first part of the trial focused on housing discrimination, including its effect on school segregation, while the second phase was directed at decisions of the Detroit school board and the state defendants that purportedly created and perpetuated the segregated system. Dimond recalls that this two-part strategy developed out of necessity. "We had no choice but to concentrate the first part of the hearing on proof of community discrimination and housing segregation; that was the only part of the case that was ready." Their intent for this phase was to show that racial discrimination in housing by officials in the public and private sectors resulted in residential segregation such that black families did not have free choice about where to live or to send their children to school. The theory was that this evidence could persuade the judge that "school authorities should not get off scot-free by arguing that they only incorporated residential segregation through an allegedly neutral system of neighborhood pupil assignments" and that school authorities made decisions that took advantage of or even perpetuated housing segregation. This, according to the plaintiffs, made school officials "willing partners — not neutral observers — in the process of segregation."

Despite having what they believed to be a strong housing case, plaintiffs' counsel worked diligently, nonetheless, to develop the second phase of their argument—that specific decisions and actions by the Detroit board and the state defendants amounted to unlawful segregation under the Fourteenth Amendment. This was necessary because a key Sixth Circuit precedent from 1966, *Deal v. Cincinnati Board of Education*, distinguished between de jure and de facto segregation and assessed how neighborhood schools and segregated housing fit into that framework. In *Deal*, the plaintiffs alleged that the Cincinnati school board's policy of maintaining neighborhood schools perpetuated a racially segregated school system in violation of equal protection, and they called for an end to school construction decisions that built on the neighborhood school concept. The Cincinnati board rejected claims that it maintained an unconstitutional system of racial segregation and argued that the plaintiffs simply were seeking a policy of racial balancing in the school system.

Both the district court and circuit court of appeals agreed with the board's arguments. In his opinion for the three-judge circuit panel, Chief Judge Paul Wieck pointed to an Ohio law that prohibited segregation in public schools, and he contended that *Brown v. Board of Education* (1954) did not require schools to be racially balanced but merely prohibited enforced segregation. He was emphatic in concluding that neighborhood schools are segregated solely because of private housing decisions or other factors; thus they do not present the same type of constitutional violation condemned in *Brown*. Wieck further insisted that "while a particular child may be attending a school composed exclusively of Negro pupils, he and his parents know that he has the choice of attending a mixed school if they so desire, and they can move into the neighborhood district of such a school." Simultaneously, however, he refused to allow this "free choice" theory to be tested by evidence. "The District Court correctly excluded evidence of alleged discrimination in the public and private housing markets. Such discrimination is caused, if in fact it does exist, by persons who are not parties to this case and the Board has no power to rectify that situation."

In addition to the *Deal* precedent, plaintiffs' job was made difficult because the Supreme Court had not yet reviewed cases concerning this "free choice" theory and the link between housing discrimination and school segregation, nor had it decided any case involving a desegregation plan that included both city schools and those in surrounding suburban districts. "To take on the issue of metropolitan desegregation at this stage," according to Dimond, "was beyond the existing state of the law and our resources." Plaintiffs' counsel were hopeful that a case being tried by Lou Lucas in Richmond, Virginia, a city already under orders to desegregate, would become the vehicle for tackling the metropolitan issue — but at a much later point. They moved forward in *Milliken*, hoping that this issue could be put off for a few years, but as the trial moved along, so did the issue of metropolitan relief.

The Plaintiffs' Housing Case and Defendants' Response

Following Lucas's opening statement, but before plaintiffs began presenting their housing case, Lucas called on a former school board member, Roy Stephens, to testify about board policies that promoted segregation. Stephens, who served from 1959 to 1966, testified that a Citizens' Advisory Committee on Equal Educational Opportunities, which studied the school system from 1961 to 1963, had substantiated allegations that the board gerrymandered school boundary lines. He claimed also that the board created optional attendance zones and established open enrollment policies, knowing full well that they would maintain segregation. Having laid the groundwork for the school case to be presented later, plaintiffs moved to presenting the housing case, led primarily by Nick Flannery and Paul Dimond, with assistance from Robert Pressman.

Although the plaintiffs called several witnesses to testify about the roles of the public and private sectors in perpetuating housing segregation, perhaps the best witness was a huge map of the city. It was prepared by William Lamson, an architect working in city planning, who had joined the plaintiffs' team before the trial began. Dimond recalls that the map was placed on a wall in the courtroom behind defense counsel "to Judge Roth's right, where he often stared when contemplating an issue or looking away from a witness." The 10 x 20-foot map, depicted "in vivid color, the almost complete residential segregation of Detroit. There was not much territory that was other than virtually all-black or all-white." Lamson also used overlays that showed how high school boundaries coincided with the residential boundaries. William Grant later described this map as the "most eloquent witness to the facts."

The housing case, which took ten days, began with Dimond's request to Judge Roth to enter into the record copies of Michigan Supreme Court decisions that upheld restrictive covenants. In 1948 in *Shelley v. Kraemer* (St. Louis, Missouri) and *McGhee v. Sipes* (Detroit), the U.S. Supreme Court held that restrictive covenants were unenforceable. George Bushnell, lead counsel for the school board, strongly objected to including these documents. He contended that the *Deal* precedent rendered evidence of housing discrimination irrelevant to school desegregation cases and also pointed to the recent passage of fair housing laws, which he said provided minority families with choice in housing. Judge Roth informed counsel for both the plaintiffs and defendants that he would take a liberal approach to the inclusion of evidence and would sort everything out later because there was no jury that could be unduly influenced by inappropriate testimony or documents. He refused Dimond's request to include the actual opinions in the restrictive covenants cases but nevertheless agreed to take them under "judicial notice."

Dimond introduced another map, this one showing the areas of Detroit where restrictive covenants had operated, demonstrating that those areas still were all-white. He called Allen Priestly, the vice president and chief title officer of an abstract and title company in the city, to testify about racial covenants in the city and suburbs that had continued even after the 1948 Supreme Court ruling. As noted in Chapter 2, the *Shelley* decision had not invalidated restrictive covenants themselves but only their judicial enforcement. Priestly stated that racial covenants were contained in nearly all new subdivisions in the Detroit metropolitan area from 1910 to 1950; this practice had been encouraged by the Federal Housing Administration (FHA). Although FHA reversed its policy in 1950, he said that "racial restrictions contained in deeds continued to be reported" by his company in its abstracts and title insurance policies until December 1969. His company finally discontinued including these restrictions because of a letter from the Department of Justice indicating that the practice violated Title VIII of the Civil Rights Act of 1968.

The plaintiffs called Richard Marks, research director for the

Detroit Commission on Community Relations, to discuss the development of housing segregation in the Detroit metropolitan area. Marks focused on the Lamson map and — looking at changes from 1940 until 1970 — described what he termed a "containment" pattern for blacks in Detroit. That is, black families initially were concentrated in the central city and a few other "isolated pockets," but even as they moved outward from the center they continued to be contained in communities away from the white population. A breakthrough by blacks across one line, said Marks, simply created a new barrier. When asked whether this pattern was the result of economic factors, suggesting that African Americans simply could not afford housing in other areas, Marks responded that there was "plenty of range of economic levels in the black community, a range that made these individuals eligible to purchase housing anywhere in the City of Detroit." Asked whether suburban housing was too expensive for black purchasers, he added that some of those areas "contained properties that might range anywhere from what might be called rural slum . . . all the way up to some of the most expensive and valued property."

Judge Roth was quite skeptical and asked Marks whether this pattern was similar to that of earlier immigrant ethnic groups who concentrated themselves in certain areas because of language and customs. Roth also suggested that a similar pattern might be relevant for "big pockets . . . of people who have come up from the South," referring to the large numbers of African Americans who moved from the rural South to the urban North during the Great Migration. Marks answered in the negative, noting that ethnic groups, as well as southern whites, after establishing themselves in the city, were dispersed in other areas. This containment pattern, Marks said, was the result of several factors: the location of public housing, restrictive covenants, federal urban renewal projects, FHA policies, and the real estate code of ethics. (All of these are discussed extensively in Chapter 2.)

Dr. Karl Taeuber, a sociologist and demographer, was called by the plaintiffs as an expert witness on urban residential segregation. In his research, Taeuber utilized what he termed a "segregation index," which calculates the degree of segregation of racial and European ethnic groups in a city. The scale for the index, calculated using census data, ranges from 0 to 100. A score of 0 means that every block in the city is racially or ethnically mixed, so there is no segregation. A value of 100 denotes that no block in the city is racially mixed, representing complete segregation. After studying census data covering the period from 1900 through 1970, Taeuber calculated the index for European ethnic groups versus the rest of the population and for blacks versus whites. The national range for various European ethnic groups ranged from 10 to 50, and it decreased over the decades. By contrast, the national range for blacks versus whites was 70 to 90, and it continued to persist at high levels for many years. Nick Flannery asked Taeuber about the black/white index for Detroit; it was 84.5.

Flannery went further, requesting the index for the Polish community in Detroit in order to challenge Judge Roth's view that the black community's experience with housing was no different from that of ethnic immigrant groups. Roth, whose family immigrated from Hungary when he was 10 years old, was aware that Detroit's Polish community was one of the largest and most tightly knit ethnic communities in the city. The judge was skeptical of the question but permitted the witness to answer. Taeuber replied that the segregation index for the Polish community was less than half of that for blacks. In his later account of the trial, Dimond notes that Roth "seemed startled by the answer," and he views this exchange as an important turning point for the plaintiffs. As noted in Chapter 4, in pretrial rulings and statements, Roth had expressed serious doubts that the plaintiffs would be able to make their case. By the time that Taeuber illustrated the different segregation patterns for blacks and for white ethnic groups, the judge already had spent days staring at the large map delineating a racially segregated community, and he had heard substantial testimony about the policies and practices contributing to that division.

The plaintiffs called several additional witnesses with expertise on governmental housing policies and practices. Perhaps the most important to the later development of the case was Martin Sloane, a former director of the housing staff at the U.S. Civil Rights Commission and former staff attorney at the Department of Housing and Urban Development (HUD). Sloane testified about the federal government's support of housing segregation through policies of the FHA and other agencies. He noted especially FHA's underwriting manuals, which advised underwriters about the factors to be used in their appraisals of houses for the purpose of FHA insurance, including race. One section of the 1935 manual, "Protection from Adverse Influences," read: "Important among adverse influences . . . are the following: Infiltration of inharmonious racial or nationality groups." Sloane, following up with a provision from the 1938 manual, then made a specific connection between residential segregation and school segregation. It read: "If the children of people living in such an area are compelled to attend schools . . . [where] a considerable number of the pupils represents a far lower level of society or an incompatible racial element, the neighborhood under consideration will prove far less stable and desirable than if this condition did not exist."

It was during Sloane's testimony, as he was being cross-examined by Alexander Ritchie, that the idea of a metropolitan remedy for school segregation initially was raised. Ritchie, counsel for the white Detroit parents included as defendant-intervenors, noted that the white population of Detroit had been steadily moving away, and he suggested that a movement toward desegregating the schools would simply drive those who remained in Detroit toward the suburbs. Given that, he asked Sloane whether a desegregation plan limited to Detroit would be at all effective. Judge Roth picked up on this question in an exchange with Sloane:

> *Judge Roth.* Well, taking [Mr. Ritchie's question] in that light and applying what you know about a city, any city in the United States with the same problem and with the same color makeup, do you have an opinion as to what would happen to what are depicted there on the map [of Detroit] as now white areas? Would they, as Mr. Ritchie suggests, lead really to an abandonment in large numbers of white folks so that when you ended up with the city you'd have a city that was no more integrated than when you started. Do you have an opinion on that?
>
> *Sloane.* The same principle has been discussed in a conjecture with respect to residential population. Experience in Washington is perhaps instructive. [The] Washington metropolitan area has not changed by more than one percentage point in terms of the per cent white and per cent black in the last seventy years. It's always been roughly 75 percent white, 25 per cent black. The distribution of the population by race in the Washington metropolitan area has changed very dramatically to the point where

the Northern Virginia suburbs has something like 6 per cent black and 94 per cent white. The Maryland suburbs and suburb of Montgomery County has something like 4 per cent black and 96 per cent white, whereas 60, 70 years ago there was an even distribution.

But talking about integrating the schools of Washington, of course Washington Public Schools are now in excess of 90 per cent black, and it's very difficult to talk about achieving school integration with that kind of percentage. But if you think in terms of the metropolitan area as a whole, the problem becomes a good deal less difficult because then we're dealing with a school population as well as a residential population which is roughly 75 per cent white and 25 per cent black.

I think in a situation like that you have to talk in terms of metropolitan wide desegregation, residentially as well as in education. And it is, in fact, I think an exercise in futility to think in terms of integrating a school system which is already so predominantly black as to make racial integration an impossibility. It is, however, not an impossibility if you talk in terms of the metropolitan area as a whole.

Now, I feel rather uneasy about—

Judge Roth. Well, I don't know whether fortunately or unfortunately this lawsuit is limited to the City of Detroit and the school system, so that we're only concerned with the city itself and we're not talking about the metropolitan area.

In Dimond's account of the case, he says that the plaintiffs were reluctant to press a metropolitan remedy at this early stage, but Flannery did inform the judge that with the State as a defendant, plaintiffs were "not prepared to concede . . . that a metropolitan solution would not be viable or would be inappropriate."

John Humphrey, a black real estate broker in Detroit, provided some of the most riveting testimony for the plaintiffs. He noted that black brokers were referred to as "realtists"; they were not permitted to use the term "realtor." They also were excluded from the city's main realtors' association. Humphrey told story after story of the discrimination and harassment he and his black clients faced when he tried to help them purchase housing in all-white neighborhoods. The most serious incident, he recalled, involved two families who moved into homes across the street from each other in 1952:

> The first one lived a year without incident, and when we sold the second family, black that had children, and the man was a factory worker, apparently the neighbors objected and thought that this was going too far, and at that time they broke out all the windows in the house and harassed the family. And subsequent to this, a police car was placed there around the clock. And while the policeman was there, they threw snakes in the basement and frightened the people to the point that they — the lady had a nervous breakdown and had to move out.

Humphrey recounted his own experiences searching for a home in Detroit's suburbs in 1968. He followed up on a newspaper advertisement, only to be immediately discouraged from purchasing the home. "I don't know why you'd want to buy this house because it floods every time it rains, a good heavy dew and things flooded all over." On another occasion, after attending an open house and being told by the owner that the home price was $65,000, he learned from another salesman that the house had been listed for only $45,000. Several additional black "realtists" shared similar stories of discrimination and harassment.

Shortly after the testimony from the "realtists," Ritchie announced that he no longer could ignore the obvious. "The white citizens of the City realistically recognize the significance of this map [the big map on the wall]. I don't think I, on their behalf, would deign to argue that we do not have a segregated city in Detroit. . . . It is quite possible for any litigant to lose a case." Judge Roth's admonition about the limitation of the lawsuit to the city aside, Ritchie used Sloane's testimony to take every opportunity to recommend a metropolitan remedy, were the judge to rule that there was unlawful segregation of the Detroit public schools. There is some debate about whether Ritchie had experienced a transformation from his earlier opposition to desegregation generally, and busing specifically, or merely was pressing for a metropolitan remedy in order to protect his clients. They initially were very skeptical of his strategy, but he convinced them that a metropolitan remedy would ensure that their children would not become a minority in the schools if they lost the case. In accepting this strategy,

Ritchie's clients also believed that a metropolitan remedy would bring in suburban antibusing interests, thereby increasing their political clout in opposing the desegregation efforts.

Despite downplaying the idea of a metropolitan remedy and emphasizing that the lawsuit was limited to the Detroit public school system, Judge Roth permitted counsel for the plaintiffs to elicit testimony from witnesses demonstrating that the residential exclusion of blacks extended to the suburbs. He reiterated his position that he would give fairly wide latitude to counsel to develop the record, and then he would "separate the wheat from the chaff." Robert Pressman began to question the head of the housing section of the Michigan Civil Rights Commission about incidents of vandalism, harassment, and intimidation of a black family who had moved to Warren, a suburb located next to Detroit.

George Bushnell and Gerald Young, representing the Detroit school board and state defendants, respectively, objected strongly to this line of questioning, arguing that events outside of the Detroit city limits were irrelevant. Pressman responded that incidents in suburbs discouraged black Detroiters from trying to obtain housing in integrated or all-white communities, whether in Detroit or the surrounding suburbs. He claimed that the state, as a defendant in the case, "has a responsibility under the Constitution to insure that black students in Detroit receive equal educational opportunities, and . . . it may be necessary in terms of relief to involve areas other than simply Detroit."

After Judge Roth permitted the questioning to continue, Donald Bauder, the commission official, focused specifically on the exclusion of blacks from two additional suburbs — Sylvan Lake and Shelby Township. During cross-examination by Alexander Ritchie, Bauder confirmed that some blacks actually worked in the suburbs, but they did not live there. The most prominent example was Warren, where around 20,000 blacks worked, while only five to seven black families were city residents.

The defendants did not present a separate case on the housing issue; their defense consisted of cross-examinations as well as objections to including testimony on this subject. They attempted to discredit the plaintiffs' testimony by showing that although the witnesses claimed to be troubled by racial segregation in housing, their agencies seemed to have done little to fully investigate or remedy charges of segregation. For example, in cross-examining Jim Bush, assistant director of the Detroit Commission on Community Relations, George Bushnell asked questions designed to demonstrate that, despite powers granted it under local ordinances, the commission had prosecuted only a small number of people for violations. Counsel also tried to show that witnesses were negligent in obtaining important information that could lead to different interpretations of the evidence. Gerald Young focused on Bush's discussion of the realtors' national code of ethics, which contained a provision promoting racial discrimination. But Young asked Bush whether he had made an attempt to determine whether that code had actually been adopted as an official state regulation. When Bush conceded that he had not done so, Young requested Judge Roth "to take judicial notice of the fact that the Code of Ethics has never been in the Michigan Administrative Code as part of the legally enforceable administrative rules of the . . . Michigan Corporation and Securities Commission."

At one point, Judge Roth, still unsure about the relevance of housing segregation to the question of whether unlawful school segregation existed, prodded defense counsel to stipulate to at least some of the proof of housing segregation, but they continued to make objection after objection. As a response, the plaintiffs' attorneys brought in a parade of witnesses. According to the later accounts of both Dimond and Grant, this was one of the main reasons that the plaintiffs were able to build such a comprehensive and detailed record of housing segregation. When the pattern of objections by defense counsel continued into the school case later in the trial, an exasperated Judge Roth showed his impatience:

I have tried to indicate at the beginning of this case that we will go a little faster if you are fairly sparse with objections. I'm going to let both sides make a full record in this case. We don't have a jury here, so I don't have to worry about their receiving some hearsay that might misdirect. Even in areas where people testify on matters that relate to what I have to do eventually and decide eventually I'm going to be fairly generous in letting them express themselves. I have made this observation before. It hasn't borne much fruit. But, I make it again.

As the plaintiffs' housing case drew to a close, the U.S. Supreme Court, on April 20, 1971, issued an important decision regarding desegregating urban school systems in the South. In *Swann v. Charlotte-Mecklenburg Board of Education*, the federal district judge supervising efforts to desegregate schools in Charlotte, North Carolina, ordered several remedies, the most controversial of which concerned busing African American children to schools in white neighborhoods and vice versa. This plan involved busing only within a single school district and, in Charlotte, the schools in the city and surrounding suburbs are part of the same district. The public school system in Charlotte had been operating under a court-approved desegregation plan since 1965, but the schools had remained firmly segregated, with 14,000 of the 24,000 black students still attending schools that were all- or nearly all-black. In its 1968 ruling in *Green v. County School Board*, the Supreme Court held that *Brown II* gave school boards "the affirmative duty to take whatever steps might be necessary to convert [a dual school system] to a unitary system in which racial discrimination would be eliminated root and branch." Judge James McMillan concluded that more needed to be done in Charlotte to comply with *Green*. In addition to evidence of racially discriminatory school board actions, McMillan found that segregated residential patterns in the city resulted from the actions of federal, state, and local governments, and he stressed the relationship between segregated housing and segregated schools. After the school board repeatedly failed to develop a meaningful desegregation plan, Judge McMillan developed a busing program to reach a 71:29 white-to-black ratio in the various Charlotte schools. This ratio represented the proportions of white and black students in the school system at the time.

When McMillan's controversial plan reached the Supreme Court, a unanimous Court upheld his order, but the reasoning behind the decision was muddled. Responding to assertions that school busing was somehow new and exotic, Chief Justice Warren Burger noted that "bus transportation has been an integral part of the public education system for years." While concluding that "the very limited use of mathematical ratios was within the equitable remedial discretion of the District Court" in this case, he warned that meaningful desegregation did not require every school in a community to reflect the system's racial composition. Burger also appeared to affirm the connection between residential segregation and segregated schools. "The construction of new schools and the closing of old ones are two of the most important functions of local school authorities and also two of the most complex. . . . People gravitate toward school facilities, just as schools are located in response to the needs of people. The location of schools may thus influence the patterns of residential development of a metropolitan area and have important impact on composition of inner-city neighborhoods."

Simultaneously, however, Burger praised the virtues of neighborhood schools and expressed dismay that federal judges in desegregation cases may be too concerned with achieving "racial balance." Another critical aspect of Burger's opinion related to whether evidence of housing segregation created or maintained by government policies could be used to require desegregation in cases where there was no proof of specific acts of discrimination by school authorities. On this question, the opinion was unclear. Burger suggested that school officials should not be held responsible, because there are "myriad factors of human existence which can cause discrimination in a multitude of ways on racial, religious, or ethnic grounds." But, he continued, "this case does not present that question and we therefore do not decide it."

The unanimous vote in *Swann* also masked serious divisions on the Court over the issue of school busing for purposes of desegregation. The struggle for unanimity was based on the Court's longstanding record of handing down unanimous decisions in school desegregation cases that began in *Brown* and continued throughout the Warren Court. As the new leader, Burger wanted to show that he could produce unanimity in these cases just as his predecessor had. The original vote apparently was 6-3 against the busing plan. Each justice then drafted a separate opinion to be shared with the others, prompting some to switch their votes. The 6-3 vote against busing eventually became 6-3 in favor, with Burger and Justices Harry Blackmun and Hugo Black as the dissenters. When these three acquiesced to the majority, Burger then wrote the unanimous ruling, using much of the language drafted by the pro-busing justices. The serious division later would reappear when the Richmond and Detroit cases reached the Court.

Plaintiffs' School Case

After the housing case, the plaintiffs moved to the second phase, attempting to prove that the Detroit public school system was segregated because of actions by the Detroit school authorities and the state defendants. Dr. Robert Green, an education expert and director of the Center for Urban Studies at Michigan State University, was the first witness. Green testified about the quality of education provided in black and white schools based on achievement test scores and community perceptions, and he discussed the harmful impact of school segregation in teaching young people concepts of white superiority and black inferiority. These lessons have consequences in the development of the community as young people become adults:

> We did not educate the white adults who went to the Detroit Public School system who are now living in [the suburbs]. . . . I see [white] flight being significantly related to what we have not done in our public schools. . . . The fact blacks can't buy houses in Warren is a failure of the Detroit Public School system. Livonia was sticks and woods when I was a kid. That suburban community was built because the Detroit Public School system did not perform its functions. It was built because we had all white elementary schools, all white junior high schools and all white high schools.

Bushnell was taken aback by Green's statement attributing responsibility to the school system for this "catalogue of discrimination and horror" and asked for clarification. Green reiterated that "a major share of the responsibility must be placed at the foot of the Detroit Public School system" and suggested that "the public educational system can go a long way in offsetting these kinds of negative attitudes," but he complained that this had not happened because of the segregated structure of the Detroit system.

Following Green's testimony, William Caldwell and Lou Lucas conducted plaintiffs' efforts to demonstrate official acts of segregation by the school authorities. They utilized information from school board records and depositions taken from school officials and made extensive use of census maps and various overlays illustrating neighborhood and school boundaries. Most of this phase of the trial involved painstaking testimony about specific policies and practices that established or maintained segregation. These included optional attendance zones, open enrollment and school transfer policies, feeder patterns (the assignment of elementary school attendance zones for junior high schools and junior high attendance zones to high schools), gerrymandering of attendance lines, school transportation policies, and school construction decisions, including the selection of sites for new schools.

Reviewing the trial transcript, one quickly sees that this was not riveting testimony. William Grant, *Detroit Free Press* reporter, described it simply as "boring." Day after day the witnesses responded to questions about the numbers and percentages of black and white students in various schools, decisions about where to draw attendance zones, the number of students affected by optional zones and transfer policies, the number of new schools built in certain locations and why they were built, the busing of students to relieve overcrowding, and the like. As Dimond later describes, the plaintiffs wanted "to show a pattern of conduct that 'naturally, probably and forseeably' resulted in segregation in the face of available desegregation alternatives." Their goal, he said, "was not to prove that Detroit school authorities were subjectively motivated by racial animus, but that objectively they were not immune to the community custom of racial segregation and discrimination." With respect to faculty segregation, plaintiffs tried to demonstrate a pattern of assigning black teachers to schools that were predominantly black and excluding them from predominantly white schools.

Although the bulk of the testimony in the plaintiffs' school case focused on the Detroit defendants, counsel also argued that the state defendants shared responsibility for the system of de jure segregation. They made both constitutional and statutory arguments. Counsel claimed that under the Fourteenth Amendment states are required to ensure equal protection of the laws, which they had failed to do by permitting racial discrimination against black students by the Detroit school district. In questioning Dr. John Porter, the State Superintendent of Public Instruction, plaintiffs asserted that education is a state function under both the Michigan constitution and state law, with local school districts under the "plenary power" of the state and the "supervisory" control of the state superintendent and state board of education. As such, counsel asserted, the segregation policies and practices of the Detroit defendants also were state actions and, therefore, the state was responsible. Furthermore, the argument went, the state had funded deliberate acts of segregation by the Detroit board, and the state board violated state guidelines in approving the board's construction program that built racially segregated schools. In passing Act 48, counsel added, the state legislature and executive repealed the board's April 7 plan to integrate its schools and made provision for creating eight segregated regions, instead of the alternative decentralization plan proposed by the school board's president that would have resulted in at least some desegregation of the district's schools.

Maintaining that the state could provide relief for the constitutional violation, plaintiffs tried their best to avoid discussing a metropolitan remedy. Concerned that legal precedent was not yet on their side and that appellate courts might be troubled by metropolitan relief because the suburbs had not been involved in the trial process, they argued that since the state board of education was responsible for public education, it could provide the necessary remedy, including "supervision of transfers across school district lines." But with Judge Roth and Alexander Ritchie pressing the question of a metropolitan solution, counsel moved forward, hoping that questions about "areawide liability or suburban wrongdoing" could be dealt with later in an amended complaint or additional hearing.

After the plaintiffs rested, but before the Detroit defendants began presenting their defense against plaintiffs' claims of de jure segregation by local and state officials, Assistant Attorney General Eugene Kraskicky filed a motion requesting Judge Roth to dismiss the state defendants from the case "on the ground that upon the facts and the law plaintiffs have shown no right to relief." As the hearing proceeded the next day, Kraskicky said to the judge, "Unless the Court wishes us to be here further, we would like permission to leave." Judge Roth, visibly upset, responded tersely, "You may leave. That is a matter entirely within your judgment." A month later, on June 25, in the absence of the state attorneys, he denied their motion for dismissal and observed:

I think that those who are involved in this lawsuit ought to be preparing for [all] eventualities, the maximum and minimum, so that if the time comes for judicial intervention . . . , it would be well for all parties to be prepared . . . the State Defendants too. I don't think the State Defendants should hide, put their heads in the sand and avoid considering what may happen if certain developments already made plain in this case take shape. Mr. Ritchie has made some points along this line, and I have. . . . How do you desegregate a black city or a black school system. . . . Now State Defendants . . . ought to be thinking in these terms indeed if that's what develops.

Even with Roth's admonition, state attorneys did not provide a defense. In an interview for this book nearly thirty-five years later, Attorney General Frank Kelley reiterated his belief that the plaintiffs had not introduced any evidence showing that the state was a party to discrimination. He concluded, therefore, that no defense was necessary because there was no obligation for the state to produce evidence against itself.

Another significant legal development occurred shortly after the plaintiffs wrapped up their school case, this time involving the Sixth Circuit Court of Appeals. The case involved the school district in Pontiac, Michigan, a city near Detroit that also experienced a strong pattern of residential segregation. In 1969, an African American federal district judge, Damon Keith, ordered an extensive busing plan to begin at the start of the 1971 school year. On May 28, 1971, the Sixth Circuit upheld Judge Keith's ruling, which had relied on evidence of de jure segregation by school officials.

Defendants' Case

George Bushnell and Carl von Ende, his co-counsel, began their defense in early June. They called Merle Henrickson, the school planner, as their chief witness. He testified about population trends, pupil populations, pupil transportation, and school construction within Detroit. Henrickson earlier had admitted that previous boards took actions to deliberately segregate the schools. In testifying for the defendants, he stressed that more recent board policies and practices, particularly beginning in the mid-1960s, reflected the board's attempt to deal with the changing demographics in the city, specifically the increasing proportion of black students in the district and the reality of residential segregation. These demographic factors affected a number of things, from overcrowding in schools to attendance boundaries to decisions about pupil transportation and school construction. In questioning from Bushnell, Henrickson described changes in the board policy on transporting students to relieve overcrowding:

> *Bushnell.* So in 1960, integration was not part of the policy but in 1966 it became part of the policy, is that correct?
>
> *Henrickson.* The policy appears to be neutral in 1960. In fact, and in view of the demographic movement which was occurring, it was in fact the circumstance that the nearest school with available capacity was in virtually all conditions a white school and the overcrowded school was virtually in all situations a school with black students and that the effect of the 1960 policy in almost all instances as it came to be applied in the years following that was to move black students into white schools a few miles out, farther out.
>
> *Bushnell.* And thus integrate the white schools?
>
> *Henrickson.* Yes.
>
> *Bushnell.* And reduce the number of blacks in the sending schools?
>
> *Henrickson.* Yes, . . . and [the Board] felt that the superintendent should have discretion to bypass . . . a school if the increase of black students by transportation, in his judgment, would be detrimental to integration or detrimental to the transition occurring within the community.

Henrickson discussed several incidents involving transportation of black students to white schools to relieve overcrowding, for which Bushnell credited the district with "leaping [the] boundary established by housing patterns and bringing black kids into the white areas."

With respect to school site selection and construction decisions, Henrickson rejected the notion that more recent decisions were made with the purpose of building one-race schools. He noted that some critics had claimed that certain schools were built for white students, but those schools were nearly all black at the time of the trial. Bushnell also asked questions designed to demonstrate that board changes in school attendance zones since 1960 "show[ed] an attendance of black students in schools outside and beyond their normal attendance areas with the effect of integrating an increasing number of schools." He elicited testimony from Henrickson indicating that the April 7 plan, which the state legislature had repealed, would have provided both white and black students with an integrated experience, although the school planner acknowledged that the plan did not affect black students in the center city schools. Defendants viewed these facts as proof that school authorities no longer were guilty of de jure segregation and should not be held responsible for residential patterns over which they had no control.

In general, the defendants' school case, like that of the plaintiffs, consisted of long days of technical testimony about board decisions about specific schools, school attendance zones, enrollment policies, feeder patterns, school construction, and other matters. Henrickson also claimed that a plaintiffs' witness was mistaken in his conclusions that the board had rejected available desegregation alternatives in favor of plans that either maintained or increased segregation.

In addition to arguing that the Detroit board increasingly had taken steps toward integration, counsel's other strategy was to shift blame to the state. Bushnell introduced evidence charging that the state discriminated against Detroit schools while favoring those in the suburbs by providing funds to transport suburban students and denying them to pupils in Detroit. He also pointed to the state's subsidization of school construction projects in the suburbs, where schools served an overwhelmingly white student population. The board's secretary and business manager testified that until the previous session of the state legislature, the Detroit board's bonding authority for raising funds was lower than that of other districts in the state. He also discussed the district's difficulty in raising sufficient operating funds compared to their suburban counterparts. Because of higher property values, suburban residents could tax themselves at lower rates and still obtain adequate revenue, while those in Detroit taxed themselves at higher rates but still could not acquire sufficient funding because of low property values. To illustrate, "the equalized value of property in Detroit was $22,838 per student, compared to $44,740 per student in Grosse Point Farms, $45,517 per student in Birmingham, and $68,873 in Dearborn."

The Detroit defendants recognized that the district's fiscal problems would only increase as the industrial base continued to leave the city along with its more affluent residents. They called on their primary education expert, Dr. Robert Guthrie of Stanford University, who testified that any desegregation plan should not be limited to Detroit, but should cover the metropolitan area. Only a metropolitan remedy, Guthrie said, would provide "maximum educational opportunity." Guthrie's testimony, along with that of other education experts, pushed the case in the direction of examining the factors affecting educational achievement rather than the question of racial segregation of public schools. And, as Dimond noted later, "a battle between various expert witnesses ensued over the relevance and impact of disparities in diverse educational 'inputs' and 'outputs' for black as compared to white schools."

Following the board's defense, counsel for the Detroit Federation of Teachers (DFT) presented the case against claims of unlawful faculty segregation. Ted Sachs and his co-counsel called primarily on two witnesses: Mary Ellen Riordan and John Elliott, president and vice president, respectively, of the DFT. Riordan testified that the DFT "has had a policy of favoring integration and promoting integration as far back as I have ever been able to trace any history of the organization." She indicated that in the early 1960s a teaching shortage in Detroit had a substantial effect on promoting the integration of the teaching staff among schools, in that many teachers took positions in the suburbs or other systems rather than risk being assigned to inner-city schools. Responding to Sach's question of whether there were, in fact, problems in schools in the inner city, she highlighted large class sizes, high student turnover, the age of buildings, the inability of families to organize parent groups to raise money for extra equipment and supplies, and the lack of sufficient communication with parents about their children's progress. The latter, she claimed, was difficult because in many families, having both parents working outside the home made it difficult to set up meetings, and because teachers were wary of visiting unsafe neighborhoods.

One explanation given for segregated teaching assignments was that in the 1950s and early 1960s, black teachers were not being hired by suburban districts, and, according to Riordan, many of them preferred black schools because they "categorized movement into previously all-white schools as having their chance to be either a guinea pig or missionary, and they didn't care much for either one." She credited Detroit school officials with engaging in a major project to recruit black teachers from southern colleges and universities, resulting in the doubling of their numbers over a ten-year period. Riordan also noted that in the 1960s, the DFT confronted the school board about racial policies affecting the assignment of teachers.

In his testimony, Elliott picked up on Riordan's introduction of the DFT's "balanced staff" concept used in the assignment of teachers. Adopted by the board in 1962 and included in the collective bargaining agreement, the balanced staff concept uses the criteria of race, sex, and experience and seeks to have schools that include blacks and whites, men and women, and both new and experienced teachers. Sachs asked Elliott whether he believed that the balanced staff policy should require a "precise mix "of each of the three criteria in each school in the district. Elliott responded that "the city . . . is or can be a series of communities of varying degrees, socially, economically, religiously, anything you can name and their needs are different and therefore school staffs may have to differ from city to city and community to community and from school to school." He also indicated his opposition to reassigning teachers in order to have each school reflect the systemwide racial proportion of the faculty, claiming that this would be counterproductive because "you need flexibility in assigning any teacher to a school."

Waiting for Judgment Day

Following final testimony and closing statements from counsel, on July 22, 1971, the trial ended, and the parties anxiously awaited Judge Roth's decision. Meanwhile, preparations for the 1971–1972 school year were under way. In Pontiac, the pot was beginning to boil over with the pending implementation of Judge Keith's busing order. Local white parents had formed an antibusing group known as the National Action Group (NAG), which organized protests against the plan, including a rally that attracted 5,000 attendees and featured as a keynote speaker Alabama's segregationist governor, George Wallace. Historian David Riddle described the city as being "in a state of near rebellion the week before the busing plan was to go into effect." Some protestors turned to violence. On the night of August 30, ten school buses in the district's parking lot were blown up. Six members of the local Ku Klux Klan were arrested. One was Robert Miles, the grand dragon of the Michigan Klan, who lived in the nearby community of Howell. A week after the bus burning, six women protested by chaining themselves to a fence in the school bus parking lot, and a week after this busing opponents used Pontiac's General Motors Fisher Body plant to stage another protest. Five hundred picketers blocked the gates to the plant, and, despite pleas from UAW officials, workers refused to cross the picket lines.

Judge Roth's Ruling on Segregation

The tension and hostility surrounding the busing issue soon would extend from Pontiac to Detroit and its suburbs. On September 27, 1971, Judge Roth issued his first ruling, finding for the plaintiffs on the claims that the Detroit public schools were illegally segregated because of both housing segregation and de jure school segregation by the local and state defendants. "Residential segregation within the city and throughout the larger metropolitan area is substantial, pervasive and of long standing," said Roth, and "is, in the main the result of past and present practices and customs of racial discrimination, both public and private, which . . . restrict the housing opportunities of black people." He declared that government policies, particularly those of FHA and VA, combined with practices of "loaning institutions, real estate associations, and brokerage firms, to establish and to maintain the pattern of residential segregation in the Detroit metropolitan area." Noting that it would be unfair to charge the school authorities with what other governmental units had done, Roth concluded that they nevertheless bore some responsibility for the segregated housing conditions. "Just as there is an interaction between residential patterns and the racial composition of the schools, so there is a corresponding effect on the residential pattern by the racial composition of the schools."

Turning to the question of how the decisions of local school authorities worked to create and maintain segregation in the public school system, Judge Roth pointed to the use of optional attendance zones; transportation policies for relieving overcrowding in schools; the alteration of attendance zones, grade structures, and feeder patterns; and school construction decisions. Beginning in the 1950s, the creation of optional attendance zones in neighborhoods experiencing

racial transition and between high school attendance areas of opposite racial compositions had the "natural, probable, foreseeable, and
actual effect" of allowing white students to "escape identifiably 'black'
schools." The school board, Roth noted, admitted to busing black students past closer white schools with available space to black schools,
a practice that continued despite the board's 1967 adoption of a policy to use transportation to increase integration. Furthermore, Roth
declared, except for a situation involving the burning of a white
school, the "Board has never bused white children to predominantly
black schools . . . despite the enormous amount of space available in
inner-city schools." On attendance zones and feeder patterns, he drew
these conclusions:

The Board admits at least one instance where it purposefully and
intentionally built and maintained a school and its attendance zone
to contain black students. Throughout the last decade (and
presently) school attendance zones of opposite racial compositions
have been separated by north-south boundary lines, despite the
Board's awareness (since at least 1962) that drawing boundary lines in
an east-west direction would result in significant integration. The
natural and actual effect of these acts and failures to act has been the
creation and perpetuation of school segregation. There has never
been a feeder pattern or zoning change which placed a predominantly white residential area into a predominantly black school zone
or feeder pattern. Every school which was 90% or more black in
1960, and which is still in use today, remains 90% or more black.
Whereas 65.8% of Detroit's black students attended 90% or more
black schools in 1960, 74.9% of the black students attended 90% or
more black schools during the 1970–71 school year.

On school construction decisions, Roth criticized the Detroit
board — and the state defendants — for not following a policy statement
issued jointly by the State Board of Education and the Michigan Civil
Rights Commission in 1966. "Local school boards must consider the
factor of racial balance along with other educational considerations in
making decisions about selection of new school sites, expansion of
present facilities. . . . Each of these situations presents an opportunity
for integration." Similarly, the state board's "School Plant Planning

Handbook" calls for taking "care in site locations" if housing patterns would result in schools largely segregated by race. Board decisions on school construction since 1959, however, had created virtually all-white and all-black schools which "contain[ed] the black population and perpetuat[ed] and compound[ed] school segregation.

Judge Roth held that the state defendants were, in fact, responsible for public education in the state, and he determined that they "acted directly to control and maintain the pattern of segregation in the Detroit schools." He based their liability on these factors: (1) funding decisions and financial arrangements that favored "neighboring, mostly white suburban districts" and which "created and perpetuated systematic educational inequities," (2) state approval of school construction that was consistent with "discriminatory practices" that "advanced . . . racial segregation," and (3) passage of Act 48, which repealed the local board's April 7 desegregation plan, required neighborhood schools, and reorganized the Detroit system into eight regions along racial lines. Act 48's purpose and effect, according to the judge, was to maintain segregation.

By contrast, Judge Roth actually praised the Detroit board's decisions on hiring and assigning faculty as one of "many fine steps . . . taken to advance the cause of quality education for all in terms of racial integration and human relations." He concluded that black teachers and administrators were not hired during the time period in question because they "were not readily available." He credited the board and the teachers union (DFT) for following "a most advanced and exemplary course in adopting and carrying out . . . the 'balanced staff concept' which seeks to balance faculties in each school with respect to race, sex and experience, with primary emphasis on race." Among a number of positive findings, Roth cited the board's success in recruiting black teachers and administrators in the decade between 1960 and 1970: an increase from 23.3 percent to 42.1 percent among teachers and 4.5 percent to 37.8 percent among administrators.

After issuing his findings of fact, Judge Roth announced the legal principles prescribed by the Supreme Court to be applied in determining whether the state can be found guilty of de jure segregation: (1) state agents, including state and local authorities "have taken . . . action with a purpose of segregation," (2) the "action . . . [has] created or aggravated segregation in the schools," and (3) "a current condition of segregation exists." Applying this test, Roth found that the state of Michigan and the Detroit Board of Education had "committed acts which have been causal factors in the segregated condition of the public schools of the City of Detroit." In summing up the violations and the relationship between housing and school segregation, he also criticized the de jure/de facto distinction in segregation law:

> The principal causes undeniably have been population movement and housing patterns, but state and local governmental actions, including school board actions, have played a substantial role in promoting segregation. It is . . . unfortunate that we cannot deal with public school segregation on a no-fault basis, for if racial segregation in our public schools is an evil, then it should make no difference whether we classify it *de jure* or *de facto*. Our objective, logically . . . should be to remedy a condition which we believe needs correction.

Finally, a few days before the trial ended, Alexander Ritchie, attorney for CCBE, in his quest for a metropolitan remedy, had filed a motion with the court to include as additional defendants the other eighty-five districts in the tri-county area — Wayne, Macomb, and Oakland counties. (Detroit is in Wayne County.) He described them as largely "white segregated school districts" and included a detailed chart containing data on the racial composition of the student body in each district. Ritchie asserted that if Judge Roth were to rule in favor of the plaintiffs, "complete relief cannot be awarded" without the inclusion of the proposed districts, and an unconstitutional burden would be imposed on the intervening defendant "in that the resulting school district of the City of Detroit . . . will remain . . . an inferior school district." None of the other defendants joined Ritchie's motion, and the plaintiffs also opposed it. At the end of his opinion on the issue of segregation, Judge Roth announced that he would not rule on Ritchie's motion to add the suburbs at that time, because "the circumstances of the case require judicial intervention and equitable relief, and it would be improper . . . to act on this motion until the other parties to the action have had an opportunity to submit their proposals for desegregation." In concluding, he invited Ritchie to amend the motion and to "resubmit it as a comprehensive plan of desegregation." The state and local defendants did not wait for Roth to issue a remedy before appealing to the Sixth Circuit.

One week after the ruling, Judge Roth held a meeting with counsel to determine how to proceed. Unlike previous hearings on the case, on October 4, 1971, the courtroom was packed with reporters, other spectators, and attorneys representing the interests of suburban school districts. Roth indicated his skepticism regarding a Detroit-only remedy, opining that "perhaps only a plan which embraces all or some of the greater Detroit metropolitan area can hope to succeed in giving our children the kind of education they are entitled to constitutionally." He ordered the Detroit board to submit within 30 days a progress report on the magnet school plan that he had ordered at the start of the trial. In addition, he ordered the Detroit officials to submit a desegregation plan within 60 days; state defendants were given 120 days to submit a metropolitan plan for desegregation. The other parties were allocated 30 days to object to the plans of the local and state officials or to offer their own alternatives. Finally, he reaffirmed his earlier decision to put off the question of joining the suburban districts as defendants.

————

Reactions to Roth's Segregation Ruling

Roth's ruling was remarkable, especially given his attitude and demeanor when the plaintiffs first began the case. Paul Dimond observes, "In the yearlong battle over the segregation of the Detroit public schools initiated by Act 48, we had witnessed a dramatic conversion. We saw a man — who only eight months before had invited us to leave — listen and hear and think and feel for forty-one trial days. In the course of the drama in his courtroom, Judge Roth came to know the color line of racial ghettoization in his own state." Others, however, reacted differently. Based on the reaction of some segments of the Detroit metropolitan community, outside observers might have thought that Judge Roth was guilty of murder or some other unspeakable crime. For months after the decision, the attacks on him were relentless. "ROTH IS A FOUR-LETTER WORD." "PITH ON ROTH." "Judge ROTH IS A CHILD MOLESTER." All of these appeared on bumper stickers throughout the Detroit area. The case was derisively referred to as the "Roth case." In the suburb of Wyandotte, during a boisterous rally, protestors hung him in effigy at the end of a mock trial. In the face of numerous death threats, federal marshals and the local police had to be called on to protect the judge and his family.

While no remedy had yet been ordered, the mere specter of a school busing plan involving the suburbs was too much for many. Within a few days of the October 4 hearing, Michigan's Republican junior senator Robert Griffin introduced into the U.S. Congress an amendment to the U.S. Constitution to prohibit busing as a remedy for school desegregation. He was quickly joined by his Republican colleagues from Michigan in the House of Representatives. This initially posed a dilemma for Michigan's white Democratic house members because many of them previously had supported civil rights, including passage of the Civil Rights Act of 1964 and the Voting Rights Act of 1965. But because they represented all-white suburbs, concerns about reelection led them to join the call for a constitutional amendment to ban busing. Philip Hart, Michigan's Democratic senior senator, was the only white member of its congressional delegation to support busing. Responding to questions about a recall effort initiated against him by citizens in the suburb of Roseville, Hart said, "Of course I'm concerned. If you like the Senate — and I do — then you don't like to see those you work for so terribly upset." But, he noted further, "Whenever there was a finding of deliberate school segregation in the South, I supported busing if that was the only way to correct it. If I were to change my position now that the issue has come home, Michigan would have a fraud for a senior senator." The recall movement eventually died, and Hart led a successful Senate filibuster against the constitutional amendment.

Democratic officials at the state level also found themselves caught between their traditional support for civil rights, on the one hand, and local party leaders and their constituents who adamantly opposed busing for desegregation, on the other. Two days after Roth's ruling, by a 67-40 vote, the Democratic State Central Committee adopted a lukewarm endorsement of busing. "We accept busing as an imperfect and temporary mechanism to help erase the imbalances in our educational system." Even this mild statement failed to satisfy some officials from metropolitan Detroit; for example, delegates from Macomb County voted 7-1 against it, with one abstention.

White suburban opposition to school busing for desegregation continued through the next several months. While residents in suburbs throughout the metropolitan area protested the possibility of cross-district busing, it was the city of Warren that became the hotbed of protest activity. Especially critical to whipping up the antibusing frenzy was the *Macomb Daily*, a newspaper published in Macomb County. According to historian David Riddle, "it would overstate the case to say that the *Macomb Daily* created the antibusing movement in Macomb County," but the editors, particularly Mitch Kehetian, editor at the Warren desk, clearly were opposed to cross-district busing. An editorial in the October 1 edition bears this out. "We do not subscribe to the theory that forced integration through busing across district lines is helping the cause. . . . We feel such long distance busing will, ultimately, defeat the proper purpose for which it is designed because . . . penalizing the suburbs for the failings of the core city does nothing but fan the flames of discontent." "The paper," Riddle continues, "kept the topic in front of the news stories when there were no new developments to report. It created a special busing section in the letters to the editor. It also took care to announce upcoming antibusing rallies."

The Quest for a Remedy

Two important personnel changes occurred on the Supreme Court during the fall of 1971. On October 22, President Nixon nominated William Rehnquist and Lewis Powell to succeed Justices John Marshall Harlan and Hugo Black, respectively, and they received Senate confirmation in early December. Harlan retired on September 23 after sixteen years of service, while Black died two days later, having served thirty-four years. Powell, a Richmond, Virginia, attorney and former president of the Richmond Board of Education, was credited with resisting the efforts of segregationists during the 1950s to close down the public school system in defiance of the *Brown* decision. Powell's appointment was part of President Nixon's "southern strategy" to win reelection by appealing to white southerners who had become disillusioned with the Democratic Party over its support of civil rights. His attempt to appoint a white southerner to fill the vacancy created by Justice Abe Fortas's resignation had failed. Nixon's first nominee was rejected primarily because of ethical improprieties. The second was attacked because of his weak credentials, but claims of racial bias also had surfaced. Powell, however, was a well-respected partner at a prestigious law firm and was perceived as carrying very little racial baggage. This was so despite the fact that in *Swann* he had submitted an antibusing amicus curiae brief on behalf of Virginia, and no meaningful desegregation of Richmond schools occurred during his tenure as board president.

More important, perhaps, was that most of the attention went to Rehnquist, who had a more controversial record. Rehnquist, who served as a law clerk to Justice Robert Jackson when *Brown* was first argued, had drafted a memorandum in 1953 arguing for maintaining *Plessy v. Ferguson*'s "separate but equal" doctrine. In 1971, Rehnquist denied that these were his views, claiming that he simply was following Jackson's directions to draft a pro-segregation memo. Adding fuel to claims of racial insensitivity were charges that he had harassed black voters when he was coordinator of the Republican Party's poll-watching activities in Arizona in the 1960s. At the time of his nomination, Rehnquist was serving as head of the Office of Legal Counsel in Nixon's Justice Department, and he was recommended by colleagues who touted him as a strong conservative and strict constructionist who would help the president to move the Court in a more conservative direction.

In early November 1971, the Detroit board submitted its evaluation of the magnet plan; it showed that very little desegregation had taken place. The authors reported a survey revealing that students, parents, staff, and board members believed that the magnet program was providing a better education, and they concluded that it achieved greater success at the middle school level than in the high schools. But they acknowledged that the nonmagnet schools remained heavily segregated, and, especially at the high school level, the "Magnet Plan accelerated the movement of white students out of majority black schools." Nonetheless, the report recommended continuing the magnet approach while admitting that it would "require greater inputs of money to build and maintain high quality in staff and program and community support." The authors also concluded that to reach Detroit's students on a larger basis, the "Magnet Plan . . . will have to cross district boundaries."

As the parties prepared their remedy plans in Detroit, federal district judge Robert Merhige announced his ruling in the Richmond case, which had been brought by the NAACP-LDF and argued by Lou Lucas and Norm Chachkin the previous year. In January 1972, Judge Merhige ordered a metropolitan desegregation program that included Richmond public schools and also those in Henrico and Chesterfield County. It was still unclear, however, whether the increasingly conservative Fourth Circuit would accept such a plan. The next month, the Sixth Circuit dismissed the appeals of Judge Roth's ruling by the Detroit board and the state defendants. The appellate court held that since no remedy had yet been granted or denied, there was nothing to review.

On March 15, 1972, Judge Roth accepted petitions to intervene from a white citizens' group and from suburban school districts. The suburban white citizens' group was represented by Robert Lord, who had been active in the antibusing campaign in Macomb County. William Saxton, a well-respected trial lawyer at one of Detroit's oldest, most prestigious firms, represented forty of the districts. Dr. Fred Davenport, superintendent of the Wyandotte school district, contacted Saxton, who had successfully represented Wyandotte years earlier in a challenge to the district's expulsion of a student for violating its grooming code. Saxton reluctantly agreed to represent Wyandotte and the other districts but only if they would agree to a joint arrangement, with three to five representatives working directly with him. The rationale for a consortium was twofold. First, it would be too difficult and inefficient to handle forty cases separately, but, more importantly, he was concerned about potential conflicts of interest. As he described in an interview, he did not want to have the districts play each other off against the others, so he cautioned that they would have to be of one mind in opposing cross-district busing on legal grounds. Only a few other suburban districts — Grosse Pointe, Southfield, and Royal Oak — chose to retain separate counsel. While these other districts had their own attorneys, they did not make arguments or file briefs; that work was left to Saxton.

Judge Roth accepted the petitions for intervention on the condition that the intervenors would not focus on factual or legal issues already decided. Saxton filed a motion rejecting these conditions on the grounds that his clients were not involved in the previous hearings, and he stressed that there had not been proofs presented that these districts were guilty of independent segregative acts. Counsel for the other suburbs seconded Saxton's complaints.

The hearings on the Detroit-only plans were held March 14–21, with testimony from local and state school officials, education scholars, and transportation experts. After these hearings, but before ruling on the plans, on March 24, Judge Roth issued a ruling declaring that it would be appropriate to consider metropolitan plans if that were deemed necessary to remedy the constitutional violation. He rejected the state defendants' arguments that no " 'state action' has had a part in the segregation found to exist" and that the state had delegated authority over education to local governmental bodies whose "sovereign powers . . . may not be disturbed by either the State or the court." These claims, Roth said, "we cannot accept. Political subdivisions of the states have never been considered sovereign entities, rather 'They have been traditionally regarded as subordinate governmental instrumentalities created by the state to assist it in carrying out of state governmental functions.' " He also pointed to the passage of Act 48 as evidence of the state's power over education and concluded that the state could not "evade its constitutional responsibility by a delegation of powers to local units of government."

Rejecting Saxton's claim that the suburban districts could not be considered in developing a remedy "absent a finding of acts of segregation on their part," Roth conceded that the Supreme Court had not yet ruled directly on the issue. But he pointed to the 1968 decision in *Green v. County School Board*, which called for desegregation plans to be evaluated on the basis of their potential effectiveness and their "promise realistically to work now and hereafter to produce the maximum actual desegregation." He then quoted from the *Brown II* implementation ruling, which held that in fashioning remedies, "courts may consider problems related to administration, arising from the physical condition of the school plant, the school transportation systems, personnel, *revision of school districts and attendance areas* into compact units to achieve a system of determining admission to the public schools on a nonracial basis, and *revision of local laws and regulations* which may be necessary in solving the foregoing problems" [emphasis added].

On March 28, in rejecting the Detroit-only desegregation plans, Roth criticized the proposals offered by both the Detroit board and the NAACP plaintiffs, each of which had critiqued the other. He joined the plaintiffs in concluding that neither of the proposals offered by the board—"free transfers" that would basically expand the existing magnet school program or a part-time desegregation plan that would involve only a few grades for two and one-half days per week—"are legally sufficient because they do not promise to effect significant desegregation." Similarly, he agreed with the board that the plaintiffs' plan should be rejected. Plaintiffs proposed that school attendance boundaries be redrawn along the lines of the April 7 plan, with some pairing and clustering of schools. With pairing, two schools of opposite race would be joined; for example, all students in grades K–3 would attend one school, with those in grades 4 to 6 attending the other. Clustering entails joining three or more schools in a similar fashion: K–2, grades 3 and 4, and grades 5 and 6.

The defendant board continued to deny that it was guilty of any act of segregation, but it argued that if desegregation were to take place, a metropolitan plan was preferable to the plaintiffs' Detroit-only remedy. A plan limited to Detroit, the board claimed, would only increase white flight from the Detroit schools, resulting in a virtually all-black Detroit district surrounded by all-white suburban districts. The plaintiffs stressed that the issue was not that majority-black schools were inherently "educationally or legally unsound" but that the schools were the result of state-imposed segregation. They contended further that a Detroit-only plan would at least begin the desegregation process, rather than having to wait for years for metropolitan relief.

Roth sided with the board defendants on this point. Although acknowledging that the "Plaintiffs' plan would accomplish more desegregation than now obtains in the system, or would be achieved under [defendants' two plans]," Roth concluded that it "would clearly make the entire Detroit public school system racially identifiable as Black." The district at that point was 70 percent black, and under the plaintiffs' plan, there would no longer be all-black or all-white schools. Moreover, black students would constitute a majority in each of the schools, with percentages ranging from 55 to 75 percent. Roth also seconded defendants' claims of the likelihood of increased white flight and maintained that the plaintiffs' plan would not lay a proper foundation for metropolitan relief were that to be necessary. He concluded: it is "inescapable that relief of segregation in the public schools of the

City of Detroit cannot be accomplished within the corporate geographical limits of the city. The State, however, cannot escape its constitutional duty to desegregate the public schools of the City of Detroit by pleading local authority."

Another set of hearings was held between March 28 and April 14 on the various metropolitan "plans" that were submitted by the state defendants, the Detroit board, the NAACP plaintiffs, and the Ritchie-led white parents' group from Detroit (CCBE). The hearings focused on a number of organizational and planning issues, including appropriate methods of pupil reassignment; quality and capacity of school facilities; transportation needs; the effects of new school construction on desegregation efforts; the reassignment of faculty; temporary and permanent administrative and financial arrangements; and appropriate community, parental, staff, and pupil involvement in the process. The state board submitted six "proposals" but refused to offer a preference: (1) remedial education programs as an alternative to desegregation, (2) a one-way plan that would send black students to suburban schools but not white suburban pupils to schools in the city, (3) a "free choice" program, (4) the magnet school approach, (5) a part-time program similar to that proposed by the Detroit board, and (6) reorganization of thirty-six districts similar to a proposal suggested by former Detroit board chairman Abraham Zwerdling in 1969. Judge Roth concluded that none of the proposals would effectively desegregate the Detroit school system. The other state defendants, Governor Milliken and Attorney General Kelley, filed objections to the six "plans."

The Detroit board's plan was to include reassignment of students at all grade levels in sixty-nine of the eighty-six districts in the tri-county area, while the CCBE recommended a sixty-two-district plan, with desegregation to begin after the fourth grade. The NAACP plaintiffs suggested plans similar to those of the Detroit board and CCBE but covering a smaller area — fifty-four districts. During the hearings, however, William Saxton, representing the suburban districts, continued to argue that a plan involving the suburbs was inappropriate. He pressed the idea that the 1971 *Swann* decision affirmed the concept that "the nature of the violation determines the scope of the remedy." Thus, Saxton contended, the remedy must be limited to the Detroit school district because that was where the de jure segregation was found — not in the suburban schools. To counter this claim and bolster their argument of state responsibility for a metropolitan remedy, the plaintiffs offered additional evidence. They demonstrated that the pattern of one-race school construction and faculty assignments was not limited to Detroit but extended throughout the metropolitan area. They also included state board computer printouts to show the massive amount of school construction that took place in the suburbs after 1950, and they provided statistics on the current racial composition of the student body and staffs in suburban schools to illustrate the extent of segregation there.

During the two-month period between the end of the hearings and Judge Roth's June 14 ruling on the metropolitan plans, the school busing issue drew increased state and national attention. To the chagrin of Democratic Party officials, in mid-May, George Wallace, campaigning on a strong antibusing platform, won the Michigan Democratic presidential primary. He received overwhelming support from voters in Macomb County, as well as the predominantly white wards in Detroit.

After Wallace's victory, President Nixon directed his aides to "hit the busing issue stand in a strong, unequivocal way," especially in Michigan. National public opinion polls were showing significant public opposition to busing. Ironically, polls from the late 1950s through the 1960s had shown increasing support for integrated schools, even in the South, but support for integration clearly did not mean support for busing. According to a 1972 Harris Survey, busing opponents outnumbered supporters by nearly three to one. Gallup polling from 1970 and 1971 showed even more opposition, as less than one-fifth of the respondents supported busing.

President Nixon already had called for a moratorium on busing and for a law to restrict busing if a constitutional amendment could not gain adequate support. In a special message to Congress in March 1972, he said that busing was "a classic case of the remedy for one evil creating another evil," and he insisted "rather than require the spending of scarce resources on ever-longer bus rides . . . we should encourage the putting of those resources directly into education." In memoirs about his years as one of Nixon's chief aides, John Ehrlichman claims that the president was against busing for desegregation because he believed that African American children were *"genetically inferior* to whites. All the Federal money and programs we could devise could

126   { *Chapter 5* }

not change that fact, [Nixon] believed. Blacks could never achieve parity — in intelligence, economic success or social qualities" (italics in original). Whatever the source of his opposition, Nixon instructed his attorney general to intervene in the Detroit case to oppose any metropolitan busing plan. Judge Roth denied the local U.S. attorney's request to intervene, but he invited him to participate as amicus curiae.

Judge Roth Issues His Ruling on the Remedy

In his June 14 ruling, Roth began by emphasizing that after finding de jure segregation in the Detroit public schools, the task for the court, in keeping with *Brown*, was about how to desegregate those schools. He conceded that "the court has taken no proofs with respect to the establishment of the boundaries of the eighty-six school districts in the Counties of Wayne, Oakland and Macomb, nor on the issue of whether, with the exclusion of the city of Detroit school district, such school districts have committed acts of *de jure* segregation." But, Roth added, "the remedy upon finding *de jure* segregation is prompt and maximum actual desegregation of the public school by all reasonable, feasible, and practicable means available." Emphasizing that the "legal effects of racially discriminatory confinement *to* a school district are not different from the effects of such containment *within* a district," he said the court's obligation was to "eliminate the continuing effects of such violation" [emphasis added]. For Roth, the racial segregation that existed between the schools in Detroit and those in the suburbs was no different from segregating black and white students in schools inside Detroit.

During the hearings on the metropolitan plans, one of Saxton's arguments focused on educational theory and research related to the effects of various factors on achievement test scores. Based on this research, he argued that the factor most correlated with achievement is socioeconomic status; in effect, recasting the issue as one of educational quality rather than government-imposed segregation. Roth rejected this line of reasoning: "Insofar as pupil assignments are concerned, the system of public schooling in every state must be operated in a racially non-discriminatory, unified fashion . . . . The adoption of an education theory having the effect of maintaining a pattern of *de jure* segregation is therefore clearly impermissible."

Turning to the proposals offered by the state defendants, the Detroit board, the CCBE intervenors, and the plaintiffs, Roth concluded that none of these was sufficient by itself to achieve desegregation of the Detroit public schools. He was especially critical of the state defendants, chiding them for refusing to make a recommendation about the appropriate area for desegregation and for "their stubborn insistence that under their self-serving, and therefore self-limiting, view of their powers they were free to ignore the clear order of this court." Roth viewed the state defendants as the "primary defendants" responsible for initiating an effective proposal because the authority of the Detroit board did not extend beyond the city's geographical limits. The state, however, had shirked its responsibility.

Judge Roth discussed several matters to be dealt with in developing a feasible and effective desegregation plan. First, to determine the appropriate geographic area, he examined the proposals offered by the various defendants and the plaintiffs, focusing on time and distance limitations for pupil transportation, the ability to eliminate racially identifiable schools, and the possibility for "maximum feasible desegregation." The plaintiffs' proposal, affecting fifty-four of the eighty-six school districts in the tri-county area (including Detroit), was accepted as "practicable, feasible, and sound." The other districts were excluded either because they were too far from the city—beyond an approximately forty-minute bus ride—or because their schools already were not racially identifiable. Responding to criticism that the proposed forty-minute guideline would pose a hardship on students, Roth held it to be reasonable, given that one- to one-and-one-half-hour rides one-way already were standard practice in some districts. He emphasized bus transportation of students as a "long-standing, sound practice in elementary and secondary schools," and added, "For school authorities to now object to such transportation practices raises the inference not of hostility to pupil transportation but rather racially motivated hostility to the desegregated school at the end of the ride."

Judge Roth pointed to data showing that in the tri-county area 42 to 52 percent of students were transported by bus to their schools, compared to the 40 percent to be affected within the proposed desegregation area. Concerned about a potential disproportionate effect of reassignments and busing on black students, he encouraged that efforts be made to ensure a "two-way," fair application to both races.

"Although the number of black and white children transported and reassigned at the outset will be roughly equal, it is inevitable that a larger proportion of black children will be transported for a greater proportion of their school years than white children, if transportation overall is to be minimized." To help in this regard, he suggested randomizing the location of grade centers and utilizing "under-capacity inner-city schools" in the short term and adding new schools in Detroit in the long term.

In discussing the issue of school construction, Roth reiterated his earlier findings of the two-way interaction between housing segregation and school segregation in the entire Detroit metropolitan area, the effect of school construction in the tri-county area on the racial composition of schools, and the state's role in funding construction that "advanced or perpetuated racial segregation in these schools." He called for reevaluation of new school construction based on the state's School Plant Planning Handbook, which cautioned care in decisions on site selection in order to avoid maintaining segregation. Faculty and staff reassignment was deemed necessary to an effective desegregation process, and the judge gave directions to base such reassignments on qualifications for subject and grade level first, and then to add the factors of race, experience, and sex. The focus should not be on quotas or racial balance in each school, he stressed, but efforts to hire additional black faculty and staff should continue.

The state defendants, particularly the state board of education, were given the task of investigating and reporting on recommendations about the various governance, financial, and administrative arrangements necessary for implementing desegregation on both an interim and a permanent basis. Judge Roth suggested several additional factors for implementing an effective plan: the creation of biracial councils composed of parents, staff, and students to participate in the process; reevaluation of curriculum content, materials, and student codes; development of in-service training for faculty and staff for multiethnic studies and human relations; and a review of the grading, reporting, counseling, and testing program.

Judge Roth's ruling did not constitute an actual desegregation plan. He appointed and charged a special panel to prepare a student assignment plan and transportation plan within the parameters established in the opinion. The membership of this panel included a designee of the state superintendent, the transportation supervisor in the state Department of Education, three representatives of the Detroit board, an education expert selected by the plaintiffs, one representative each for the CCBE defendant-intervenors and the suburban defendant-intervenors, and a member of the Michigan Civil Rights Commission. Two additional members from teachers unions were added later — representatives of the DFT and the Michigan Education Association (MEA). The panel was directed to report back within forty-five days of the June 14 ruling with a specific plan to proceed. The Detroit board, state defendants, and suburban defendant-intervenors all immediately appealed the ruling to the Sixth Circuit Court of Appeals.

The Battle over Busing Continues

As the legal proceedings continued, public outrage against busing as a remedy for school segregation did not wane, particularly in the suburbs. In June, Congress passed an amendment to the Higher Education Act calling for a moratorium on busing. The amendment was introduced by Michigan congressional representative William Broomfield, a Republican from the suburb of Royal Oak, but the bill did not directly affect the Detroit case because it did not apply to cases already in the federal courts. School busing continued to have major repercussions on electoral politics beyond the Wallace victory in the Michigan Democratic presidential primary. In the 1972 elections, state Republicans included an antibusing resolution in their platform at the state convention in order to gain support from antibusing Democrats. Their strategy met with some success; for example, the mayor of Warren subsequently became a "Democrat for Nixon." The Democratic Party found itself in a bind, with local, state, and national party officials disagreeing over the issue. In a visit to a Detroit-area suburb shortly before the Michigan presidential primary, George McGovern, the frontrunner for the Democratic presidential nomination, announced his willingness to implement Roth's busing ruling despite his own opposition to cross-district busing, and he characterized busing as "an overblown issue." The busing issue became a major sticking point at the Democratic National Convention. Although a national resolution called for busing to be available as "another tool to accomplish desegregation," many local and state Democratic officials, including a majority of the Michigan delegation, were adamantly opposed.

The 1972 race for U.S. Senate between the incumbent Robert Griffin and his challenger, Attorney General Frank Kelley, demonstrates vividly the power of the busing issue in electoral politics. As noted earlier, almost immediately after the October 1971 hearing where Judge Roth indicated the possibility of a metropolitan remedy, Senator Griffin introduced a constitutional amendment to prohibit busing. In late July 1972, Griffin published in the *Macomb Daily* a one-page letter to Kelley titled "What Is Your Position on Busing?" In it, Griffin touted his fierce, consistent opposition, highlighting his introduction of the amendment, his support of a moratorium on busing, and his introduction of an amendment to the Higher Education Act seeking to withdraw the jurisdiction of federal courts to issue busing orders. He criticized Kelley both for his handling of the Detroit case and for making inconsistent statements on the busing issue. Pointing to the fact that Kelley signed the state party's lukewarm endorsement in October 1971 and then expressed disapproval of the national party's plank on busing in July 1972, Griffin taunted him: "I am at a loss to understand how you could support one and reject the other." The letter then requested Kelley to "answer, directly and forthrightly, some questions which Michigan voters have on their minds" about his position on busing and the proposals to prohibit it.

Although antibusing groups received most of the publicity for their protest activities, there were attempts to cool down the rhetoric and take a more open position on the subject. Even in Warren, a group called the Northeast Interfaith Center for Racial Justice appealed for moderation and calm. A broader organization, the Metropolitan Coalition for Peaceful Integration, consisting of religious, civic, and labor groups, suburban and city residents, and blacks and whites, came together to provide leadership and direction on the issue. The Catholic Diocese in Detroit, led by John Cardinal Dearden, called for restraint. Most importantly, he declared that Catholic schools would not be permitted to become partners in the fight against integration.

Parents, who have demonstrated no previous interest in Catholic education but now seek to enroll their children in a Catholic school, must expect to be questioned carefully regarding their motivation at this time in seeking a Catholic school education. Because it is important to eliminate any possibility that our schools become or even seem to become places of refuge for people who are seeking to avoid integrated education, it is to be expected that these people will not automatically be permitted to enroll their children in the Catholic school.

On July 5 the desegregation panel reported to Judge Roth that additional buses would be needed to implement the plan. Subsequently, Roth added the state treasurer as a defendant and ordered that funds be issued to purchase the buses requested by the panel. Nearly two weeks later, the Sixth Circuit granted the state defendants' motion to stay the order. On July 20 Judge Roth certified the major issues for appeal to the Sixth Circuit. The circuit court invited the U.S. attorney general to participate in order to defend the constitutionality of the federal busing moratorium.

The Sixth Circuit Court of Appeals Weighs In

A three-judge panel of the Sixth Circuit heard oral argument on August 24, 1972, in Cincinnati. The panel included Chief Judge Phillips and Judges Peck and Edwards; Phillips and Peck had participated in the *Deal* case. In *Deal*, the Sixth Circuit had rejected housing segregation as grounds for ordering school desegregation. Because of *Deal*, the plaintiffs placed more emphasis on the acts of de jure segregation by the Detroit board and state defendants, although they did not completely ignore the evidence of housing segregation. Attorney General Kelley argued that the state defendants were not guilty of any segregative acts, while the Detroit board emphasized that if the board were determined to be responsible for school segregation, the suburbs were in the same boat and a metropolitan remedy was necessary. By this time, George Roumell, a labor lawyer and arbitrator, had replaced George Bushnell as attorney for the Detroit board. William Saxton continued to argue that the constitutional violation extended only to Detroit, so the suburban districts, which had not even had their day in court, should not be included in the remedy. The assistant attorney general who arrived to defend the busing moratorium, argued instead against the metropolitan remedy, generally echoing Saxton's arguments.

While the panel deliberated, a new school year began amid the uncertainty about the future. Busing continued to be an important election issue in Michigan politics and in the presidential election. On November 4, President Nixon was reelected by a landslide vote, and Kelley lost to Griffin. Nixon received a substantial number of votes from traditional Democrats in the tri-county area affected by the busing plan, especially the rank-and-file members of the UAW. Although the UAW leadership supported "busing within reasonable limits" to bring about integration, its members refused to go along. Some scholars point to Nixon's success with this constituency as laying the groundwork for the emergence of what nearly a decade later became known as the Reagan Democrats in Macomb County.

Kelley remains convinced that he lost the election primarily because of voter opposition to busing. He recalls a particular television advertisement as key to his defeat: the screen opens to yellow school buses around 4:00 in the morning, with children being sent out in the darkness. The voice-over says: "Is this what you want for your children? Vote for Robert Griffin." Kelley says that the ads were even run in Michigan's Upper Peninsula (UP), hundreds of miles from the Detroit metropolitan area, and when UP residents were polled, many assumed that their children were going to be affected by the cross-district busing plan. Douglas Fraser, chair of the UAW's political action committee, invited Kelley to speak at an event shortly after the election. He recalled Kelley's words: "I got hit by a yellow bus on my way to Washington." The irony is that during the campaign, Kelley, as a defendant in *Milliken*, was arguing against Judge Roth's finding of illegal segregation against the state and Detroit board and against the metropolitan plan.

On election day another event of tremendous significance took place: Judge Roth suffered a massive heart attack. While some area residents sent get-well wishes, some of his critics were relentless, phoning the hospital to say, "I hope the bastard dies."

On December 8, as Roth continued recuperating at home, the three-judge panel unanimously affirmed his findings of de jure segregation of Detroit public schools by the Detroit school board and the state of Michigan and the impropriety and inadequacy of a Detroit-only remedy. The panel did, however, vacate portions of his ruling. The remedy was put on hold to give the state legislature time to fashion a remedy voluntarily, and the panel held that in the event of inaction by the legislature, the district court must hear every suburb affected by a cross-district remedy before ordering it. The panel also vacated the portion of the ruling designating the geographic desegregation area, but the court affirmed the standards for determining relief that Judge Roth had applied. Most significantly, the panel refused to consider relevance of proof of housing discrimination because this would have required overruling *Deal*. The justification was that the situation in Detroit was different from that in Cincinnati — the trial revealed evidence of de jure segregation by the Detroit board and state defendants, so the panel simply distinguished *Deal* as not relevant.

Paul Dimond writes that the plaintiffs were heartened by the ruling, but they were concerned because around the same time, the Fourth Circuit reversed Judge Merhige's decision that created a metropolitan remedy in Richmond, Virginia. The court specifically held that the segregation existing in the city of Richmond and its neighboring suburbs were the result of de facto housing segregation and the "root causes of the concentration of blacks in the inner cities of America are simply not known." Later, when the Supreme Court split 4-4 in the *Richmond* case, it became clear that the unanimous vote in *Swann* in 1971 had been misleading: the justices were much more divided on the issue of busing than it had appeared. (Justice Powell did not participate because he previously had served as president of the Richmond school board.) The 4-4 vote left the circuit court's decision standing, and it was not accompanied by an opinion offering specific guidance either to lower courts or other affected parties. The per curiam opinion stated simply: "The judgment is affirmed by an equally divided Court."

The defendants immediately sought en banc review of the three-judge panel's *Milliken* decision (meaning that all the appellate judges in the circuit would rehear the case) rather than appealing immediately to the Supreme Court. En banc review was granted on January 16, 1973, and on February 8 oral argument was heard before all nine judges. The plaintiffs and defendants generally reiterated the arguments they had presented to the three-judge panel, with one major exception. George Roumell, attorney for the Detroit board, announced that he would not argue against Judge Roth's finding of segregation but would recommend a metropolitan remedy: "Four distinguished judges of this Circuit—Judges Roth, Phillips, Peck, and Edwards—have reviewed the segregation findings against Detroit and the State. Although I may not be happy with their judgment, I do not intend to argue any further on that score. Instead, I want to explain the compelling reasons supporting a metropolitan remedy."

Four months later, on June 12, 1973, by a 6-3 vote, the Sixth Circuit, largely in agreement with the three-judge panel, affirmed Judge Roth's ruling on the issue of segregation and the need for metropolitan relief. In the majority opinion, Chief Judge Phillips reviewed the prior proceedings, with substantial attention to Judge Roth's finding of segregative acts by the Detroit board and state defendants. Phillips's opinion included key parts of the trial testimony concerning the drawing of attendance zones and pupil assignment practices, optional attendance zones, and building construction by the Detroit board, along with state responsibility for public education, the state's role in school construction and transportation decisions, and the passage of Act 48. He concluded that the "record in this case amply supports the findings of the District Court of unconstitutional actions by public officials at both the local and State level." But like the three-judge panel, the entire appeals court refused to review *Deal*. "In affirming the District Judge's findings of constitutional violations . . . we have not relied at all upon testimony pertaining to segregated housing except as school construction programs helped cause or maintain such segregation."

After reviewing Judge Roth's finding that a Detroit-only plan would not achieve desegregation of its public school system, Phillips noted that this case was different from the "classical school segregation case" in that his court had not previously dealt with a finding that anything less than a "metropolitan area plan would result in an all black school system immediately surrounded by practically all white suburban school systems." He appeared to accept the plaintiffs' emerging "containment" theory, writing that the "record reflects a present and expanding pattern of all black schools in Detroit (resulting in part from State action) separated only by school district boundaries from nearby all white schools. We cannot see how such segregation can be any less harmful to the minority students than if the same result were accomplished within one school district." Furthermore, given the findings of state responsibility, particularly that the state board's approval

of school construction in Detroit and the suburbs promoted segregation throughout the metropolitan area, the majority upheld Roth's call
for an areawide remedy:

> In the instant case, the only feasible desegregation plan involves
> the crossing of the boundary lines between the Detroit School Dis-
> trict and adjacent or nearby school districts for the limited purpose
> of providing an effective desegregation plan. The power to disre-
> gard such artificial barriers is all the more clear where, as here, the
> State has been guilty of discrimination which had the effect of cre-
> ating and maintaining racial segregation along school district lines.

In addition, Phillips expressed the majority's concern that to hold that
school district boundaries could not be crossed "would be opening a
way to nullify *Brown v. Board of Education*" and revive *Plessy v. Ferguson*'s "separate but equal" doctrine.

While agreeing that a metropolitan plan was both necessary and
within the power of the federal courts to grant equitable relief, the
court vacated Judge Roth's areawide remedy orders and remanded the
case to the district court for further proceedings. Phillips held that
the suburbs affected by his orders had the right to be heard on the
issue of metropolitan relief, but the district court did not need to
rehear the issues of the ruling on segregation and the insufficiency of
a Detroit-only remedy. Finally, the majority vacated Roth's July 11
order directing the purchase of school buses in preparation for implementation of the desegregation plan.

Each of the three dissenters wrote separately. Judge Wieck, the
author of *Deal*, attacked the majority for punishing innocent suburban white children and characterized the metropolitan plan as "ill-
conceived" and a "legal monstrosity." He assailed his colleagues for
distinguishing *Deal*, maintaining that school segregation was the result
of private housing choices. He also complained that there had been
no proof of de jure segregation by the suburban school districts, and
he asserted that the doctrine of sovereign immunity insulated the state
defendants from this lawsuit. Wieck called for a new trial to be
focused solely on a Detroit-only desegregation plan. Judge Kent, in
less bitter language, agreed that there were no findings of segregation
against the suburban districts. He argued, therefore, that the case

should be remanded, with all of the suburban districts in the tri-county area given the opportunity to participate in a hearing on all of the issues, "with particular attention to the necessity for finding a constitutional violation which would justify the imposition of a metropolitan remedy." Judge Miller thought the court's decision on the merits of the case was premature and "ill-advised." For him, the most appropriate action was to remand the case for a new trial on all the issues, including the issue of segregation, with full participation by all of the suburbs.

The state and suburban defendants then filed a petition of certiorari requesting review by the U.S. Supreme Court. It now was 1973; nearly three years had passed since the plaintiffs originally filed the case, and a resolution was yet to be determined. The fate of the public schools in metropolitan Detroit was in limbo as the parties waited to hear from the Supreme Court.

Getting Off the Bus

Milliken in the Supreme Court

On September 6, 1973, the state defendants and suburban school district defendant-intervenors filed petitions for certiorari, requesting Supreme Court review of the Sixth Circuit's en banc ruling. Under the high court's rules, in order for the petition to be granted, at least four justices must agree, a concept referred to as the "Rule of Four." At the time that cert petitions are filed, the terminology for referring to the parties in a case changes. When the losing party at the court below asks the Supreme Court to review the case, that party then becomes the "petitioner"; the prevailing party becomes the "respondent." In this case, therefore, the state defendants and the suburban school districts become the petitioners, while the original plaintiffs become the respondents. Here, although the Detroit school board lost in the trial court and court of appeals, it also became a respondent because it opposed the petition for review.

Briefs on the Petitions for Certiorari

The state defendants disputed the trial and appellate courts' findings of state liability for the segregation that existed in the Detroit school system. The brief challenged the ruling of state liability for metropolitan segregation, contending that "school districts are local state agencies of legislative creation exercising plenary discretionary power over student assignment within their respective districts." Consequently, the state could not be held vicariously liable for the actions of the Detroit school district. Moreover, the governor, attorney general, and state treasurer should be dismissed from the case, petitioners argued, because the lower courts had made no finding of unconstitutional conduct against them. The state defendants also argued that the court of appeals erroneously held that a Detroit-only desegregation plan could not remedy the unconstitutional segregation found in Detroit.

The briefs for both the state defendants and petitioner suburban school districts emphasized that a multidistrict remedy could not be imposed since no evidence was introduced showing that they had engaged in acts resulting in de jure segregation of their school systems. Furthermore, they contended, the suburban districts had been denied due process because they had not been included in all phases of the trial and early appeals.

In opposition to granting the cert petitions, the school board and NAACP argued that there was no specific desegregation plan before the Court for review, since the en banc court had vacated the remedy portion of the district court's ruling and remanded it for development of a metropolitan plan, with full participation from the affected suburbs. Upon remand, respondents asserted, the lower court would resolve issues concerning the extent and type of transportation to be utilized, the precise method of crossing school district boundaries to exchange students, the number of students to be included, and faculty transfers, if any. On the question of state liability for de jure segregation in the Detroit district, the school board brief stated that under Michigan law the state is responsible for education, and local school districts are "mere instrumentalities of the state." Consequently, because the de jure actions of the Detroit district are binding on the state, the state also has committed de jure acts of segregation and it alone "must provide a remedy."

School Desegregation Cases in Richmond and Denver

The arguments in the Supreme Court briefs in *Milliken*, particularly the merits briefs, which are filed after review is granted, were shaped significantly by two cases decided around the time that the Sixth Circuit made its en banc decision. On May 21, less than a month before the en banc ruling, the Supreme Court decided *Bradley v. School Board of Richmond* (1973), discussed in the previous chapter. The petitioners in *Milliken* picked up on the Fourth Circuit's argument that Judge Merhige was concerned simply with achieving racial balance in the school systems, and they consistently attributed similar motives to Judge Roth.

Keyes v. Denver School District No. 1 (1973), the second case bearing directly on *Milliken*, was decided on June 21, only nine days after the Sixth Circuit's ruling in *Milliken*. This was the first Supreme Court ruling to involve segregation in northern schools, and it concerned situations where segregation existed but was not imposed specifically by state law. The case involved two sets of schools in the Denver school system—those in the Park Hill community in the northeast section of the city and those in the core city area. After finding that the school board had taken deliberate actions to segregate the Park Hill schools, a federal district court ordered desegregation. But it refused to order desegregation of the entire district on the basis of the findings in Park Hill. The court of appeals affirmed this decision.

The Supreme Court upheld the order to desegregate the Park Hill schools but remanded the case for reconsideration of the issue of desegregating the entire district. Justice Brennan's majority opinion held that a finding of deliberate segregation in a significant part of a school system presumes intentional segregation by school authorities in other schools in that system. Most importantly, Brennan's opinion maintained the distinction from *Swann* between de jure and de facto segregation, stating that the relevant inquiry is the "purpose or intent to segregate." Brennan directed the district court to permit the school board to demonstrate that the Park Hill schools were separate from the other schools in the district and should be treated as an isolated entity. If the board failed, then the court was to examine whether the board actions regarding the Park Hill schools had the effect of creating a dual system. If so, the board had "the affirmative duty to desegregate the entire system 'root and branch.'" But even if the court determined that the board's actions in Park Hill did not create a dual system, the board nonetheless must prove that the core city schools were not intentionally segregated. Absent such proof, the lower court was authorized to "decree all-out desegregation of the core city schools."

The 7-1 vote in this case, like the unanimous decision in *Swann*, was misleading, with the justices much more divided than the vote made it appear. Burger concurred only in the result, without issuing an opinion. Douglas joined Brennan's majority opinion but wrote separately to argue that "there is no constitutional difference between de jure and de facto segregation, for each is the product of state actions or policies." In his opinion concurring and dissenting in part, Powell also criticized the de jure/de facto distinction, but he saw it as an example of northern hypocrisy:

> There is segregation in the schools of many [northern] cities fully as pervasive as that in southern cities prior to the desegregation decrees of the past decade and a half. The focus of the school desegregation problem has now shifted from the South to the country as a whole. Unwilling and footdragging as the process was in most places, substantial progress toward achieving integration has been made in Southern States. No comparable progress has been made in many nonsouthern cities with large minority populations primarily because of the *de facto/de jure* distinction nurtured by the courts and accepted complacently by many of the same voices which denounced the evils of segregated schools in the South. But if our national concern is for those who attend such schools, rather than for perpetuating a legalism rooted in history rather than present reality, we must recognize that the evil of operating separate schools is no less in Denver than in Atlanta.

His disagreement with the de jure/de facto distinction notwithstanding, Powell was not in favor of expansive judicial action in desegregating schools. He saw the "fundamental problem [as] residential segregation," which "result[s] from purely natural and neutral non-state causes." Powell sharply attacked busing as a means for desegregating schools, asserting that extensive student transportation was too disruptive and diverted resources necessary to provide the best quality education for all students. Simultaneously, he praised neighborhood schools as the foundation for a successful school system and healthy communities:

> Neighborhood school systems, neutrally administered, reflect the deeply felt desire of citizens for a sense of community in their public education. Public schools have been a traditional source of strength to our Nation, and that strength may derive in part from the identification of many schools with the personal features of the surrounding neighborhood. Community support, interest, and ded-

ication to public schools may well run higher with a neighborhood attendance pattern: distance may encourage disinterest.

Powell's position was not surprising. Two years earlier in *Swann*, before his appointment to the Supreme Court, he submitted an amicus brief on behalf of Virginia that made these very same arguments against busing and in favor of neighborhood schools: "The unique educational advantages of the neighborhood school system . . . result in the accomplishment of the ultimate goal of [the Equal Protection] clause: the best possible education for all children. Pursuit of absolute racial balance in major metropolitan areas through the use of extensive busing of students deprives the school system of the singular advantages of the neighborhood concept, and . . . thwarts the attainment of equal educational opportunity."

In his dissent in *Keyes*, Justice Rehnquist criticized the majority for its "drastic extension of *Brown*" (and *Green*) to school systems with no recent history of segregation mandated by law. He concluded, moreover, that the lower courts were correct in ruling that unconstitutional segregation in the Park Hill area did not imply that the entire district was unconstitutionally segregated.

Certiorari Granted and Merits Briefs
Filed in *Milliken*

On November 19, 1973, two months after the petitions were filed, six justices voted to accept review—Burger, Stewart, White, Blackmun, Powell, and Rehnquist—while Brennan, Douglas, and Marshall voted to deny it. Despite this strong vote, the question of the finality of the Sixth Circuit's ruling appears to have been of some concern. An unsigned typewritten memo dated November 6, probably from a law clerk, noted that "in the strict sense, there is no final decision in this case," but a handwritten note at the bottom offered a justification for review. "Someone will have to fudge a bit on the finality p[oin]t, but regardless it would probably be difficult for the [Court] to not take the case now. [The Sixth Circuit Court of Appeals] did say that a Detroit-only plan was 'unacceptable' so to that extent there is a final order on the general question of a metropolitan wide plan."

{ *Chapter 6* }

After review was granted, oral argument was scheduled for February 27, 1974. Oral argument is the only point in a Supreme Court case where counsel for the parties have the opportunity to address the justices directly. At this point, there actually were three cases to be considered, and they were consolidated into one, with *Milliken v. Bradley*, the original suit, as the lead case. *Allen Park Public Schools et al. v. Bradley* referred to the suit filed by William Saxton on behalf of forty suburban districts, while the third case, *Grosse Pointe Public School System v. Bradley*, concerned only that school district. After certiorari is granted and the date for oral argument set, petitioners and respondents must file new briefs arguing the merits of the case.

Petitioners' Briefs

The briefs for the state and suburban petitioners repeated and expanded on the arguments made in support of their cert petitions, especially the underlying theme that the lower courts' decisions, especially Judge Roth's rulings, were based on their desire to achieve a social goal of racial balance. The state brief cited a statement from Judge Roth during a pretrial conference at the remedy phase of the hearings: "In reality, our courts are called upon, in these school cases, to attain a social goal through the educational system, by using law as a lever."

Then, emphasizing that *Keyes* requires proof of intent to segregate, the state petitioners maintained that they had not engaged in any purposeful acts resulting in de jure segregation either within Detroit or between Detroit and other school districts in the tri-county area. They disputed the trial court's findings regarding state responsibility for segregation, labeling them as clearly erroneous. (These findings were related to discrimination in transportation funding, decisions about school construction, passage of Section 12 of Public Act 48, and the transportation of black students in the Carver district past nearby white schools in an adjacent district, to a black school in Detroit.) Because Section 12 had been held unconstitutional by the court of appeals, they argued, there was no other state action amounting to de jure segregation. They also disputed the segregation findings against Detroit school officials, asserting that "the cause of segregation in Detroit's public schools is racial residential concentration, not the de jure conduct of the Detroit Board of Education."

The petitioners' briefs also focused on the claim that the suburban school districts had been denied due process and that an interdistrict remedy was not appropriate. In the brief for the suburban districts, William Saxton hammered away at the latter point, using *Swann*'s language that "the nature of the violation determines the scope of remedy." Since the violation was only in Detroit, he contended, the remedy could not extend to suburbs.

Petitioners' briefs appeared calculated to appeal particularly to Justice Powell, whose opinions in earlier cases emphasized local control of education, criticized busing for purposes of school desegregation, and condemned racial balance. In the landmark case of *San Antonio Independent School District v. Rodriguez* (1973), decided three months before *Keyes* and the Richmond case, a group of Hispanic parents had challenged the Texas school financing system as a violation of the Equal Protection Clause. They contended that their children and other poor children in the state were provided an inferior education because of the state's use of property taxes as the primary basis for funding its schools. Powell's majority opinion held that despite serious disparities in funding among school districts, the property tax system for financing education was not an equal protection violation. Powell rejected the parents' claim that education was a fundamental right that must be provided equally to all students, and he wrote approvingly of the financing scheme as "assuring a basic education for every child in the State . . . and encourag[ing] a large measure of participation in and control of each district's schools at the local level." The state's brief highlighted this position from *Rodriguez* and quoted verbatim from Powell's *Keyes* opinion about the importance of neighborhood schools. Powell's focus in *Keyes* on the transportation costs connected with busing for desegregation and the diversion of monies for this purpose also was reflected in the petitioners' brief. After noting the amount of money estimated to be necessary for the purchase of new buses for the multidistrict remedy in *Milliken*, petitioners wrote, "The limited funds and resources available for public education are far better spent in educating children than in transporting children out of their school districts to other school districts for racial balance." Finally, petitioners' statement that "the compulsory transportation of any child to a distant school solely for racial balance purposes impinges upon the liberty of that child" also was similar to language in Powell's *Keyes* opinion.

Respondents' Briefs

The NAACP and Detroit board respondents reiterated their claim that the case never should have been accepted for review since no desegregation plan actually was before the Court. No issue of massive busing was presented, the NAACP argued, because " 'walk-in' desegregation [was] possible across the borders of the [Detroit school district] between all-black Detroit schools and contiguous, all-white suburban schools." The crux of the NAACP's argument was its "containment" theory of the constitutional violation. Paul Dimond later described their approach:

> We tried to envision just what it was that persuaded Judge Roth not to limit relief to the Detroit school district. That led us back to our original characterization of the violation as the containment of blacks in a set of separate, *de jure* black schools. During forty-one trial days on violation and sixteen more on remedy, Judge Roth had seen how a core of blacks-only schools had expanded dramatically over a twenty-year period but always within a state-created racial line of containment.

The brief summarized this containment theory and the need for a metropolitan remedy:

> Since *Brown*, and in direct violation of their constitutional rights, black children in Detroit have been intentionally confined, by various *de jure* devices, to an expanding core of black schools always separated by a line from immediately surrounding white schools. Because of the continuing nature of that constitutional violation, reflected in the expansion of the state-imposed core of black schools, [state and suburban defendants] seek to interpose as the new dividing line the existing boundaries of the Detroit School District. If that dividing line is permitted to stand without breach to perpetuate the basic dual structure, the intentional confinement of black children in schools separate from whites will continue for the foreseeable future. The violation of constitutional rights will continue without remedy. Such a result [would] repeal *Brown* and return these children to *Plessy*.

State responsibility for the segregation violation was the essence of George Roumell's brief on behalf of the Detroit board. In fact, according to Elwood Hain's account of the case, the board "somewhat awkwardly abandoned its claims of innocence" and shifted blame to the state. To support his claim about the plenary authority of the state over education, Roumell pointed to: (1) the state superintendent's and state board's power to remove local board members without election, (2) state power to consolidate school districts without consent from the local electorate, (3) state authority to transfer property from district to district without the districts' consent, (4) the existence of school districts that "are not coterminous" with other political boundary lines, (5) the provision of "massive state financial aid," and (6) state laws and state board regulations governing many of the day-to-day operations of local schools. Given this pervasive state control of education, the argument continued, the state was responsible for both the de jure actions of the Detroit school board and for providing a remedy that is "effective, eliminates the vestiges of segregation 'root and branch,' establishes 'schools, not a White and a Negro school, just schools,' and prevents resegregation."

Turning to the remedy issue, the board brief argued that an interdistrict remedy was appropriate because the Detroit metropolitan community is strongly interrelated politically, socially, and economically. In challenging allegations of excessive transportation costs of a metropolitan plan, Roumell noted the record indicated that the tentative proposal included reasonable distances and travel times. In many cases, the brief noted, "cross district transportation would be shorter than present intra-district transportation."

Amicus Briefs

U.S. Solicitor General Robert Bork submitted an amicus brief that turned out to be influential to the outcome and reasoning of the Supreme Court's opinion. The solicitor general, appointed by the president, represents the federal government before the Supreme Court. In cases where an executive branch department or agency loses in the federal courts of appeals, the solicitor general decides whether to seek Supreme Court review, and this official personally argues most of these cases when certiorari has been granted. The Court also permits the solicitor general to file amicus briefs where the government is not a party to the litigation and to give oral argument in such cases. In this role, the solicitor general, often referred to as the "tenth justice," works to identify important cases for the justices and to present legal arguments that assist them in making decisions.

Simultaneously, however, solicitors general are expected to represent the political and ideological goals of the presidents who appointed them. Given the Nixon administration's staunch opposition to busing for desegregation purposes, Bork's intervention in this case was no surprise. In a 1972 address to Congress, President Nixon said that busing was not conducive to providing a good education and had "been a classic case of the remedy for one evil creating another evil" and said that the school bus, which previously had been a "symbol of hope," was becoming a "symbol of social engineering on the basis of abstractions." He accused federal courts of adopting "extreme remedies" and encouraged proponents of busing to "end the hardship caused . . . for some poor children and recognize that the largest urban ghettos could never be desegregated." The resources spent on busing, Nixon said, should be spent more directly on education.

In early 1973, President Nixon had nominated Robert Bork, a professor at Yale Law School, to the position of solicitor general. Bork's writings had captured the attention of conservatives in the Nixon administration, who were impressed by his approach to constitutional interpretation. Bork espoused a philosophy of original intent, which stresses that the Constitution's provisions must be interpreted according to the intentions of the framers. This approach explicitly rejected a more expansive view of constitutional interpretation that had been the hallmark of the Warren Court. Bork gained notoriety only two months after being named solicitor general for his role in what became known as the "Saturday Night Massacre." During the Watergate scandal, the attorney general and his deputy resigned rather than follow President Nixon's order to fire the special prosecutor who was investigating the matter. Solicitor General Bork agreed to serve as acting attorney general and carried out the order.

After reviewing the lower court proceedings, Bork began with the language from *Swann* indicating that "the nature of the violation determines the scope of the remedy." Referring to the Court's decision in *Spencer v. Kugler* (1972), a case from New Jersey, he said that the mere fact of adjacent school districts having disparate racial compositions does not imply a constitutional violation. Citing the federal government's amicus brief from *Richmond*, Bork asserted there can be no interdistrict remedy without an interdistrict violation. For example, if racially discriminatory acts of the state or local school districts have been a direct or substantial cause of interdistrict school segregation, then an interdistrict remedy would be appropriate. Even then, he contended, the remedy should "be tailored to fit the violation, particularly in view of the deference owed to existing governmental structures." Echoing Justice Powell's comments, the solicitor general noted that even proof of some interdistrict violations does not always justify extensive interdistrict busing because time or distance of travel may be so great that children's health would be at risk or the educational process would be harmed.

Applying these principles to *Milliken*, Bork concluded that the metropolitan remedy was not warranted because the record "does not show that constitutional violations have directly altered or substantially affected the racial composition of schools in districts outside of Detroit." While acknowledging the lower courts' conclusions regarding the pattern of residential segregation throughout the Detroit metropolitan area and the interconnections between residential segregation and school segregation, he insisted that the findings of constitutional violations were limited to Detroit. Furthermore, he minimized the findings of state violations, concluding that only one of them — the transportation of Carver students — had an interdistrict impact. Bork described this as an "isolated instance" that could not "support a metropolitan-wide interdistrict remedy involving 54 or more school systems."

Characterizing the prediction that a Detroit-only plan would lead to white flight as merely speculative, he turned to the government's brief from *Richmond* to argue that it was not relevant anyway. "The desire to preserve the existing racial character of the City of Richmond or of its school system is not of constitutional dimensions and does not warrant including within the scope of relief other school systems that are uninvolved in Richmond's violation. Petitioners may prefer a consolidated school system with a large, stable white enrollment; the Constitution does not." Similarly, Bork labeled Judge Roth's findings of housing discrimination as "general remarks," claimed them not to be the basis of the court's decision, and concluded that they did not support an interdistrict remedy. Furthermore, he cited the government's brief in *Richmond*, which asserted that even more specific evidence of housing discrimination and other state acts did not justify the interdistrict relief contemplated there.

Bork concluded by recommending that the case be remanded to the district court for new hearings with full participation by all of the school districts in the tri-county area. The purpose would be to determine whether the suburban districts committed any constitutional violations or whether the Detroit violations had an interdistrict segregative impact. Based on these findings, the district court then would be able to "fashion appropriate relief to remedy the particular violations found."

The court received additional amicus briefs, most of them reiterating the arguments made by the petitioners, respondents, and solicitor general. The state of Indiana filed because it was involved in a similar case which was pending in the Seventh Circuit. In that case, a federal district court determined that the Indianapolis Public School System was guilty of de jure segregation and subsequently ordered an interdistrict remedy to include twenty-three other school districts in eight counties. The main factual difference between the two cases was that in Indianapolis additional hearings were held to determine whether the other districts also had committed acts of de jure segregation: the court found that they were not de jure segregated systems. The court, nonetheless, issued the cross-district order, primarily on the basis of the Sixth Circuit's decision in *Milliken*. Counsel for the State of Indiana contended that if the lower court rulings in Indianapolis and Detroit were to be upheld, the cases "would instigate a more major political and social upheaval than the progression . . . from the 'separate but equal' doctrine of *Plessy v. Ferguson* (1896), to the 'separate is inherently unequal' doctrine of *Brown I.*"

The broad political and social impact of a ruling affirming a metropolitan remedy was not lost on the justices. One of Justice Blackmun's law clerks made this point quite clearly in a memo dated several days before oral argument:

This will be the critical case for the future of northern school desegregation. Detroit's situation is probably typical of every northern city in that the whites are abandoning the city schools for the suburbs and leaving them for the blacks who remain behind. The rather tortuous policy choice before the [Court] is whether to reverse the [court of appeals] and thereby preclude the only effective means of achieving actual integration (i.e. racial balance) in the urban context or to affirm the [court of appeals] and open the door to massive busing decrees in all northern cities and thereby bring the wrath of the nation and I suppose Congress down on the [Court]. Although there is probably some room for middle ground compromises, whatever the [Court] does, it will be hard to limit any opinion that is written so as to avoid affecting other northern cities.

Blackmun expressed the same sentiment in his own statement written after he received the memo. Noting that the result obviously would affect northern cities, he suggested that it would "bring criticism on the Court however it decides" and observed, "This case ain't easy. It's another that the Court cannot 'win' in the sense of popular approval."

Oral Argument

Under the Court's rules, the general time limit for oral argument is one hour — thirty minutes per side. Here, however, the Court extended the time to one and three-quarter hours. Each side was allotted forty-five minutes to make its case, and Solicitor General Bork was granted fifteen minutes to represent the United States as amicus curiae.

When the day of oral argument arrived, the courtroom was packed with members of Detroit and national media, black and white spectators, and even the justices' wives, who were seated in private boxes. Paul Dimond later wrote that the section reserved for official dignitaries was filled by antibusing congressmen from Michigan and other states, many of whom had earlier introduced constitutional amendments to ban busing in case the Court ruled in favor of the respondents. Dimond maintained that the president and Congress clearly were united in opposition to busing such that "No Court could be blind to [the] political backlash to what had become the Roth case."

THE STATE AND SUBURBAN PETITIONERS

The petitioners' argument began with a brief appearance by Michigan attorney general Frank Kelley. Because Kelley had not been in court during the trial and therefore did not know the details of the case very well, he agreed that William Saxton would carry the bulk of the argument. Saxton had met with both Kelley and Solicitor General Bork in preparation for their appearance. Kelley asserted that the respondents' "containment" argument was not made at earlier phases of proceedings and that their amended complaint gave no evidence of school boundary manipulation for segregation purposes nor evidence of de jure segregation by other districts. He called this a "classic case of a remedy in search of a violation." Kelley received no probing questions from the justices, escaping, as Dimond later described it, "not only unscathed but triumphant."

William Saxton picked up on Kelley's argument that the suburban districts inappropriately had been brought into the case. "You will search this record in vain to find one whit of evidentiary material that any suburban school district committed any de jure act of segregation, either by itself, in complicity with the State, or complicity with anyone else." (In an interview for this book, he said that he had cautioned his clients to be certain they had no policies in place to lure white students from Detroit to enroll in their schools as nonresident, tuition-paying students. If they had done so, he warned, this would have been enough for the Supreme Court to hold them liable for de jure segregation.) He concluded with a forceful and passionate defense of the suburbs:

> In *Swann*, this Court said that the task is to correct the constitutional violation by balancing the individual and collective interest. That means that the interest of those one million parents and children who live outside Detroit, who have paid taxes to support their school district, who have considerable investments in homes, who have input into the local school, who desire to continue the concept of local schools, also have interest in this case, equally as well as the plaintiffs. And if those interests are to be balanced, the rights of these people may not be sacrificed on the altar of racial balance in order that their children may be judicially conscripted and interchanged with students in Detroit.

{ *Getting Off the Bus* }   151

When Solicitor General Bork took to the lectern, he asserted that, despite respondents' claims to the contrary, an extensive interdistrict remedy had been contemplated, "almost certainly, including busing." Reminiscent of Justice Powell's prior statements, he claimed that the contemplated remedy would be costly to school children in the Detroit metropolitan area and would involve "widespread disruption of governmental units." Unlike Kelley and Saxton, Bork suggested that if respondents wanted an interdistrict remedy, the case should be remanded for trial and findings concerning whether there were constitutional violations that "directly altered or substantially affected the respective racial composition of the Detroit school system and the specific suburban school systems." But rather than have them begin a new lawsuit, he suggested they could be permitted to amend the existing complaint. Bork insisted that respondents must demonstrate specific evidence of racial discrimination that affected cross-district lines before an interdistrict remedy could be ordered. Otherwise, he said, the remedy is not designed to remedy the violation but rather to interfere with the consequences of changing demographic patterns. Finally, disputing the Sixth Circuit's description of school district lines as artificial lines, Bork declared that "people have arranged governmental units, bonding financing, control of local schools; they have arranged their lives according to where those lines are."

NAACP: NICK FLANNERY AND NATHANIEL JONES

Nick Flannery and Nathaniel Jones argued on behalf of the respondents. Flannery began by announcing that he would focus on the nature and scope of the violation "as a predicate for proposed interdistrict remedies" and the opportunity for suburban districts to be heard, while Jones's task was to discuss the "practicalities of interdistrict desegregation, including Michigan law and practice." Paul Dimond later wrote that after petitioners completed their argument, Jones "knew that plaintiffs faced an uphill struggle in their battle against a color line that was coming to coincide with the boundaries of the Detroit school district."

Flannery summarized the conclusions of the lower courts as finding "conventional segregative practices" by the state and the Detroit board "affecting . . . the Detroit district," along with a "variety of other governmental, private, and quasi-governmental practices which caused housing segregation and school segregation to be mutually supportive, mutually interlocking devices." This was not, Flannery emphasized, "the State's role in isolation today and the Detroit Board's role in isolation tomorrow," but a number of factors, "especially the segregated school practices, operated in lockstep with an areawide metropolitan policy of confining by housing discrimination . . . black families to an identifiable core in Detroit." The result, he said, was that state policies favoring suburban schools served as a lure for white families, while black families were excluded from these same opportunities because of residential segregation in the metropolitan area outside Detroit. Flannery observed that the "culminating contribution of the state" to the de jure segregated Detroit district was Act 48, which was passed just as the district had begun to change its segregative practices.

He directly answered the claim that respondents' containment theory and the possibility of an interdistrict remedy were last-minute ideas, pointing the justices to the trial transcript to illustrate that early in the trial seven or eight witnesses had testified to a containment pattern in the entire metropolitan area. Flannery stressed that during the first week of the trial, plaintiffs suggested the potential inadequacy of a Detroit-only remedy; this, even as the district court advised counsel not to ask witnesses questions about metropolitan relief. He summarized counsel's response to Judge Roth: "Your Honor, we'll have to see what the record will show. It may develop, on the basis of the record made in this case . . . that Detroit-only relief may be found insufficient." Flannery said this was clear evidence that their containment theory was not a "Johnny-come-lately objective," and a metropolitan remedy was not an "eleventh-hour" concept. Interestingly, NAACP records contain a letter from Flannery to Jones, dated September 4, 1970, less than a month after the case originally was filed, about this issue:

I am suggesting that a conventional desegregation suit in a system the size of Detroit will absorb resources like the Pyramids and that its principal effect will be to accelerate white flights to Warren and similar havens. If I am correct, the result will be a segregated, under-financed school system. . . . Because the educational and housing discrimination facts support it and because the State has already intruded itself, I recommend that you consider metropolitan relief. In candor, I think that we may well lose on that issue through the Supreme Court, but I think for several reasons that we should do it.

Flannery pleaded with the Court not to vacate and remand the case after three-and-a-half years of litigation because this "would cost a great deal and gain nothing."

Flannery's discussion of the state's responsibility for the areawide violation as the basis for Judge Roth's metropolitan remedy prompted an interesting exchange with Justice Blackmun. Flannery insisted that given the containment pattern created by the mutually supportive connection between school and housing segregation in the metropolitan area, Roth was determined not to allow school district boundaries to thwart appropriate relief. Blackmun jumped in and asked whether the same artificial line principle would apply to situations between states. Flannery responded by distinguishing between local district boundaries and those of states, noting the latter "have a form of sovereignty, a form of autonomy, ceded to them by the Constitution," which local school districts do not enjoy. Blackmun pressed further, asking whether the situation would be different if the states had made some arrangements between themselves that resulted in school segregation. Flannery answered, "I would think that the federal courts would sit as a forum to vindicate those rights, but I have not thought through the jurisdictional questions." Blackmun's concern about federal-state issues and school district boundaries is reflected in his personal notes about the case from two days before oral argument:

I have always been concerned, of course, with an approach that would completely ignore long-established and innocently drawn boundary lines. Once we cross that barrier, we open the way to doing the same thing in all possible types of situations. . . . What then, do we do about the District of Columbia? If the district lines go by the board, is not the next step to enforce a plan across state lines? If Detroit can be desegregated on a metropolitan basis by getting into surrounding districts, why may not the city of Washington be desegregated by getting into adjacent portions of Maryland and Virginia? Mr. Coleman, when I asked this question of him in the Richmond argument, flatly stated that state lines would never be crossed. I didn't believe him then and I don't believe him now, once this barrier is overcome.

Jones began his portion of the argument by emphasizing that the district court acted with restraint and caution, taking great efforts to examine the evidence offered, and he noted that Judge Roth's decisions were affirmed both by a three-judge panel and by the court of appeals sitting en banc. Roth, according to Jones, was guided by Supreme Court decisions that obligated him to direct educational authorities to develop a plan to convert the state educational system to a unitary system, "a plan that promised realistically to work now and hereafter." This led Roth to proceed toward a metropolitan remedy, and he initiated an inquiry into the practicalities that would be involved in such relief — the relevant area, boundaries, law, and practice. He defined the relevant area as the tri-county area consisting of Wayne, Oakland, and Macomb counties, constituting a standard metropolitan statistical area under U.S. census criteria. This tri-county area represented a "community of interest" . . . "bound together by economic interests, recreation interests, social concerns and interests, governmental interests of various sorts, and a transportation network." To illustrate, he gave examples of work and housing patterns of residents in the three counties.

Jones attempted to demonstrate the authority of the state over local school districts by focusing on financial bonding rules, but some of the justices appeared skeptical, and Justice Powell specifically stressed instead the authority of local districts over real estate taxes and budget-making. When Justice Brennan asked Jones whether the costs for operating local districts would increase if the metropolitan plan went forward, he said he could not answer because there was no actual plan before the Court. "All that is before the Court now is the narrow question of whether or not these [school district] boundaries, these geographical boundaries are permeable. . . . There is no plan of government finance; these are the matters that are poised for determination by the [district] court based upon the remand of the Sixth Circuit."

The Conference and Opinion Assignment

The justices took up the case at their conference on March 1, five days after oral argument concluded. Although oral argument is open to the public, the conference is confined to the justices only—no secretaries, law clerks, or staff of any kind. During the conference, the justices discuss the case in order of seniority and take a preliminary vote, the outcome of which determines who writes the majority opinion. If the chief justice is in the majority, the chief assigns the opinion to him/herself or another member of the majority. If, however, the chief is in the minority, the most senior justice in the majority assigns it.

Based on the records of the justices in previous school desegregation decisions, it was assumed that *Milliken* would be decided by a 5-4 vote, but the substance of the ruling was the mystery. Justice Douglas, who joined the Court in 1939, had been a consistently strong supporter of school desegregation and of federal remedial power in this area since the *Brown* decisions. And, although agreeing with Justice Powell that the de jure/de facto distinction should be abandoned, he had strongly supported busing in the Charlotte and Denver cases as an appropriate remedy for desegregating schools. Justices Brennan and Marshall, appointed to the Court in 1956 and 1967, respectively, also were strongly in favor of school desegregation and of federal court efforts to compel recalcitrant school districts to implement meaningful desegregation plans, including the use of busing. Brennan wrote the *Green* majority opinion in 1968 calling for an end to "all deliberate speed" and for eliminating segregation "root and branch." After carrying out the NAACP's litigation strategy to end Jim Crow, including segregation in public schools during the 1950s, Marshall pushed his colleagues on the Court to resist local efforts to delay and evade school desegregation orders. Justice White, who joined the Court in 1962, also supported providing federal judges with broad discretion to implement school desegregation, including busing plans. From his arrival on the Court in 1958, Justice Stewart had also voted in favor of school desegregation, particularly where there was evidence of de jure segregation and actions to delay implementation. By the time of the *Swann* decision involving the schools in Charlotte, however, he appeared to become increasingly hesitant about permitting federal courts to order expansive implementation plans, especially large-scale busing programs. As the justices negotiated with Burger over the *Swann* majority opinion, Stewart expressed a belief that busing was appropriate at the junior high and high school levels, but not for elementary school students.

Despite writing to uphold most of Judge McMillan's sweeping desegregation plan in *Swann*, Chief Justice Burger really did not favor extensive federal judicial intervention in school desegregation cases. In his first term, the justices decided *Alexander v. Holmes County Board of Education* (1969), where the Fifth Circuit Court of Appeals had granted a request from thirty-three Mississippi school districts to postpone desegregation for yet another year. The request had the support of the Nixon administration. Before the Court issued a per curiam ruling overturning the circuit court, Burger drafted an opinion viewed by his colleagues as too solicitous of the districts' attempts to delay implementation. His position in *Keyes*, concurring only in the result, also illustrated his opposition to broad desegregation orders.

Justices Powell and Rehnquist joined the Court in 1972, after the *Swann* case, and it was not a surprise when both expressed their disdain for busing in *Keyes*. Powell's amicus brief on behalf of Virginia in *Swann* and his opinion in *Rodriguez* extolling the virtues of neighborhood schools and local control of education made it clear where he stood on the issue. Rehnquist's sterling conservative credentials had led to his appointment as assistant attorney general in the Nixon administration, and he was viewed as a "strict constructionist" who would help to slow down and perhaps reverse the Court's desegregation decisions. Also, Rehnquist purportedly helped to draft the administration's proposed antibusing constitutional amendment. Following his appointment in 1970, Justice Blackmun supported the rulings in *Swann* and *Keyes*. During deliberations behind the scenes, however, Blackmun indicated his reluctance to uphold expansive judicial intervention in school desegregation matters, especially if school boards had not been proven responsible for causing the segregation.

These general patterns fueled speculation that the 4-4 vote in *Richmond* broke down this way: Chief Justice Burger and Justices Blackmun and Rehnquist — all Nixon appointees — voted to affirm the circuit court and strike the metropolitan remedy, while Justices Douglas, Brennan, and Marshall — all holdovers from the Warren court —

voted to reverse the appeals court and reinstate the trial judge's decision ordering it. Paul Dimond, attorney for the respondents in *Milliken*, later wrote, this "meant that one of the five remaining members of the Warren court, probably Justice Stewart or Justice White, had joined the Nixon appointees in rejecting cross-district relief in Richmond." This was especially intriguing because a year earlier, Dimond noted, "Stewart had written an opinion for the five Warren holdovers, including White, to reject a proposed splintering of existing school districts that would have hindered desegregation."

Blackmun's thinking about the potential impact of *Richmond* is revealed in his statement of the issues in *Milliken* before oral argument. He noted that the way the Court handled *Richmond* was crucial to the outcome of *Milliken*, and the position of Justice Powell on this was key. Blackmun wrote, "If Detroit is affirmed, then the Richmond case ought to be reversed. Its not being reversed is then due to the historical accident of the disqualification of Justice Powell. If Detroit is to have a metropolitan plan, then Richmond does not deserve not to have one." That is why, Blackmun continued, some of the justices wanted either to hear the two cases together or deny review in Richmond, decide Detroit, and then decide Richmond in a future year. He also observed that Powell "is in a bit of a box because of his long opinion in the Denver case arguing that the *de jure-de facto* distinction is not a valid one. That substantially weakens his position here if he is at all inclined to reverse."

Justice Brennan's notations on his docket sheet for *Milliken* show that Rehnquist and Powell voted to reverse and vacate the court of appeals's decision outright, while Blackmun, Stewart, and Burger voted to reverse and vacate in line with the solicitor general's argument — remand to the district court to determine whether there is an interdistrict violation before deciding on the remedy. Marshall, White, Brennan, and Douglas voted to affirm the district and appeals courts. Justice Douglas's notes on the conference discussion are sketchy and his writing difficult to decipher, but they nevertheless provide some insight about various justices' thinking. Burger began by arguing that the case was just like *Richmond*, so it required reversal, but Blackmun said it was weaker than *Richmond*, where only three counties were involved and each had been guilty of segregation. Therefore, he was inclined to go along with the solicitor general's position. White saw the state as guilty of de jure segregation, so in his view, a remedy beyond Detroit would be appropriate, and he rejected the argument that racial balance was the overriding concern. Powell said the case involved open-ended jurisdiction with as many as eighty-four districts affected and noted that the Court had never permitted such a far-reaching remedy. He termed the case a "monstrosity on its face" with potential to wreak chaos on local school districts. Subsequently, Burger took on the majority opinion himself, and in a letter to Douglas that same day Marshall volunteered to write the principal dissent.

Boston

As the opinion writing commenced, meanwhile, in June, another battle over busing in the North was beginning in Boston. During the 1971–1972 school year, the NAACP filed a suit in federal district court against the Boston School Committee, which had refused to comply with the Racial Imbalance Act, passed by the Massachusetts legislature in 1965. Under the act, school districts were prohibited from operating any schools with more than 50 percent minority students. Hearings conducted by Judge Arthur Garrity found that in a system where 61 percent of public school students were white and 32 percent black, 84 percent of the white students attended schools that were more than 80 percent white, and 62 percent of black students attended schools more than 70 percent black. Garrity determined that the school committee caused or contributed to the segregation through policies related to feeder patterns, maintenance of overcrowded white schools and under-utilized black schools, school site selection and construction decisions, teacher assignments, and, to a lesser extent, districting and transfer policies.

In his June 1974 opinion, issued one month before the Supreme Court decided *Milliken*, Garrity ruled that the school committee's policies and practices "had intentionally brought about and maintained a dual school system" that was unconstitutionally segregated at all grade levels. He dismissed the school committee's claim that it simply was following a policy of protecting neighborhood schools, maintaining that this was "a reality only in areas of the city where residential segregation is firmly entrenched." As an example, he noted that the elementary schools "were not located near the center of regular compact districts, but rather near the edges of irregular districts requiring some students to attend a relatively distant school when there is another school within one or two blocks" of their homes.

As an interim remedy, Garrity adopted a desegregation plan developed by state education officials to comply with the Racial Imbalance Act. The plan would require half of the system's 94,000 students to change school assignments, including the busing of more than 18,000 students, 8,500 of them white. He noted that roughly one-third of Boston's students already were being bused or were taking public transportation to school, including some elementary school pupils. The plan was controversial, however, primarily because nearly 800 black children would be bused into South Boston, a working-class Irish neighborhood with a history of hostility to African Americans, while an equal number of white students would be sent to school in Roxbury, a black neighborhood regarded as the heart of the ghetto.

Judge Garrity was attacked for his order sending black children into "Southie." The opposition was led by antibusing activists, including Louise Day Hicks, a prominent member of the school committee. Indeed, two months before the busing order, 3,000 protestors had demonstrated at the Boston Commons, singing "Over there, over there, our kids aren't going over there." Opposition to Garrity's order was not limited to citizens in Boston but included President Gerald Ford, who had become president in August 1974 after Richard Nixon was forced to resign. Ford, a former Michigan congressman, had represented the Grand Rapids area in western Michigan for twenty-five years. Nixon selected him to succeed Spiro Agnew as vice president after Agnew's resignation in late 1973 following a financial scandal. Ford was a popular congressman, having served as House minority leader from 1965 to 1973. He later declared of Garrity's order: "The court's decision . . . in my judgment was not the best solution to quality education in Boston. I have consistently opposed forced busing to achieve racial balance as a solution to quality education. And, therefore, I respectfully disagree with the judge's order." As Peter Irons noted in his account of this controversy, Ford's statement assured the protestors that "the federal government would not help the Boston police keep order when the buses rolled into South Boston from Roxbury."

The Decision and Opinions in *Milliken*

On July 25, 1974, five months after the case was heard, the Court issued a 5-4 decision, upholding the finding of de jure segregation of the Detroit school district but rejecting an interdistrict remedy for the segregation violation. The case was remanded to the district court to develop a Detroit-only remedy. While there was clear agreement among the five to strike the interdistrict remedy, writing the opinion proved a difficult task, and it took several drafts and intense behind-the-scenes negotiations for Burger to gain consensus. He did not circulate his initial draft opinion until May 31, nearly three months after oral argument. The struggle began on June 5, when Justice Powell wrote an eleven-page memo indicating that Burger's analysis was essentially incorrect. Powell characterized *Milliken* as presenting two issues: (1) identifying the conditions that would justify a federal court to consolidate two or more school districts, or parts thereof, for the purpose of achieving desegregation and (2) determining the limitations on the power of a federal court to order extensive interdistrict busing to achieve desegregation. Burger, he said, addressed the first question only in part and did not examine the second question at all. Powell directed Burger to Solicitor General Bork's amicus brief for guidance, reminding him that those who voted at the conference to reverse "expressed a significant degree of approval of the S[olicitor] G[eneral]'s analysis."

Powell criticized Burger's emphasis on the racial balance issue, arguing that the district court might have ordered a consolidation remedy without requiring racial balance at all. Thus racial balance was immaterial because the basic question was "whether and under what circumstances a federal court may order a consolidation of school operations in disregard of established school districts." Powell acknowledged that Burger's draft opinion did recognize that there was no interdistrict violation justifying an interdistrict remedy, and he encouraged Burger to strengthen that section. Declaring that the Court never before had held a constitutional violation in one district to justify including other districts in the remedy, Powell called for the majority to say explicitly that "the Constitution requires no such extra district or interdistrict remedy." He emphasized that in *Richmond*, even with the two adjacent districts having formerly practiced segregation, four members of the Court concluded that no consolidation or interdistrict remedy was automatically justified in that case.

Powell referred to Bork's brief for examples of situations where interdistrict relief would be appropriate, and, most importantly, held that in determining whether unlawful segregation had occurred, federal courts must apply the *Keyes* standard, requiring intentional and de jure action by school authorities. This was interesting in light of his earlier criticism of the de jure/de facto distinction. He reiterated the importance of the *Swann* principle that the nature of the violation determines the scope of the remedy. He encouraged Burger to tighten the section minimizing state authority over education in Michigan and to emphasize the importance of local control of public education, pointing particularly to his own opinion in *Rodriguez* and to the difficulties of decision making and the operation of schools he thought inherent with consolidation or interdistrict remedies. He claimed the court of appeals' characterization of school districts as lines drawn on a map for political convenience denigrated them and was "nonsense."

Powell then urged Burger to de-emphasize his focus on the violation of the suburban districts' due process rights because "it conveys the impression that we are more concerned about failure to afford hearings to the suburban districts than we are about the fundamental issues." He also argued for reversing the case outright, asserting that "little purpose will be served by our taking this case merely to remand it for a full rehearing with all parties before the court." Powell also referred Burger to his opinion in *Keyes* and to Bork's brief to show that the Constitution does not require busing to achieve desegregation. Finally, he concluded with the observation that even if racial balance were constitutionally required, it would be impossible to achieve and maintain it in each school, given demographic shifts.

Burger made a few changes in his next draft circulated on June 11, although he apparently ignored most of what Powell had suggested. In a memo the next day, Robert Richter, one of Blackmun's clerks, told his boss that the clerks for Powell and Stewart agreed that the three justices should "make some attempt individually or collectively to bring the Chief around." They believed the opinion was preoccupied with racial balance, when the real issue was whether the district court could remedy the de jure segregation in one district by ordering relief crossing district lines. Richter's memo also indicated his fear that Burger's attack on racial balance could undermine desegregation orders in the South, where judges used rough mathematical ratios within districts as goals for eliminating dual systems there. And once more he raised the larger political implications of the Court's decision:

> It might be nice if the Court made some gesture to the overriding commitment to integration, even if the case is being decided against the plaintiffs. It is one thing if the politicians choose to make noise about the undesirability of forced desegregation. When the Court goes out of its way to treat desegregation as a necessary evil that should be avoided if possible, it abdicates the role of moral leadership that only it, as a nonpolitical branch, can provide. . . . This is an important case of first impression that touches almost every city in the country in a significant way. It is important therefore that the Court issue a single majority opinion that speaks for a majority of the Court. Under normal circumstances it would seem advisable to hold this case over [to another term]. The need to take this issue out of the political arena before the fall precludes this course I believe and therefore I think it is important that the Chief's opinion be cleaned up.

On June 13, the day after Richter's memo, Justice Marshall sent a memo specifically requesting the case be held over to the 1974 term. Claiming that it was not possible to complete his dissent before adjournment of the current term, he noted that while the conference had voted on March 1, the initial majority opinion draft was not circulated until May 31. In his memo, Marshall set out the issues he intended to address in his dissent, but his request for delay failed.

Justices Powell and Stewart sent memos to Burger on June 14 and 17, respectively, again requesting him to de-emphasize his racial balance discussion. Powell sent Burger another letter on June 18, chiming in on Stewart's arguments to de-emphasize racial balance and urging him to focus more on the remedy aspect of the case. That same day, Burger sent Powell and the other three (including Rehnquist) a memo contending that their differences were "essentially semantical," although his comments showed that they were not. He said he had stripped down the discussion of racial balance to "one page in which

I recite the uncontrovertible [*sic*] fact that the desire for racial balance was the fulcrum from which the District Court proceeded to the error that followed, i.e., mandating an inter-district remedy with no showing of an inter-district violation."

Burger's next draft, on June 19, began to minimize the focus on racial balance, although still not enough to satisfy the other members, and the discussion of the denial of due process to the suburbs issue also remained. The other justices had stressed earlier that, given the conclusion that the suburbs could not be included in the remedy without evidence of segregative practices on an interdistrict level, it was unnecessary to discuss the procedural problems of excluding them from earlier hearings. On June 20, Powell wrote to Burger, stressing the need for a solid majority, and Burger's subsequent June 21 draft, which deleted more of the objectionable racial balance language and removed the due process discussion, gained support. Powell, Stewart, and Rehnquist sent memos officially joining Burger's opinion on June 24, and Blackmun did so the next day. The final touches were made to the opinion while Stewart worked on a concurrence, and Justices Douglas, White, and Marshall drafted their dissents.

On July 10, two weeks before the ruling was announced, Judge Roth suffered his third heart attack in eighteen months; he died the next day. An article in the *Detroit Free Press* by William Grant summarized his background and career, focusing especially on the attacks he endured because of his decisions in *Milliken*. "Judge Roth never publicly acknowledged the criticism and he seldom discussed it even with his closest friends. But it bothered him, deeply, and he privately seethed when resolutions from American and state bar associations recognizing his judicial restraint and fairness received no publicity." Grant also noted that the judge was "absolutely certain his metropolitan integration order was the right thing to do." Roth's death did not go unnoticed at the Court, as Justice Stewart sent his colleagues a two-sentence memo acknowledging it, with Grant's article attached.

Burger's Majority Opinion

In Burger's majority opinion, the influence of Powell, Blackmun, and Stewart is clear. Following an extensive discussion of the facts and the record, Burger considered the equity powers of federal courts in school desegregation cases based on *Brown* and *Swann*. He completely ignored the respondents' containment theory, adopting instead the approach urged by the solicitor general and the suburban and state petitioners: under *Swann*, the nature of the violation determines the scope of the remedy. Thus Burger declared that a federal court could not properly impose an interdistrict, areawide remedy to a single-district de jure segregation problem unless it first was established that unconstitutional racially discriminatory acts of the other districts had caused interdistrict segregation, that district lines had been deliberately drawn on the basis of race, or that the single-district violation had an interdistrict impact. "Without an interdistrict violation and interdistrict effect, there is no constitutional wrong calling for an interdistrict remedy." Applying that principle to this case, he concluded that the remedy must be limited to the Detroit school district and accepted William Saxton's argument that the containment theory was an "eleventh-hour consideration":

> The record before us, voluminous as it is, contains evidence of *de jure* segregated conditions only in the Detroit schools; indeed, that was the theory on which the litigation was initially based and on which the District Court took evidence. With no showing of significant violation by the 53 outlying school districts and no evidence of any interdistrict violation or effect, the court went beyond the original theory of the case as framed by the pleadings and mandated a metropolitan remedy.

He continued: "The constitutional right of the Negro [students] residing in Detroit is to attend a unitary school in that district." Burger also insisted that both lower courts "shifted the primary focus from a Detroit remedy to the metropolitan area only because of their conclusion that total desegregation of Detroit would not produce the racial balance which they perceived as desirable." But he greatly reduced the focus on racial balance, a primary criticism of his earlier drafts.

On the question of permeability of school district lines, Burger said the notion that they "may be casually ignored or treated as mere administrative convenience is contrary to the history of public education in the United States." Moreover, he espoused Powell's positions regarding the virtues of local control over education and the argument that a metropolitan remedy would give rise to numerous problems as to large-scale busing of students, financing, and administration. Burger claimed that a metropolitan remedy would require "consolidation of 54 independent school districts historically administered as separate units into a vast new super school district," and he asked a series of questions, initially raised in Powell's first memo, about who would make the necessary administrative and financial decisions. The majority also accepted the petitioners' contention that "the local school district is an autonomous political body." One legal scholar wrote that in doing so, the Court overruled two lower court judges who were "uniquely knowledgeable about the state's plenary control over its school districts"—Judge Roth, a former Michigan attorney general, and Sixth Circuit Judge George Edwards, a former justice of the Michigan Supreme Court.

While not overruling the lower court findings that the state had engaged in segregative actions through its decisions on transportation, school site selection and construction, and financial aid, Burger confined their effects within the Detroit school system. The majority concluded that with one exception, no evidence indicated that "either the State or any of the 85 outlying districts engaged in activity that had a cross-district effect." That exception was the transportation, in the late 1950s, of black students from one district, past nearby white schools to a predominantly black school in Detroit. But Burger described it as a single, isolated instance involving only one of the suburban districts and the city district. This, he said, was insufficient to justify a broad metropolitan-wide remedy. The Court also downplayed the effect of the passage of Act 48, and, more significantly, Burger dismissed the district court findings showing the connection between housing segregation and school segregation. These findings, were irrelevant because, Burger argued, the Sixth Circuit had not relied on such evidence in making its decision. Finally, as Powell urged, Burger dropped the due process discussion, having ruled that the suburban districts could not be part of the remedy. While adopting the solicitor general's framing of the issue in this case, the majority rejected his suggestion to remand it for determination of whether there were de jure violations by the suburban districts that might justify an interdistrict remedy. Thus the Court went far beyond what Bork had recommended.

Burger's opposition to a potential metropolitan busing program and his preoccupation with the concept of racial balance is not surprising, in light of his actions after writing the opinion that upheld busing in the 1971 *Swann* case. J. Harvie Wilkinson III, who later became a prominent judge on the Fourth Circuit Court of Appeals, writes that during the court's summer recess, Burger "personally paint[ed] on *Swann* a conservative gloss." In a matter concerning a Winston-Salem, North Carolina, school board, Burger's opinion cautioned the district judge that *Swann* did not require racial balance throughout the school system or in each school. "He promised personally to block any court order requiring daily bus travel approaching three hours, if closer school facilities were available." In an unusual move, federal judges throughout the country were sent copies of this opinion, marked "For the Personal attention of the Judge." Wilkinson concludes of this episode: "it was increasingly apparent that . . . Burger personally chafed at the [*Swann*] opinion bearing his name."

———

Stewart Concurrence

Justice Stewart's concurrence emphasized that the interdistrict remedy ordered here was improper because the record indicated unconstitutional racial segregation to have existed only within Detroit, and the other schools presumptively were administered in complete accord with the Constitution. He did, however, allow that interdistrict relief might be appropriate in other situations, such as state officials drawing or redrawing district lines to separate the races or "purposeful, racially discriminatory use of state housing or zoning laws." In a puzzling footnote, he ignored the connection between school segregation and housing segregation. "It is [the] essential fact of a predominantly Negro school population in Detroit—caused by unknown and perhaps unknowable factors such as in-migration, birth rates, economic changes, or cumulative acts of private racial fears—that accounts for the 'growing core of Negro schools,' a 'core' that has grown to include virtually the entire city." Also baffling was his claim that "No record has been made in this case showing that the racial composition of the Detroit school population or that residential patterns within Detroit and in the surrounding areas were in any significant measure caused by governmental activity."

Ironically, these claims seem to contradict his majority opinion in a 1968 case, *Jones v. Alfred H. Mayer Co.*, applying the Civil Rights Act of 1866 to private housing discrimination. Stewart had written, "Just as the Black Codes enacted after the Civil War to restrict the free exercise of [fundamental] rights were substitutes for the slave system, so the exclusion of Negroes from white communities became a substitute for the Black Codes. And when racial discrimination herds men into ghettoes . . . then it too is a relic of slavery." In *The Brethren: Inside the Supreme Court*, Bob Woodward and Scott Armstrong reported that by the time of the Richmond case, Stewart had become reticent about busing for desegregation purposes, in part because of mainstream opposition to it. Stewart allegedly informed his clerks that he had "ridden the bus on the Charlotte and Denver decisions, but that Richmond was different. 'It is where I get off.'" And a source close to the justice suggested that his position in *Milliken* was at least partly based on his fear that a ruling upholding Roth's decision would have led to "blood in the streets."

The Dissents

Justices Douglas, White, and Marshall each penned dissents. In a solo dissent, Douglas lamented that in "rul[ing] against the metropolitan area remedy we take a step that will likely put the problems of the blacks and our society back to the period that antedated the 'separate but equal' regime of *Plessy v. Ferguson.*" He maintained that in school desegregation cases there is no constitutional difference between de facto and de jure segregation, and, given the plenary authority of the state over education in Michigan, school districts act as agencies of the state. In Douglas's view, the district court had found ample evidence of state action in creating segregation in the metropolitan area; therefore a metropolitan remedy was proper. Stressing that no specific desegregation plan had been adopted, he concluded: "It is conceivable that ghettos develop on their own without any hint of state action. But since Michigan by one device or another has over the years created black school districts and white school districts, the task of equity is to provide a unitary system for the affected area where, as here, the State washes its hands of its own creation." Douglas also noted the negative impact on urban education created by this decision, in conjunction with the *Rodriguez* ruling a year earlier.

The inner core of Detroit is now rather solidly black; and the blacks, we know, in many instances are likely to be poorer, just as were the Chicanos in *San Antonio School District v. Rodriguez*. By that decision the poorer school districts must pay their own way. It is therefore a foregone conclusion that we have now given the States a formula whereby the poor must pay their own way. Today's decision, given *Rodriguez*, means that there is no violation of the Equal Protection Clause though the schools are segregated by race and though the black schools are not only "separate" but "inferior."

Justice White, joined by Douglas, Brennan, and Marshall, castigated the majority for allowing deliberate acts of segregation and their consequences to go unremedied "because an effective remedy would cause what the court considered to be undue administrative inconvenience to the state." He argued that the record was replete with evidence of constitutional violations, for which the state is responsible under the Fourteenth Amendment, even if those violations occurred locally. Consequently, for White, the court's precedents justified an interdistrict remedy:

I cannot understand, nor does the majority satisfactorily explain, why a federal court may not order an appropriate interdistrict remedy, if this is necessary or more effective to accomplish [the] constitutionally mandated task [of eliminating all vestiges of state-imposed segregation]. As the Court unanimously observed in *Swann:* "Once a right and a violation have been shown, the scope of a district court's equitable powers to remedy past wrongs is broad, for breadth and flexibility are inherent in equitable remedies." In this case, both the right and the State's Fourteenth Amendment violation have concededly been fully established, and there is no acceptable reason for permitting the party responsible for the constitutional violation to contain the remedial powers of the federal court within administrative boundaries over which the transgressor itself has plenary power.

Justice Marshall wrote the principal dissent, joined by the other three dissenters. He began by noting that under the Court's precedents, once state-imposed segregation has been demonstrated, the state's duty is "to eliminate all vestiges of racial discrimination and to achieve the greatest possible degree of actual desegregation." Marshall accepted the respondents' containment theory, arguing that the district court found clear and substantial evidence that black children "had been intentionally confined to an expanding core of virtually all-Negro schools immediately surrounded by a receding band of all-white schools." Racial balance was not, Marshall insisted, the basis of the interdistrict remedy proposed, "but rather the purposeful, intentional, massive, *de jure* segregation of the Detroit city schools, which under our decision in *Keyes*, forms a 'predicate for a finding of the existence of a dual school system,' and justifies 'all-out desegregation.'" He angrily accused the majority of misrepresenting the motives of Judge Roth:

> The Court has conjured up a largely fictional account of what the District Court was attempting to accomplish. With all due respect, the Court, in my view, does a great disservice to the District Judge who labored long and hard with this complex litigation by accusing him of changing horses in midstream and shifting the focus of this case from the pursuit of a remedy for the condition of segregation within the Detroit school system to some unprincipled attempt to impose his own philosophy of racial balance on the entire Detroit metropolitan area. The focus of this case has always been the segregated system of education in the city of Detroit. The District Court determined that interdistrict relief was necessary and appropriate only because it found that the condition of segregation within the Detroit school system could not be cured with a Detroit-only remedy. It is on this theory that the interdistrict relief must stand or fall. Unlike the Court, I perceive my task to be to review the District Court's order for what it is, rather than to criticize it for what it manifestly is not.

Marshall also agreed with Roth that a Detroit-only decree likely would result in the Detroit school system becoming a substantially all-black system by increasing white flight to the suburbs. And, like

Justice White, he criticized the majority for ensuring that, despite the state's control over education and its responsibility for segregation in Detroit schools, the district court became powerless to require the state to remedy its constitutional violation in any meaningful fashion. Marshall was incensed by Burger's concluding statement, ordering the case to be remanded for "a prompt formulation of a decree directed toward eliminating the segregation found to exist in Detroit city schools, a remedy which has been delayed since 1970." This was, Marshall observed, the "great irony" of the opinion and "its most serious analytical flaw," given Judge Roth's explicit finding that a Detroit-only remedy "would not accomplish desegregation."

Finally, Marshall concluded that the Court was bowing to public opinion against desegregating schools and warned of the long-range implications of this decision:

Desegregation is not and was never expected to be an easy task. Racial attitudes ingrained in our Nation's childhood and adolescence are not quickly thrown aside in its middle years. But just as the inconvenience of some cannot be allowed to stand in the way of the rights of others, so public opposition, no matter how strident, cannot be permitted to divert this Court from the enforcement of the constitutional principles at issue in this case. Today's holding, I fear, is more a reflection of a perceived public mood that we have gone far enough in enforcing the Constitution's guarantee of equal justice than it is the product of neutral principles of law. In the short run, it may seem to be the easier course to allow our great metropolitan areas to be divided up each into two cities — one white, the other black — but it is a course, I predict, our people will ultimately regret.

Milliken II and the Retreat from School Desegregation

The Supreme Court's decision against a metropolitan remedy elicited reactions ranging from relief and jubilation to anger, disappointment, and sadness. Suburban residents, the plaintiffs and defendants and their counsel, school authorities, elected officials, members of the black community, and other observers, all expressed their feelings about the ruling. Their responses illustrate the complexity of this case.

Reaction in the Suburbs

Suburban residents generally agreed with the decision, but some expressed ambivalence. As a mother from Grosse Pointe, one of the more upscale suburbs, put it, "Intellectually, I'm for equality in education, and busing. But not in the Detroit area. I'm interested in equality, but I do not want my child in the inner city and faced with the problem of the ghetto." Similarly, a twenty-one-year-old Warren resident said, "Everybody feels sorry for kids in the inner city. . . . My parents worked hard for their money so they could bring me to a better area. I could see bringing underprivileged kids to better schools, but busing was utterly ridiculous."

Some suburban residents who opposed the decision also spoke out, although they were in the minority. For example, a Rochester resident was quoted in the *Detroit Free Press* as feeling "very badly" about the ruling. "I thought it was a constructive move, and my children were willing to participate. I feel busing is an answer but I know that's not a popular view." Letters to the editor also expressed disappointment with the decision. "I was deeply saddened by the high court ruling that there will be no cross-district busing in the Detroit area. . . . The inconvenience that busing creates for parents, and the extra time that students may have to spend on buses is a small price to pay to see children mature and learn the true meaning of brotherhood and sister-hood in tomorrow's world." Another wrote, "What right has this society to expect respect for or obedience to the law by the black man after the Supreme Court decision on busing? If the decision is consistent with the Constitution, the Constitution is out of touch with justice; if the decision is not consistent with the Constitution, the high court is out of touch with the laws of the land."

The overwhelming suburban responses, however, were parents' joy and relief that their children would be spared from attending "unsafe schools" in Detroit. One mother from Warren, a hotbed of antibusing sentiment (discussed in Chapter 5), described her reaction: "I clapped my hands and said something like goodie. My kids would have been bused in a bad neighborhood. My school's here, in the back yard. That's why we moved here." Some suburbanites said they opposed busing because it was expensive and a waste of money, or they said it did not improve educational quality. Undeniably, though, some of the opposition was motivated by antipathy towards Detroit and its residents. A high school student from Warren told a reporter "My dad used to live in an integrated neighborhood, and he said he'd go to jail before he'd let them bus me."

After interviewing a group of women in the middle-class suburb of Roseville, a *New York Times* reporter concluded that there was "no way to overestimate the depth and intensity of passion that the busing controversy generated here and in other towns on the periphery of Detroit." One woman who had grown up on Detroit's east side said she moved to Roseville because she was not going to send her kids "to that school down there." "You've got your good colored and your bad, just like white. But if you could live down there and see those animals coming and going." The irony, noted the reporter, was that the school children in Roseville did not score particularly well on national tests, and some of the parents believed the schools in Detroit were better in some ways than their own. Asked about the possibility of integrated housing in the suburbs, one woman noted that her husband would immediately put out a for-sale sign. This question generated a particularly interesting response from the woman who earlier had referred to "good colored." "If it's a colored person buying the house with his own hard-earned money, and he wants better for his kids, that'd be O.K. But you get that welfare and that Aid to Dependent Children bunch." And, she noted, they "would have to prove that they had not been sent by the National Association for the Advancement of Colored People." Letters to the editor in the *Detroit Free Press* expressed similar sentiments:

> *Southfield resident*: Stop kidding yourselves that Detroit school conditions are a result of segregation. They are bad and dangerous because there is no control put on the "rotten apples." Did the NAACP and Roth really think we would allow them to experiment with our children? I think not, but they sure spent one hell of a lot of our money to have proven how preposterous and asinine a multi-city busing program would be. Clean up your act, Detroit, and earn some respect.
>
> *Warren resident*: I am anti-busing, but I feel no great victory—I feel great relief. To be forced to put my children on a bus and have them sent into an unknown or hostile area would have brought out the fight in me.

———

Responses from School Authorities and Elected Officials

Three suburban school superintendents who helped lead the opposition to an interdistrict remedy—Eugene Spencer of Clawson, Wilfred Webb of Hazel Park, and Fred Davenport of Wyandotte—were especially pleased with the decision. Davenport, who initiated the meeting with their attorney, William Saxton, felt vindicated because, he said, they knew their districts had not contributed to segregation in any way. Webb asserted that a contrary ruling "would have destroyed school districts as we know them" as well as ended the concept of neighborhood schools. In an interview for this book, Saxton indicated that his clients' opposition to interdistrict busing was not based on racial antagonism but upon concerns about difficult administrative issues that would accompany implementation.

President Gerald Ford and Governor William Milliken also praised the ruling. Ford described it as a "victory for reason" and a "great step forward to finding another answer to quality education," while Milliken said it would be "very well received in the country and in Michigan." The governor indicated his strong feeling that "to deal with integrated schools by busing is very superficial and very counterproductive." His sentiments were shared somewhat by Detroit's black mayor, Coleman Young, who did not "shed any tears for the demise of cross-district busing," but Young simultaneously noted that the issue of remedying unequal opportunity due to racial or economic discrimination remained. Young maintained, nonetheless, that if the Court had permitted cross-district busing, suburban parents would develop an interest in the Detroit schools and see the need for equal education. John Porter, the state superintendent of public instruction, was also mindful of the challenge going forward, of determining how to "provide an integrated educational setting in order that children can be equipped to effectively function as adults in a culturally pluralistic society."

Responses of the Plaintiffs and the Black Community

Not surprisingly, the original Bradley plaintiffs and their legal team were quite despondent. A *Detroit Free Press* article included reactions from Verda Bradley, whose son Ronald was the first named plaintiff, and Ray Litt, a white Detroit businessman who also was a plaintiff. Bradley said she was "in a state of shock for a few minutes" when first hearing the news but said she continued to believe in busing to achieve integration. Litt lamented the decision and noted that while busing created an "artificial social situation," he still believed it to be "worth the trouble" to create a better society. In an interview in the *Detroit News* thirty years later, in May 2004 Bradley said she did not regret her decision to participate in the case, but she worried that Ronald never recovered from the publicity and backlash that accompanied *Milliken*. "This thing messed with him. People are so cruel." As a result of the decision, Ronald was not bused. He eventually dropped out of high school in the tenth grade. In 2004, he was in his late 30s and unemployed. While expressing pride in playing a role in this landmark case, she said she no longer sees busing as the way to integrate schools.

On the day of the ruling, Nathaniel Jones, lead NAACP attorney representing the plaintiffs, lambasted the decision as a "giant step backwards toward the separate but equal doctrine." Three weeks later, the *New York Times* published his letter to editor, written in response to a *Times* editorial titled "Wrongs without Remedy." The editorial had concluded: "in refusing to fashion a remedy sufficiently broad to correct the constitutional wrong which it found, the Court's majority has made us all, not just the black children of Detroit, the losers in the long run." In his letter, Jones contended that the Court's decision sent two messages: "To whites it says that if discrimination against blacks is on a vast enough scale, remedies will prove too awesome to invoke and thus the evil can be perpetuated; and to [black] Americans it says that they have only those rights that the white majority finds convenient to concede." He implored the editors to continue highlighting the gap between the nation's promises of equality and its unwillingness to do what is necessary to achieve it.

Overall, however, the reaction in the black community was more mixed than in the predominantly white suburbs. An editorial in the *Michigan Chronicle*, the leading black newspaper in the state (published in Detroit), characterized the decision as rejecting the dream of achieving true democracy "for the sake of a misguided suburban privilege of racial privacy" and criticized the emphasis on local control as a "court-mandated maintenance of an outdated racial separatism." Likewise, one of the *Chronicle*'s regular columnists argued that the *Milliken* ruling, along with the school financing decision in *San Antonio v. Rodriguez*, reaffirmed the " 'separate and inferior' rule that was recognized as legal before 1896" and, he claimed, put blacks "back into the 19th century, one step out of slavery."

By contrast, a *Chronicle* news article indicated that many blacks were not surprised by the decision and some were relieved because they opposed cross-district busing to begin with. They also viewed the Court's directive to implement a Detroit-only desegregation remedy as a "stalling tactic" that could interfere with efforts to provide quality education in the city's schools. One parent, a member of the Detroit school board and chair of one of the district's regional boards, asserted that she never supported metropolitan busing, "but I suppose I could have lived with it. But now since this is [the Court's] decision, we have to take care of our own. We have to see to it that everybody is accountable so that our children will have the kind of education they should have." Another mother said that she had never favored busing, she was for quality education, and she did not "want [her] children to go to Livonia to school." Yet another lamented that "four years has been wasted and God knows how much money it cost to fight in the courts for our children to go to school with white children in another school district instead of putting all our efforts toward fighting the state and the federal government for the money to pay for the proper education in our own Detroit schools." But this attitude, Nathaniel Jones argued, failed to recognize that the lawsuits were necessary to establish the constitutional violations that gave the federal courts jurisdiction to order resource remedies. Another regional board chair posed a different argument against busing: "It would break up the family structure, because mothers wouldn't be able to go to the schools when their children are having problems. Far too many of our Black families are already made up of broken homes."

A *New York Times* article published two days after the decision reported on interviews with black Detroiters who resided in an area between downtown Detroit and the affluent suburb of Grosse Pointe. The author concluded that for many of them, the decision "was only a small disappointment" and did not generate the "deep emotional reaction of parents in the suburbs." One mother with children in the local schools said that busing was "okay," but she felt that if nearby schools were doing the job, there was no point in busing, and the Detroit schools were "trying to do the job." By contrast, a retiree who had paid for his granddaughter to attend a private school in Grosse Pointe but no longer could afford it was more critical: "I still think that kids here could get a better schooling with busing. Suburban schools have the better teachers, and kids will learn more, and they wouldn't be as crowded." In interviews with *Free Press* reporters, black Detroit high school students agreed, asserting that they wouldn't mind busing if it improved their school. "If they're going to bus us, they might as well bus us to Grosse Pointe. Out there we'd get better education, no second or third class teachers."

Reactions from Other Observers

One of the harshest critiques of both the decision and busing opponents came from William Serrin, a former *Free Press* reporter, in a guest column in the *New York Times*. He charged suburban officials with abandoning the city of Detroit after Detroit taxes and capital had been used to subsidize suburban life—from roads and expressways to public parks and home and commercial construction. Serrin blasted Burger's majority opinion for failing to acknowledge that school segregation between the city and its prosperous suburbs was the result of mortgage discrimination, suburban zoning and home buying practices, and unequal education funding by the state. In a particularly strident passage, he lambasted busing opponents who maintained that the issue was not busing at all, but quality education:

Will the leaders—liberals like Democratic Representatives James G. O'Hara and John D. Dingell, who jumped on the antibusing bandwagon; the members of the Legislature; the Governor; the corporate leaders—will these men fight for more money for Detroit? No.

Will school tax revenues be apportioned on the basis of need, so that Detroit and other poor children will get the money they deserve? No. Will Detroit's housing and unemployment problems be addressed? No. Will suburban housing segregation be combated, so blacks can move to suburbs? No. Will artificial boundaries be ended? No. Will wealth assume its responsibilities? No.

Nothing will happen. Integration is now a matter for Detroit only. Thus it will be of little concern to the people of wealth and power, who live elsewhere.

Serrin concluded by comparing the busing controversy in Detroit with controversies over integration in the South in previous decades. He complained: "The problem was the same. The hatred was the same. The same epithets, the same code words were used. The same cowardice was demonstrated by normally responsible people. The matter was handled in the same way by the press, from the white view. Everywhere we are the same."

Tom Wicker, a southerner and regular *Times* columnist, also saw the irony of northern controversies over school integration. The decision, said Wicker, confirmed southerners' beliefs that once northerners were affected, desegregation efforts "would be quickly stopped." He also pointed to a connection between governmental actions and segregation in public schools in northern cities and suburbs, as well as the likely impact of the decision in maintaining the status quo. Wicker, nevertheless, was sympathetic to concerns raised in Burger's opinion about the "administrative, financial and logistic" difficulties that would accompany interdistrict busing. In addition, he questioned the effectiveness of busing, noting that some studies of integrated school districts had demonstrated little evidence that test scores for minority students had improved. Finally, he highlighted increasing black opposition to busing, asserting that many African Americans "are offended by the notion that sitting in the classroom with white pupils will improve their children's education."

Derrick Bell, a black law professor at Harvard and former member of the NAACP legal team that had litigated many civil rights cases, made a similar argument: "The insistence on integrating every public school that is black perpetuates the racially demeaning and unproven assumption that blacks must have a majority white presence in order to either teach or learn effectively." Similarly, Ronald Edmonds, director of the Center for Urban Studies at Harvard's Graduate School of Education, claimed that the focus on integration can actually disadvantage black children. Because integration almost always places them in the minority, Edmonds said, black parents are diverted from establishing community control of their schools or from making those schools more responsive to the needs of their children.

In a journal article published a year after the ruling, William Grant, the *Free Press* education writer who followed the case from the outset, reflected on the criticism directed towards the NAACP and other integration proponents. He rejected the argument that they were proceeding on the assumption that majority-black schools were inherently inferior. Grant said in the cases leading to *Brown*, counsel easily could have proved that the black schools were not equal, as required by the "separate but equal" doctrine. Thus the strategy could have been to seek only financial equality, but, he noted, the NAACP decided to mount a "frontal attack on segregation itself," partly because of skepticism that predominantly white communities really would provide "permanent equity" for black schools. With this strategy, he continued: "The way to assure an equal education for minority children is to have them attend school with white children—not because blacks and other minorities must sit next to whites to learn but because it is the parents and grandparents of the white children who control the school boards and the state legislatures that run the schools." In the years since *Milliken*, Bell and others have continued to argue that the better approach would have been to focus on requiring financial equity between white and black schools, rather than on the ill-fated efforts to desegregate them.

––––––

Back to the Drawing Board: *Milliken* Returns to the District Court

After *Milliken* was remanded to the district court, NAACP officials announced the possibility of amending the complaint in order to provide evidence of unconstitutional segregation by suburban school districts. Such evidence would be grounds for an interdistrict remedy. Plaintiffs' attorneys determined, however, that it would be difficult for this effort to be successful. Furthermore, according to Nathaniel Jones, the time and resources necessary to pursue interdistrict relief in *Milliken* likely would have hampered his legal team's ability to handle future single-district cases that also needed to be litigated. The focus on whether suburban school officials established or promoted segregation obscured a key point. There was no need for such actions in the suburbs because the rigid housing segregation that existed there ensured that few, if any, black students were available to attend these schools.

Meanwhile, the district court initiated proceedings to develop a Detroit-only desegregation plan, as the Supreme Court had ordered. With Judge Roth's death, this task now fell to Judge Robert DeMascio, who had been assigned to the case by a blind draw on January 7, 1975. DeMascio, a Nixon appointee recommended for his seat on the federal bench by Senator Robert Griffin, had a reputation as a "law-and-order" judge in Detroit's criminal court. Judge DeMascio faced a daunting task. As many observed at the time, how does one integrate a school system that is 70 percent black? Indeed, the district had become even more black than it was when the case originally was filed, leading to arguments that putting together a plan under these circumstances was like shooting at a moving target. And, given the rigid housing segregation within Detroit, the increase in white flight to the suburbs, and the ban on including white students from the suburbs, developing an effective integration plan in Detroit without using busing was next to impossible. Also, Judge DeMascio reportedly was opposed to busing and was quite fearful that a busing plan would lead to the type of unrest that rocked Boston after Judge Garrity's busing order a few months earlier.

Ironically, years later in an interview for an oral history project, DeMascio said that significant school desegregation could have occurred without busing if the suburbs had been included in the remedy, given the proximity of some white suburban schools to black schools in Detroit:

> If I could have used the suburbs, I could have had children walking to school. For example, Dearborn was 100 percent white. Detroit schools that were very close to the border, 70 to 90 percent black. It would have been so easy to reduce that by having children walk to the schools.
>
> In Grosse Pointe, there were schools at Alter Road, which was the borderline of Grosse Pointe Park. Totally white. And here was a school a block and a half away in Detroit, 90 percent black. Well, those children could have had a desegregated education by simply walking. No busing involved. And there were communities like it.

Ironically, this is essentially what the plaintiffs originally proposed — walk-in desegregation — after Judge Roth had rejected various Detroit-only plans. In further reflections, Judge DeMascio speculated whether the state could have solved the problem by creating zones to divide up the Detroit system, the Dearborn system, and others, rather than permitting each community to run its own school system. He asserted, nonetheless, that school districts like Grosse Pointe were not guilty of any actions that created segregation in Detroit schools. Yet he wondered aloud whether "the state superintendent . . . could have worked out something, and saved [Judge] Roth a lot of trouble, by just working out something with the closely related schools on the border of Detroit."

Complying with the Supreme Court directive, nevertheless, DeMascio ordered the Detroit school board and the Bradley plaintiffs to submit their own desegregation proposals on April 1, 1975. Before the plans were submitted, many observers assumed that some level of busing in Detroit would be included, but this sparked a major controversy. The Detroit Board of Education was wary of Detroit-only busing, although it had supported a metropolitan-wide busing remedy. Shortly after the Supreme Court's decision, Cornelius Golightly, president of the board, said that he was opposed to a Detroit-only remedy because, given the 70 percent black student population, shifting around the remaining white students would not create any meaningful integration. In January 1975, he said sarcastically, "It is both a joke and a hoax that a Board of Education with a majority of black members is required by law to integrate a minority of white students into a majority of black students in order to bring those black students into the mainstream of American life." (Between the original case filing in 1970 and the high court's decision in 1974, the board had shifted from majority-white to majority-black control—nine of the thirteen seats.) Recognizing, however, that the board was under a direct order to integrate, Golightly's goal was to adopt the most minimal plan that could receive court approval. Some board members—black and white—still were in favor of voluntary integration plans, such as magnet schools and student transfer programs.

The idea of adopting a Detroit-only busing plan split other segments of the black leadership in Detroit. Some labor activists, political leaders, and officers in the local branch of the NAACP pushed the national body to drop the idea of busing. They saw it as counterproductive, as did a group called New Detroit. New Detroit officials believed that white flight was dissipating and that some whites could be persuaded to return to the city, but a plan that bused white and black students a considerable distance would upset this possibility. They expressed approval of a minimal busing plan that would involve some white and black junior and senior high schools located near each other, but which would leave elementary schools untouched. Local leaders engaged in discussions with Nathaniel Jones, Lou Lucas, and other NAACP officials who supported busing. The national NAACP sought to avoid a repeat of Atlanta, where local and national NAACP officials had become embroiled in a dispute over desegregation proposals in that city. William Grant concluded that national officials felt they could not back away from busing in Detroit because this could harm other cases where de jure segregation had been found. Grant also questioned New Detroit's claim that having no busing would keep whites in Detroit, arguing that this was unlikely, given that white flight had preceded the issue of busing.

In the midst of these conflicts, the Detroit board was faced with the reality that 84 of 290 city schools were majority-white although the student body was 71.5 percent black. Golightly and deputy superintendent Aubrey McCutcheon tried to come up with a plan that would not "tear the city apart." The board presented a draft proposal at a public hearing on March 24, eight days before the April 1 deadline set by Judge DeMascio. The proposal included busing of students at 120 elementary schools and a number of junior high schools in five regions, and it used pairing of schools within regions to achieve racial balances around 30–70 percent white or black. Some of this pairing resulted in placing first through third grade students in one school, and fourth through six graders in another, but it was unclear the extent to which high school students would be included in busing plans.

The four-hour meeting was contentious, with serious opposition from Detroit parents who were especially concerned about segregating children by age groups. They also complained about restrictions on existing freedom-of-choice plans, and they criticized the board for using money for busing rather than for hiring better teachers. Board members pushed back, however, reminding the community that desegregation was not a choice; it was required by court order. At a final public hearing two days later, a sizable group of Latino parents presented their concerns about the potential impact of the proposal on bilingual education. Specifically, in one of the regions, schools that had bilingual services were being paired with those without such programs. These parents also requested that Latino students be classified separately from blacks and whites in the plan.

Former Wayne State law school professor Elwood Hain provided a detailed account of the proceedings surrounding submission of the desegregation proposals, Judge DeMascio's rulings, the implementation of an eventual plan, and court of appeals decisions on DeMascio's orders. Hain's description of the events was enriched by interviews he conducted with Judge DeMascio, NAACP attorney Lou Lucas, and Detroit school board officials. The school board and plaintiffs took drastically different approaches in their final proposals. The board plan was aimed at desegregating about 60 percent of the district, focusing on the eighty majority-white schools and only some of the black schools. The board utilized attendance zone changes, new feeder patterns, noncontiguous zoning, pairing and clustering schools, and revised grade structures. Each school in the district would have roughly the same proportion of black and white students as there was systemwide—a 71:26 ratio, with 3 percent other minorities. All grade levels would be covered; 51,000 of 257,000 students were to be transferred; and regional boundaries would remain intact, with little crossing by students. This proposal also recommended thirteen educational components "designed to improve education or to smooth the transition to a desegregated system" and requested that the state be required to pay for the plan. The estimated cost was $54.9 million, including $11.1 million for 425 buses. Within a month, this estimate was modified to $49.9 million, with $9 million for 335 buses—ninety fewer than the original estimate.

NAACP PROPOSAL

NAACP attorneys presented the plaintiffs' proposal, which covered almost every school and reassigned about 20,000 more students than the board's plan. Using information from Gordon Foster, their education expert who had testified during the trial, plaintiffs sought to have each school mirror the racial composition of the district, plus or minus 15 percent, such that the ideal range was between 57.5 percent and 87.5 percent black. But Foster's plan could not strictly follow this, so he ended up with a plan with schools ranging from 41.4 percent to 89.8 percent black. The plan ignored regional boundaries and did not include any "educational components."

JUDGE DEMASCIO'S DECISION

After receiving the plans, Judge DeMascio appointed three "experts" to assist him in reviewing them—a former Secretary of HEW, an education professor who had authored the student assignment plans used in Charlotte and Denver, and a former U.S. Commissioner of Education. DeMascio tried, unsuccessfully, to get the board and plaintiffs to find areas of consensus and agree to a single plan. After conducting a series of hearings with each side, on Saturday, August 16, DeMascio announced his ruling (written opinion actually dated

August 15). He rejected the NAACP proposal altogether, and he also rejected portions of the school board plan. He ordered the school board to revise its plan according to the guidelines provided in his ruling. DeMascio did not, however, provide a specific date for implementing a desegregation plan. Hain characterized the court's plan as "openly solicitous of the fears of Detroit's remaining white population," "requir[ing] much less actual desegregation than even the [board] thought was legally required," and "putting the burden of that desegregation mainly on the black children."

DeMascio's ruling contained several key provisions. First, he ordered a very limited Detroit-only busing plan – one that included only 27, 524 of the 247,774 students – with the three regions in the entire central city school area omitted. The overall result was that 80 percent of the city's black students were excluded. DeMascio also ordered "ancillary relief," consisting of educational components for all schools, whether segregated or not. These components, based in part on the board's proposal, included: (1) a remedial reading program, (2) in-service training for faculty and staff, (3) vocational education, (4) a testing program, (5) a new uniform code of student conduct, (6) a school community relations program, (7) a counseling and career guidance program, (8) co-curricular activities, and (9) bilingual/bicultural and multicultural studies. The plan did not include any provision regarding faculty reassignments, except to the extent required to deal with changes in grade structure (from K–6, 7–9, and 10–12, to K–5, 6–8, and 9–12). In addition, a monitoring commission was established to oversee programs and make reports to the court, the parties in the case, and the public. Finally, DeMascio ordered the school board to institute specific plans and programs to fulfill the educational components.

In the weeks and months that followed this initial decision, Judge DeMascio issued a series of supplemental rulings and orders modifying the plan's components and its implementation. In doing so, he dealt only with the school board. NAACP counsel announced their displeasure with being excluded from these additional proceedings. DeMascio justified his actions in an October memorandum: "The adversarial phase of this litigation ended with the August 15, 1975 partial judgment; the issue of the conformance of the revised plan with our guidelines was an issue solely between the defendant Detroit

Board and the court. Thus, our failure to include plaintiffs in the process of shaping the details of the transportation plan was not motivated by indifference to their views, but rather reflected the fact that the adversarial phase of this litigation had ended." This explanation, however, did not end the conflicts between the plaintiffs' counsel and the court.

Implementation of Busing in Detroit

As negotiations between Judge DeMascio and the school board over the educational components continued, his minimal busing plan was implemented peacefully in January 1976. Joseph Radelet's and Elwood Hain's later accounts of *Milliken* point to the work of local groups in preparing the public as the primary reason that implementation went smoothly. The Coalition for Peaceful Integration (CPI) and Pro-Detroit (People and Responsible Organizations for Detroit) spearheaded these efforts. The CPI was formerly the MCPI (Metropolitan Coalition for Peaceful Integration), a collaboration between city and suburban organizations, created when interdistrict busing appeared likely. MCPI consisted of church groups, social agencies, and unions (including the DFT), but efforts to attract the business community failed. After the Supreme Court foreclosed the interdistrict remedy, the coalition dropped "Metropolitan" from its name, and suburban groups were replaced by Detroit-based community organizations. Pro-Detroit was comprised primarily of leading figures in the political and business community, including Mayor Coleman Young and former mayor, Judge Roman Gribbs.

Although some members had publicly opposed Detroit-only busing, Pro-Detroit decided to work with CPI to assure peaceful implementation. The groups sponsored radio and television announcements by various community leaders calling for public calm and cooperation, conducted citywide and neighborhood meetings to educate the public, developed resource packets for all the schools and their staffs, and recruited volunteers to assist with the actual implementation. Other groups joined their efforts, and the police department created a busing task force, with 450 officers "chosen as being the most cool-headed," and the department provided them with a special two-day training session.

Another influential factor was one over which local officials had no control – the weather. When the day of implementation arrived, snow and bitter cold had battered the city for six weeks, and rain and refreezing the day before made driving hazardous. These conditions helped keep public protests to a minimum. In addition, antibusing leaders decided against picketing at schools, opting instead to encourage parents to boycott the schools, which Hain describes as "a tactic that promoted peace by temporarily removing from school, children from the most inflamed households." Radelet notes that although implementation was peaceful, "the atmosphere was very tense. There was constant fear in the months to follow that a routine fight between students would escalate into racial conflict related to busing. But major disruptions did not happen. It was a Detroit success story."

A Return to the Sixth Circuit

Even as the busing program was successfully implemented, the plaintiffs, state, and school board continued to disagree with various aspects of Judge DeMascio's orders. The plaintiffs claimed that the busing plan, especially with the central city schools excluded, was too limited and that the educational components were not a sufficient remedy for the massive de jure segregation that had been proven. In May 1976, DeMascio directed the state to pay for half the annual costs of four of the components: the remedial reading program, in-service training, testing, and counseling and career guidance. The school board was to pay the remainder through its regular budget and federal grants. The state claimed that the inclusion of these four components was not appropriate because there was no constitutional violation justifying them; furthermore, the state contended it should not have to pay *any* of the costs for components of the plan. The school board argued that all of the components were necessary to remedy racial segregation in the Detroit public schools and that the state should be required to pay 75 percent of the costs, not just half.

The case returned to the Sixth Circuit for resolution of these issues. A three-judge panel heard arguments on June 15 and issued its decision on August 4. The panel upheld Judge DeMascio's order requiring the challenged educational components as "essential to the efforts to combat the effects of segregation." Requiring the state to pay half the costs also was within the district court's power, the panel affirmed, because state officials and agencies had "contributed substantially to the unlawful *de jure* segregation that exists in Detroit" and because of the financial crisis facing the Detroit school board. The appeals court also affirmed DeMascio's pupil assignment plan, except for his exclusion of schools in the three central city regions: "We cannot hold that where unconstitutional segregation has been found, a plan can be permitted to stand which fails to deal with the three regions where the majority of the most identifiably black schools are located." Even so, the panel did not offer any guidance to Judge DeMascio on this, because of the court's conviction that "genuine constitutional desegregation cannot be accomplished within the school district boundaries of the Detroit School District." The court then noted that the plaintiffs were taking steps to establish the basis for a metropolitan remedy within the guidelines given by the Supreme Court in its 1974 decision.

Another Trip to the Supreme Court

Subsequently, the state appealed the Sixth Circuit's ruling to the Supreme Court. The high court granted review in November 1976, heard oral arguments on March 22, 1977, and issued its decision in *Milliken II* on June 27. By a unanimous vote, the Court affirmed the Sixth Circuit on both aspects of its ruling. Chief Justice Burger wrote the opinion, joined by all the other justices except Justice Powell. Burger noted that although the Court previously had not addressed directly the question of the propriety of ancillary relief in school desegregation orders, since *Brown I* and *Brown II* "federal courts have, over the years, often required the inclusion of remedial programs in desegregation plans to overcome the inequalities inherent in dual school systems." Thus the educational components ordered by the district judge in *Milliken* "did not break new ground" but were "expressly approved" by earlier rulings. Burger wrote, "Pupil assignment alone does not automatically remedy the impact of previous, unlawful educational isolation; the consequences linger and can be dealt with only by independent measures." The Court also rejected the state's claim that Judge DeMascio abused his discretion by requiring it to share the costs of the educational components. Because state officials bore some

{ *Chapter 7* }

responsibility for unconstitutional conduct, under *Swann*, the burden is on them "to take the necessary steps 'to eliminate from the public schools all vestiges of state-imposed segregation.'" Justice Powell wrote an opinion concurring only in the judgment, asserting that the Court should have not decided the case at all, but should have dismissed the writ of certiorari as improvidently granted.

―――――

Implementation of the Remedy and Closure of the Case

The Supreme Court's decision paved the way for implementation of the remedial aspect of Judge DeMascio's plan, but it did not end the controversy. The Monitoring Commission, created to oversee the programs, found itself in continuing conflict with the school board over its reports criticizing the board's performance in implementing and evaluating the various components. In addition, in 1976, plaintiffs' counsel had sought to get Judge DeMascio to recuse himself from the case, claiming a lack of impartiality and improper exclusion from meetings DeMascio held with attorneys for the school board and teachers union. In mid-January 1977, five months before the Court issued its second *Milliken* decision, DeMascio rejected the plaintiffs' allegations and motion for recusal. While his decision was upheld by another district judge who found "no appearance of any partiality whatsoever," in 1978, the Sixth Circuit suggested that DeMascio recuse himself, given the "bitter feelings that have developed."

DeMascio removed himself from the case in August 1980 and was replaced by a panel of three district judges: Chief Judge John Feikens and Judges Avern Cohn and Patricia Boyle. For the next several years, the plaintiffs, school board, and state continued to clash over the costs of the programs, and the relationship between the Monitoring Commission and school board deteriorated further. In 1984, the panel disbanded the commission and ended its oversight of the educational components. Judge Cohn recalled the situation this way:

When we did all this, we said: "Prompted by concern over the environment in which the Monitoring Commission appeared to be operating, we are of the opinion that implementation of the educational components of the remedial orders should be an integral part of the responsibilities of the Detroit Board of Education and viewed by it in the same manner as its other responsibilities. We are of the opinion that our oversight responsibility under the remedial orders and the manner in which courts usually operate to enforce such orders might distort the political processes which govern elected boards of education."

The Sixth Circuit, however, sent the case back to the panel with an order to reinstate the Monitoring Commission and the two components concerning the school community relations program and the uniform student code of conduct. At this point (1985), responsibility for the case moved from the panel to a single judge — Avern Cohn. Judge Cohn continued his supervisory role until September of 1988, when he terminated jurisdiction over the educational components. On February 24, 1989 — nineteen years after the original suit was filed — Judge Cohn closed the case.

———

Post-*Milliken* Legal Developments: Cases in Dayton, Columbus, and Wilmington

After *Milliken I* was decided, NAACP attorneys were perplexed not only by whether and how to bring metropolitan school desegregation cases in the North but also about what it would take to bring successful federal suits involving even de jure segregation within single, large urban systems. Two significant cases of the latter type that reached the Supreme Court involved claims of systemwide segregation within the Dayton and Columbus, Ohio, school districts.

The Supreme Court first encountered the Dayton case in 1977 when it decided *Milliken II*. The Detroit and Dayton cases were heard a month apart, and the Court announced its ruling in the Dayton case on the same day as *Milliken II*. *Dayton Board of Education v. Brinkman I* (1977) arrived at the Court after protracted proceedings in the lower courts, marked by disagreements over the nature and extent of segregation violations, the legal significance of the evidence, and the scope of the remedy. The district court determined that while there was evidence of unlawful segregation, these violations were few and isolated, so the remedy should be limited to a few schools. The court of appeals ruled, however, that a systemwide plan was appropriate.

The Supreme Court, in an opinion by Justice Rehnquist, held that the systemwide remedy was disproportionate to the specific constitutional violations found by the district court, but the Court rejected the school board's request to dismiss the case. Instead, Rehnquist remanded it to the district court for consideration of all possible constitutional violations that could support a systemwide remedy. Upon remand, the district judge withdrew his previous violations findings and said that the plaintiffs had not proved their case. The Sixth Circuit reversed, concluding that a systemwide plan should be reinstated because school officials' prior acts of segregation had systemwide effects. Meanwhile, the district judge in the Columbus case found evidence of segregative intent infecting the entire system, so he also ordered a systemwide remedy. A different panel of the Sixth Circuit affirmed his ruling.

The only metropolitan case brought by NAACP officials after *Milliken I* that met the standard set in that case concerned the schools in Wilmington, Delaware and the surrounding suburban districts in New Castle County. As noted in Chapter 1, the Delaware case was one of five that had been consolidated in the original *Brown* litigation (*Gebhart v. Belton*, 1954). After *Brown*, state officials continued their resistance to desegregation for more than a decade. Ultimately, in 1971, a suit was filed in federal court against the state for its policies creating and maintaining segregation in the entire metropolitan area—both in the Wilmington schools and in the suburban white schools. Because the plaintiffs challenged the constitutionality of state law, federal rules at that time required the case to be decided by a three-judge panel rather than a single judge. Appeals from decisions of three-judge panels subsequently bypass the circuit court of appeals and go directly to the Supreme Court for review. The district panel refused to decide on the metropolitan issue while *Milliken* was pending, but after the Supreme Court's decision, the court invited suburban districts to intervene and present evidence. At the conclusion of these proceedings, the panel found a continuing areawide violation with significant interdistrict effects and held that state law was a significant contributing factor. The Supreme Court affirmed the violation ruling, remedy hearings ensued, and an interdistrict remedy encompassing the city and suburban schools was affirmed by the Third Circuit.

School officials in all three cases requested review by the Supreme Court; the Columbus and Dayton cases were accepted. In 1979 the Court handed down its decisions upholding a systemwide remedy in both cases, by 7-2 and 5-4 votes, in Columbus and Dayton, respectively. Justice White, joined by Justices Brennan, Marshall, Blackmun, and Stevens, wrote the majority opinion for each. Justice Stewart, joined by Chief Justice Burger, wrote an opinion concurring only in the result in Columbus and dissenting in Dayton. Justices Powell and Rehnquist each wrote dissenting opinions. In *Columbus Board of Education v. Penick*, White found that the board's actions in deliberately segregating some schools had a sufficient systemwide impact to justify a systemwide remedy. Moreover, he concluded, "proof of purposeful and effective maintenance of a body of separate black schools in a substantial part of the school system is itself prima facie proof of a dual system," unless the school board provides sufficient rebuttal evidence.

Similarly, in *Dayton Board of Education v. Brinkman II*, White held that a systemwide remedy was appropriate. He wrote: "Given intentionally segregated schools in 1954 . . . the Court of Appeals was quite right in holding that the Board was thereafter under a continuing duty to eradicate the effects of that system and that the systemwide nature of the violation furnished prima facie proof that current segregation in the Dayton schools was caused at least in part by prior intentionally segregative official acts."

In his opinion, Justice Stewart said the Court generally should accept the factual findings of trial courts in school desegregation cases; thus he was able to join the ruling upholding the remedy in Columbus but rejecting it in Dayton. In addition, Stewart disagreed with the majority's view that the existence of an unconstitutional dual system in 1954 (the time of *Brown*) places on school boards "a continuing duty to eradicate the effects of that system."

The dissents by Justices Powell and Rehnquist accused the majority of misreading precedents and evidence to conclude erroneously that de jure segregation was currently present in the public schools of Columbus and Dayton. According to Powell, school segregation in major urban areas "results primarily from familiar segregated housing patterns, which — in turn — are caused by social, economic, and demographic forces for which no school board is responsible." Accusing the majority of "relying upon fictions and presumptions" to uphold the systemwide remedies, he maintained that "the absence of integration in all schools cannot reasonably be attributed to discriminatory conduct." Furthermore, he asserted, the "type of state-enforced segregation that *Brown I* properly condemned no longer exists." Powell also issued his familiar call for local control of public education.

Justice Rehnquist accused the majority of "unprincipled" analysis and departing from "established doctrines of causation and discriminatory purpose." The Court, he said, improperly supported a systemwide remedy that was based primarily on racial imbalance in the Columbus and Dayton schools. Rehnquist viewed the findings of segregation in these cases as isolated acts that did not form a pattern of de jure segregation requiring a systemwide remedy.

Shortly after the rulings, both the Columbus and Dayton boards requested the Court to rehear their cases, but in October 1979 the Court rejected the petitions. Six months later — over strong objections from Justices Powell, Rehnquist, and Stewart — the Court also refused to hear Delaware officials' appeal of the interdistrict remedy ordered there. Writing for the three, Rehnquist called the "county-wide remedy more Draconian than any ever approved by this Court," and he chastised the Court for doing "a disservice to local government and the people of Delaware, and very likely in the long run to the Equal Protection Clause of the Fourteenth Amendment, by once again declining to review a case of such fundamental importance." This dissent from the denial of certiorari, along with opinions in the Columbus and Dayton cases, reflected a deeply divided Court. Indeed, the Court had moved a long way from its early school desegregation decisions, where unanimity had been the rule.

Perhaps the Court was simply reflecting divisions in the country at large, as school desegregation continued to be a controversial issue. For example, even as the Court was deliberating on the Columbus and Dayton cases in the summer of 1979, the House of Representatives was considering an amendment to prohibit the use of busing for desegregation purposes. On July 24, nearly three weeks after the decisions, antibusing advocates fell short in getting the two-thirds vote necessary for passage. The emotional debate and 216-209 final vote against the amendment illustrated, nonetheless, the continuing salience of this issue.

Milliken's Impact on School Desegregation and Education in the North

While it is difficult to determine with precision the impact of *Milliken*, it is widely accepted that the decision has had a major effect in hindering efforts to desegregate urban schools and to provide a quality education for students of color. Gary Orfield and Susan Eaton, with the Harvard Project on School Desegregation, argued that *Milliken I* "rendered *Brown* meaningless for most of the metropolitan North" and, Orfield asserted, "lock[ed] millions of minority schoolchildren into inferior, isolated schools." Jennifer Hochschild and Nathan Scovronick described *Milliken* as "the most important [school desegregation] decision since *Brown*," one that "shut off effective school desegregation for most northern cities, where more and more African Americans and Latinos were living."

MILLIKEN, WHITE FLIGHT, AND DESEGREGATION

Hochschild and Scovronick elaborated further, assessing *Milliken*'s impact on white flight:

The limits set by *Milliken* made things worse in much of the country. It prohibited movement of students, teachers, and resources across district lines unless state governments intervened, and it reinforced the effects of racial and class isolation in housing. The possibility that cities might be desegregated under *Brown* and its successors helped send whites to suburbs that *Milliken* then absolved from any role in a solution. At the same time, economic trends sent poor blacks (and later, immigrants) into the cities. As industries then moved out, cities became much poorer, resources for city schools became more limited as their need became more urgent, and urban schools got much worse. Their decline further justified whites' (and middle-class blacks') retreat into suburbia or private schools.

This is precisely what happened in Detroit. As described in Chapter 2, by the time the Court decided *Milliken*, the city already had undergone significant economic decline. The tax base was depleted, as industries relocated and working-class and middle-class whites who could afford it moved to the suburbs. Moreover, resources for schools were further eroded by numerous school millage defeats in the 1960s and 1970s, including one that occurred less than two weeks after the decision. Jeffrey Mirel notes that "when *Milliken* . . . was finally implemented, the Detroit school system was poorer and more racially isolated than ever before." He concluded that — although the busing issue was neither "the principal cause of the financial problems of the district" nor the "sole reason" for white flight — "busing exacerbated and accelerated both these developments." Others appear more skeptical of the effects of *Milliken* on white flight. Judge Avern Cohn, despite conceding that the case "set back racial integration by confining the remedy to the Detroit city limits," offered this analysis years later:

I'm not a sociologist and not an educator, but I am also not sure that the case really hastened white flight from Detroit by much. I lived in Detroit the first 55 years of my life. Detroit, because of the age of its housing stock and the layout, simply became a less attractive place to live. Those who could afford to move into the new suburban communities and partake of the amenities they offered did so. School environment was a part of that but a small part. The City had aged, and as I say, those that could escape its wrinkles did so, while leaving those who couldn't afford it behind; but not because of *Bradley v. Milliken*.

The purported connection between busing decrees and white flight became a major point of disagreement among those studying these issues. A 1975 study by sociologist James Coleman helped initiate the debate. Several years earlier, Coleman had advocated school desegregation as a useful strategy to improve urban education. In 1975, however, he concluded: "The extremely strong reactions of individual whites in moving their children out of large districts engaged in rapid desegregation suggests that in the long run the policies that have been pursued will defeat the purpose of increasing overall contact among races in schools." Another social scientist, David Armor, went further. His research showed, he contended, that ending large-scale desegregation orders actually would halt white flight and would even entice whites to move back to the city.

Questions about white flight notwithstanding, the fact remains that not much meaningful desegregation has occurred in northern schools in the wake of *Milliken*. Studies indicate that northern schools have become more segregated than those in the South. In a 2004 study, Gary Orfield and Chunmei Lee reported that the "four most segregated states in 2001 for black students . . . were New York, Michigan, Illinois and California." Other northern states included in their list of the top twenty most segregated states for black students were New Jersey and Pennsylvania. Interestingly, Delaware—a border state and the only state outside the South where urban-suburban busing had been ordered—was ranked number two on the authors' list of the most integrated states for black students in 1991-1992, with 90 percent of its black students in majority white schools. A decade later, however, five years after the state's desegregation plan had been dissolved, that number had dropped to nearly 53 percent, but the state still was ranked fifth best.

SCHOOL DESEGREGATION AND EDUCATIONAL QUALITY: ARE THEY CONNECTED?

The other question arising in *Milliken I* and its aftermath is the relationship between school desegregation and educational quality. During the trial, various expert witnesses testified about the effect of segregation on the quality of schools, and the question of whether school desegregation would increase or decrease the educational achievement of minority students was an issue during the remedy hearings, especially the consideration of metropolitan plans. The suburban districts relied extensively on David Armor's research, in which he concluded that mandatory desegregation plans exacerbated racial divisions in schools and had not resulted in increased achievement gains for minority students. According to Armor, taking minority students out of their communities with peers of the same socioeconomic background and putting them in higher income areas where they have to compete with higher achieving classmates makes them realize how disadvantaged and far behind they are. This then heightens their feelings of racism and impedes them from achieving academic success. Armor was one of the witnesses called to give a deposition by William Saxton, attorney for the suburban schools. By contrast, in advocating a metropolitan plan rather than a Detroit-only remedy, the Detroit school board took the opposite position. According to the board's counsel, the trial record showed that "the integration of poor or working class black youngsters with white youngsters of similar economic status is not as likely to provide an environment for their educational improvement as is an environment which includes a preponderance of youngsters from a middle class background."

In ruling that a metropolitan remedy was required, Judge Roth was critical of both approaches. He characterized the evidence offered by the suburban districts as speaking "mainly to educational theory and recent and sometimes contradictory research about narrowly measured educational effects." At the same time, Roth concluded:

> Citation to such research, either in support or rejection of school desegregation, misses the primary point: insofar as pupil assignments are concerned, the system of public schooling in every state must be operated in a racially non-discriminatory fashion; until that objective is met, the very system of public schooling constitutes an invidious racial classification. The adoption of an education theory having the effect of maintaining a pattern of *de jure* segregation is therefore clearly impermissible.

Judge Roth's statements did not end the discussion about desegregated schools and educational quality. Supporters and opponents of desegregation, including busing, continued to cite studies showing positive or negative effects on the achievement levels of black and white students. In addition to analyzing the impact of desegregation on black children, researchers also addressed the concerns of some that white students were harmed by it. After reviewing numerous studies conducted in the 1970s, 1980s, and 1990s, Jennifer Hochschild and Nathan Scovronick maintained that desegregation was more successful than has been assumed, especially in the South. This was partly because some southern school systems contained city, suburban, and rural communities within a single district rather than the urban-suburban district lines that marked northern schools. Based on the desegregation studies, which included data on test scores, high-school dropout rates, and college attendance rates, Hochschild and Scovronick concluded: "So far as one can tell from the evidence, desegregation succeeded not only in moving children into integrated settings but also benefitted them educationally. . . . School desegregation . . .

made black students better able to pursue and attain their dreams—and possibly even to seek competitive success against whites. Except in unusual circumstances, it did not harm the ability of whites to pursue *their* dreams" [emphasis in original].

The Retreat from Desegregation
in the Urban North

The period after *Milliken I* was marked by a retreat from efforts to desegregate schools in the urban North toward a focus on improving predominantly black schools that had been harmed by segregation. This retreat is seen in the rhetoric and actions of public officials, in the attitudes of the public, both white and black, and in the Court's *Milliken II* decision. The Nixon and Ford administrations and members of Congress, both Democrats and Republicans, continued to push for legislation to limit desegregation and to restrict the enforcement power of the Department of Health, Education, and Welfare (HEW), especially for programs involving busing. Missouri Democratic Senator Thomas Eagleton expressed sentiments shared by many: "I find no compelling reason to maintain busing as a congressionally authorized procedure in school desegregation cases when . . . in a great many cases, the social problems created by busing now outweigh the social advantages to be derived from bringing black and white students together." Solicitor General Robert Bork filed appeals pressing the Court to strictly limit busing. Campaigning during the Democratic primaries for the presidency in 1976, Jimmy Carter described busing as a "well-intentioned idea" that had proven to be too divisive and had not improved educational opportunity. And although Drew Days, Carter's assistant attorney general who served as head of the Justice Department's Civil Rights Division, worked closely with the plaintiffs in the Dayton and Columbus cases, during the first three years of Carter's presidency, the Justice Department "initiated only a handful of suits against school segregation." President Ronald Reagan, Carter's successor, advocated voluntary desegregation programs, and his Justice Department joined suits seeking to reduce or eliminate busing plans in Nashville, Tennessee, and Seattle and Tacoma, Washington. Reagan encouraged school systems to find alternatives to busing, such as magnet schools, but then decreased the grant funding available for those programs.

In 1977, the U.S. Commission on Civil Rights emphasized that because of rigid neighborhood segregation, "busing between cities and suburbs [is] the only viable way of desegregating public schools in the nation's large urban areas." But as discussed in Chapter 6, although opinion polls during the 1960s and 1970s indicated increased public acceptance of integrated schools, the public opposed busing as a means to desegregate. Some of this was due to the widely reported claims that it was too racially divisive, was too costly, and was harmful to white students. The public's concerns about racial division certainly were fueled by media coverage of the violent clashes that accompanied busing in some communities. For example, Gary Orfield reported that during October 1975, nine of twenty-six evening news broadcasts that carried stories on urban school desegregation focused on the conflicts in Boston and Louisville, and five of the reports concerned white flight from desegregation in other parts of the country. He concluded, "Few viewers could realize that in most affected communities desegregation had been accepted peacefully."

Claims that busing was inordinately expensive and resulted in students having to travel extraordinary distances were prevalent. According to Hochschild and Scovronick, the evidence, however, pointed in the opposite direction, with desegregation "sometimes reduc[ing] the amount or cost of busing and increas[ing] white students' average transportation time only marginally." The author of a 1983 *New York Times* article reported that statistics from government agencies and desegregation studies showed that 55 percent of all public-school students were bused on a daily basis, but only 7 percent of them were bused for school desegregation purposes.

Researchers have also pointed to evidence that blacks increasingly became opposed to school desegregation and busing. Christine Rossell drew extensively upon public opinion data and her research with David Armor on black and white attitudes from the 1950s through early 1990s. She concluded that there no longer were significant differences between blacks and whites on these issues: black parents, much like their white counterparts, opposed busing and preferred neighborhood schools. Given these data, she maintained, it is "time to rethink our policies on equality in education because, at least with regard to school desegregation, they have been out of sync with what black parents, and indeed parents of all races, actually believe and want for their children." Drew Days acknowledged studies indicating that some African Americans may be retreating from the "integrative ideal" established in *Brown*, but he asserted that this was because of "the burdens blacks have had to carry in the desegregation process, the degree to which integration requires assimilation and rejection of black values and institutions, and the seemingly intractable problems presented for largely black school systems."

The Supreme Court's ruling in *Milliken II* illustrated this impulse away from school desegregation and toward compensating for segregation through the use of the "educational components" approach. The decision and the philosophy and language of the time shifted from a desire to integrate public schools to what Gary Orfield and Susan Eaton termed a "false dichotomy between desegregation and educational compensation." Claiming that racial integration and quality education are not incompatible, they discussed the limits of educational compensation plans in improving education in urban communities. Because these programs are temporary and the schools already have lost revenue, additional compensation has been insufficient to make a real difference. In a 1994 interview with Orfield, former Detroit School Superintendent Arthur Jefferson said of the educational components programs: "My feeling is that they did do some good. My feeling is that while the condition of the Detroit schools is nothing to stand up and applaud, it probably would have been worse without that relief." Judge Avern Cohn agreed: "These monies were insignificant when considered in light of the school district's budget" and "were insufficient to serve as an incentive for real change." In the retrospective to his book on desegregation, Paul Dimond, counsel for the *Milliken* plaintiffs, described it as "guilt money" that has done little to improve inner-city Detroit schools and has left them "largely separate and still unequal."

The Supreme Court's "Resegregation" Decisions in the 1990s

Echoes of the *Milliken* decisions reverberated in three significant Supreme Court rulings in the 1990s, referred to by Orfield and Eaton as "resegregation decisions": *Board of Education of Oklahoma City v. Dowell* (1991), *Freeman v. Pitts* (1992), and *Missouri v. Jenkins* (1995). These cases involved school districts in Oklahoma City, Oklahoma; DeKalb County, Georgia; and Kansas City, Missouri; which had all previously been under orders to desegregate. By the time these cases arrived on the Court's doorstep, the Burger Court had become the Rehnquist Court, and the administration of President George H. W. Bush was encouraging federal courts to withdraw their supervision over school desegregation. The Court's decisions continued the de jure/de facto distinction, along with the emphasis on neighborhood schools and local control of education.

DOWELL (1991)

In a 5-3 decision in *Dowell*, with David Souter, William Brennan's successor, not yet serving, the Court authorized school districts to end busing in favor of neighborhood schools, even if it would result in a return to racial segregation. Chief Justice Rehnquist's majority opinion was joined by Justices Byron White, Sandra Day O'Connor, Antonin Scalia, and Anthony Kennedy. (O'Connor and Kennedy succeeded Stewart and Powell, respectively, while Scalia filled the vacancy created when Rehnquist was elevated to chief.) Rehnquist insisted that local control over education was paramount and that federal judicial supervision should end, once the vestiges of past de jure segregation had been eliminated "to the extent practicable." The decision, however, provided little guidance for federal courts and school districts seeking to end judicial supervision.

Justice Marshall, joined by Justices Blackmun and John Paul Stevens (Douglas's successor), dissented vigorously. In Marshall's view, the fact that "racially identifiable schools" continued to exist established that the school district had not eliminated the "vestiges of past *de jure* segregation" and thus had not remedied the constitutional violation. He pointed to the long history of segregation in Oklahoma City schools and the "nearly unflagging resistance by the [school] Board to judicial efforts to dismantle the city's dual education system." In light of these factors Marshall argued, "Because the record here shows . . . that feasible steps could be taken to avoid one-race schools . . . the Court of Appeals' reinstatement of the [desegregation] decree should be affirmed."

The following year, after Marshall's retirement but before Clarence Thomas's arrival, the justices decided *Freeman v. Pitts*, involving the DeKalb County district that since 1969 had been under a federal court order to desegregate. School officials sought dismissal of the case, contending that the system had achieved unitary status on four of the six factors established in *Green v. County School Board* (1968): student assignments, transportation, physical facilities, and extracurricular activities. A group of parents argued that federal judicial supervision should continue until unitary status was reached on the other two factors (faculty assignments and resource allocation). By a vote of 8-0, with Justices Blackmun, Stevens, and O'Connor concurring only in the judgment, the Court agreed to a partial withdrawal of the district court's control. Justice Kennedy's majority opinion authorized "return[ing] control to the school system in those areas where compliance has been achieved, limiting further judicial supervision to operations that are not yet in full compliance with the court decree." Furthermore, he emphasized, "Residential housing choices, and their attendant effects on the racial composition of schools, present an ever-changing pattern, one difficult to address through judicial remedies." Justice Scalia's concurrence called for an *immediate* end of federal court supervision of school systems that no longer practice intentional segregation. In separate concurrences, Justices Souter and Stevens cautioned that federal courts must engage in an extensive analysis of all the *Green* factors before terminating supervision, including whether decisions by school authorities contributed to racially identifiable schools.

MISSOURI V. JENKINS (1995)

In 1995, the Court decided the Kansas City case, *Missouri v. Jenkins II*. Five years earlier, a sharply divided Court had upheld a federal court order directing Kansas City school board officials to increase taxes in order to help fund a magnet school program aimed at promoting integration by attracting suburban students to inner-city schools (*Missouri v. Jenkins I*, 1990). When the case returned, Justices Ginsburg and Breyer, who had succeeded White and Blackmun, respectively, joined Justices Stevens and Souter in dissent. A five-member majority invalidated the district court's decision that ordered the state to fund salary increases for the school district's staff, as well as remedial "quality education" programs designed to improve inner-city schools and to help reverse white flight." Referring explicitly to *Milliken* as a leading precedent, Chief Justice Rehnquist held that the remedial authority of federal courts is limited to eliminating the vestiges of prior *de jure* segregation." In this case, he said, the district court's purpose was "to attract nonminority students from outside the [Kansas City] schools," but this *"inter*district goal [was] beyond the scope of the *intra*district violation" [emphasis in original].

Justice Thomas's concurrence, charging the district court with paternalism, also was critical of the reasoning in *Brown:*

> It never ceases to amaze me that the courts are so willing to assume that anything that is predominantly black must be inferior. Instead of focusing on remedying the harm done to those black school-children injured by segregation, the District Court sought to convert the Kansas City, Missouri, School District into a "magnet district" that would reverse the "white flight" caused by desegregation. . . . The court has read our cases to support the theory that black students suffer an unspecified psychological harm from segregation that retards their mental and educational development. This approach relies on questionable social science research rather than constitutional principle, but it also rests on an assumption of African American inferiority.

Elaine Jones, former director-counsel of the NAACP Legal Defense and Educational Fund, offered a different assessment of the reasoning in *Brown* that black students were harmed by racial segregation: "This is so not because all-black institutions are inherently inferior because they are all black but because of continuing structural inequities directly attributable to race." Applying this logic to the Kansas City system, she continued, "from almost precisely the moment the school district became majority black, the majority white electorate consistently voted against bond issues and tax levies, precipitating a catastrophic decline in the capital and educational resources of the school district. Without the highly controversial court ordered remedy in *Jenkins v. Missouri*, the deterioration of the school district would not have been arrested."

School Desegregation Returns to the Supreme Court: The 2007 Cases from Seattle and Louisville

After the 1995 *Missouri v. Jenkins* decision, the Court withdrew from school desegregation cases for more than a decade, although federal district courts and courts of appeal continued to hear them. At the high court, cases on race had become focused primarily on issues of employment discrimination and affirmative action policies, both in the workplace and in higher education. School desegregation returned to the Court's agenda in December 2006, when the justices heard arguments in cases from Seattle, Washington, and Louisville, Kentucky. Both districts voluntarily had adopted race-based student assignment plans aimed at maintaining integration in their public schools. The Seattle district never had been under court-ordered desegregation; its plan began after the filing of a federal lawsuit and the settlement of a segregation complaint filed by the NAACP with the Department of HEW's Office for Civil Rights. In 2000, Louisville had been released from a desegregation decree which had been ordered by a federal court in 1975. The Louisville plan operated on a metropolitan-wide basis because the city and suburban schools had been combined into the Jefferson County School System. (Louisville was one of the communities that attracted significant media attention in the 1970s because of the conflicts surrounding the merger of city and suburban systems and the implementation of an extensive busing program.)

In June 2007, the new chief justice, John Roberts, a former Rehnquist law clerk who also served in the Reagan and first Bush administrations, announced the ruling for a fractured Court. The justices split 5-4 in striking down both the Seattle and Louisville programs (cases decided in the same opinion). Roberts's opinion was joined fully by Justices Scalia, Thomas, and Alito; Justice Kennedy wrote an opinion concurring in part and concurring in the judgment. Roberts said the programs were "directed only to racial balance, pure and simple," and this was a violation of equal protection. Citing *Milliken* and *Freeman v. Pitts*, he pointed to the de jure/de facto distinction, maintaining that the "distinction between segregation by state action and racial imbalance caused by other factors has been central to our jurisprudence in this area for generations." Roberts concluded simply: "The way to stop discrimination on the basis of race is to stop discriminating on the basis of race." Justice Kennedy, although agreeing that the Louisville and Seattle plans were unconstitutional, said that his colleagues had gone too far in asserting that race may never be taken into account by school authorities. Race could be used to achieve compelling interests in achieving racial diversity, Kennedy insisted, as well as "avoiding racial isolation" and addressing "the problem of *de facto* resegregation in schooling," so long as the programs were carefully drawn. He had in mind race-conscious policies that do not identify individuals by race, such as magnet schools or decisions about where to locate schools.

Justice Breyer wrote for the dissenters—Stevens, Souter, and Ginsburg—in a lengthy opinion, portions of which he read from the bench. Breyer sharply criticized the plurality for "announc[ing] legal rules that will obstruct efforts by state and local governments to deal effectively with the growing resegregation of public schools," for provoking a new "disruptive round of race-related litigation," and for "undermin[ing] *Brown*'s promise of integrated primary and secondary education that local communities have sought to make a reality." His statement from the bench also alluded to recent personnel shifts on the Court that may have affected the decision. The justices had denied review in a similar case from Massachusetts while Justice O'Connor was still on the Court, but after the arrival of Roberts and Alito, the Court accepted review of the Seattle and Louisville appeals. In addition, given O'Connor's vote and majority opinion in favor of affirmative action in the 2003 University of Michigan Law School case (*Grutter v. Bollinger*), she likely would have voted the other way in the Seattle and Louisville cases.

Conclusions

More than thirty-five years after the first *Milliken* decision, urban education remains in crisis. After efforts at desegregation were abandoned, civil rights activists, educators, and elected officials looked to other solutions to assist urban schools in educating large numbers of disadvantaged children who remain racially isolated in webs of concentrated poverty. School choice and private school voucher programs and the creation of charter schools and single-sex academies have been among the strategies adopted to deal with this problem of unequal educational opportunity. Also, given the Court's 1973 *Rodriguez* decision foreclosing the possibility of achieving funding equity through federal intervention, some have pursued equitable funding litigation at the state level. The federal No Child Left Behind program, initiated by President George W. Bush in 2002, was touted by many as the answer to the problems of urban school districts, but nearly a decade later, there has not been much improvement. In late 2009, the administration of President Barack Obama launched its "Race to the Top" initiative, a program that allows states to compete for a share of more than four billion dollars in education funding. Whether urban schools will benefit from this program is unclear.

As for Detroit, the school district remains plagued by high dropout rates, declining enrollments, ballooning deficits, high superintendent turnover, financial scandals and corruption, and public disputes among school board members. The district's fiscal health has deteriorated so badly that in March of 2009 the state appointed Robert Bobb as an emergency financial manager to oversee the district's finances. Three months after his appointment, a former director of communications for the district wrote an op-ed in the *Detroit Free Press* calling for the state simply to abolish the Detroit public schools and replace the system with smaller districts to be monitored by the state. He offered these harsh words: "DPS is the Somalia of public education. It is the quintessential failed public school district, a diseased organizational culture. To be sure, there are a handful of schools that might be worth saving. But the majority of them fail our children." By December of 2009, despite reports of disappointing results on a nationwide test of fourth through eighth graders, there seemed to be a few positive signs. Bobb has had some success in reducing the deficit, voters approved a $500.5 million bond proposal to rebuild or renovate eighteen schools and demolish numerous others that have been closed, and more than 3,000 residents have volunteered to participate in a reading program to assist students. There also is a call to have Robert Bobb appointed as an emergency academic manager, but that would require a change in state law.

The continuing crisis in Detroit schools has led some to question whether a different decision in *Milliken* would have made a positive difference in Detroit or in other metropolitan school systems. James Patterson observed:

> We cannot conclude . . . that a decision the other way in *Milliken* would have transformed race relations or education in America's metropolitan regions. Thanks in part to the economic problems besetting the United States in the 1970s and early 1980s, cities and suburbs alike confronted deep fiscal problems that compounded existing class and cultural differences, among them the new mix caused by the arrival of a great many people of Hispanic background. There was often little political will to devise metropolitan solutions to these differences.

Arthur Johnson, who was appointed in 1966 as the first black assistant superintendent in the history of the Detroit school system, takes a different position. Reflecting on *Milliken* in his memoirs, he contended: "If the city's black children attended schools that were mostly white, there is no way that American society and leadership would have allowed the schools and educational culture to deteriorate as they have in Detroit and other urban districts that are predominantly black. The absence of a white constituency means the absence of genuine political concern in the corridors of power."

Looking back from the vantage point of the second decade of the twenty-first century, which of these assessments seems more accurate? While the fiscal, social, and political issues facing metropolitan communities since the 1970s indeed have been extremely complex, it is difficult to believe that the crisis in urban education generally, and Detroit specifically, would be what it is today had the Court decided differently in *Milliken*. It is reasonable to assume that had white and black children across metropolitan areas been required to attend the same schools, urban schools would not have deteriorated so badly. Without the opportunity to escape desegregation by further flight to the suburbs, white residents likely would have been more concerned about ensuring high quality in all the schools. State legislatures would have had a greater incentive to allocate resources in ways that served the needs of all schools in urban areas, not simply those in the suburbs. White voters may have been more inclined to support millage and bond proposals when deemed necessary. And perhaps the current emphasis on charter schools and vouchers for private schools would not be necessary.

The argument that the better strategy would have been to jettison the idea of cross-district desegregation in favor of providing more funding for urban schools seems doubtful and somewhat naive. As Judge Cohn observed of Detroit, even at the outset, the funding connected with the educational components program was not adequate to bring about major improvements because so many of the schools were in such poor shape to begin with. In that context, massive amounts of continued additional funding also would have been necessary, and, even if those extra resources were promised, what were the chances that such promises would be kept? Given the sentiments held by many whites in the Detroit metropolitan area, it is unlikely that either city residents or state legislators would have supported continual increases in funding for Detroit public schools. After all, even before the drive toward desegregation began, white voters in Detroit had begun voting against millage increases and bond proposals, despite evidence of dire financial circumstances in the district.

At the national level, policy decisions in the 1980s illustrate the difficulty of depending on public officials to provide increased funds for inner-city schools, even those under desegregation orders. At the same time that the Reagan administration decried busing and called for alternatives such as magnet schools, it was cutting the funding to pay for these programs. In 1981, the administration merged numerous categorical grant programs into one block grant program to be administered by the states according to state formulas approved by the federal Department of Education. This included an emergency school aid program for districts with desegregation problems, a program under which cities had been allowed to apply directly for the funding. Under this new Chapter 2 block grant, however, this funding was controlled by states. Cities complained that state governments were not taking into consideration the higher per-pupil costs of inner-city districts. Consequently, because many of those districts had to take money from their regular programs to pay for desegregation, they found themselves in a catch-22 situation. As a St. Louis school official described it, "we'll have to rob Peter to pay Paul." The superintendent of Buffalo, where twenty-one magnet schools had been created, made this observation: "One of the most galling things is that the president has argued for this type of desegregation magnet schools [*sic*] and we have gone in that direction. Yet he has stripped us of all the money to do this sort of thing."

The issue presented with urban and metropolitan desegregation cases was not that of racial balance, but student equity. As many noted at the time, the plaintiffs and most of their supporters were not seeking to desegregate Detroit schools because they believed that black students needed to be sitting next to white students to learn. As Verda Bradley noted in her interview in 2004, "We were upset because [Detroit's black schools] weren't getting as many materials as some other schools. We figured if it was desegregated, we would get the same."

Finally, from a theoretical perspective, it does appear that focusing solely on upgrading urban schools rather than on desegregating them would have signaled a return to the *Plessy v. Ferguson* doctrine of "separate-but-equal." This pernicious doctrine was based on the premise of white superiority and black inferiority, a theory which *Brown*, the cases that followed it, and the Civil Rights Movement of the 1950s and 1960s attempted to eradicate. Permitting a resurgence of "separate-but-equal" in metropolitan school systems would simply have legitimated what Paul Dimond refers to as "a caste system of racial ghettoization."

In the final analysis, *Milliken v. Bradley* was about far more than school desegregation and busing. It reflected differing perceptions and perspectives about several things — the origin and operation of the metropolitan color line; the political, economic, and social dynamics of Detroit and its suburbs; and the role of law and the courts in achieving social change, especially in the face of resistance from the public, as well as from government officials. But the aftermath of the decision leaves one important question unanswered: is school integration still an important value in American society? In his *Milliken* dissent, Justice Marshall wrote: "Our Nation, I fear, will be ill served by the Court's refusal to remedy separate and unequal education, for unless our children begin to learn together, there is little hope that our people will ever learn to live together." Early in this new century, it is unclear how many Americans share these sentiments.

CASES CITED

Alexander v. Holmes County Board of Education, 396 U.S. 19 (1969)
Allen Park Public Schools v. Bradley, 418 U.S. 717 (1974)
Berea College v. Kentucky, 211 U.S. 45 (1908)
Board of Education of Oklahoma City v. Dowell, 489 U.S. 237 (1991)
Bolling v. Sharpe, 347 U.S. 497 (1954)
Bradley v. Milliken
 338 F. Supp. 582 (1971)
 345 F. Supp. 914 (1972)
 484 F. 2d 215 (1973)
 540 F. 2d 229 (1976)
 402 F. Supp. 1096 (1975)
 411 F. Supp. 943 (1975)
Bradley v. School Board of Richmond
 338 F. Supp. 67 (1972)
 462 F. 2d 1058 (1972)
Briggs v. Elliott, 347 U.S. 483 (1954)
Brown v. Board of Education
 347 U.S. 483 (1954) (*Brown I*)
 349 U.S. 294 (1955) (*Brown II*)
Buchanan v. Warley, 245 U.S. 60 (1917)
Civil Rights Cases, 109 U.S. 3 (1883)
Columbus Board of Education v. Penick, 443 U.S. 449 (1979)
Cooper v. Aaron, 358 U.S. 1 (1958)
Corrigan v. Buckley, 271 U.S. 323 (1926)
Cumming v. Richmond County Board of Education, 175 U.S. 528 (1899)
Davis v. County School Board of Prince Edward County, 347 U.S. 483 (1954)
Dayton v. Board of Education v. Brinkman
 433 U.S. 406 (1977) (*Dayton I*)
 443 U.S. 526 (1979) (*Dayton II*)
Deal v. Cincinnati Board of Education
 369 F. 2d 55 (1966)
 419 F. 2d 1387 (1969)
Dred Scott v. Sandford, 60 U.S. 393 (1857)
Freeman v. Pitts, 503 U.S. 467 (1992)
Gebhart v. Belton, 347 U.S. 483 (1954)
Gong Lum v. Rice, 275 U.S. 78 (1927)
Green v. County School Board, 391 U.S. 430 (1968)
Griffin v. County School Board of Prince Edward County, 377 U.S. 218 (1964)
Grosse Pointe Public School System v. Bradley, 418 U.S. 717 (1974)

Hall v. DeCuir, 95 U.S. 485 (1878)

Jones v. Alfred H. Mayer Co., 392 U.S. 409 (1968)

Keyes v. Denver School District No. 1, 413 U.S. 189 (1973)

McGhee v. Sipes, 334 U.S. 1 (1948)

McLaurin v. Oklahoma State Regents, 339 U.S. 637 (1950)

Meredith v. Jefferson County Board of Education, 551 U.S. 701 (2007)

Milliken v. Bradley
    418 U.S. 717 (1974) *(Milliken I)*
    433 U.S. 267 (1977) *(Milliken II)*

Missouri v. Jenkins
    495 U.S. 33 (1990)
    515 U.S. 1139 (1995)

Missouri ex rel. Gaines v. Canada, 305 U.S. 337 (1938)

Morgan v. Hennigan, 379 F. Supp. 410 (1974)

Parents Involved in Community Schools v. Seattle School District No. 1, 551 U.S. 701 (2007)

Pearson v. Murray, 169 Md. 478 (1936)

People ex rel. Workman v. Board of Education of Detroit, 18 Mich. 400 (1869)

Plessy v. Ferguson, 163 U.S. 537 (1896)

Reynolds v. Sims, 377 U.S. 533 (1964)

Roberts v. City of Boston, 59 Mass. 198 (1849)

San Antonio Independent School District v. Rodriguez, 411 U.S. 1 (1973)

School Board of Richmond v. State Board of Education, 412 U.S. 92 (1973)

Shelley v. Kraemer, 334 U.S. 1 (1948)

Sipuel v. Oklahoma State Regents, 332 U.S. 631 (1948)

Spencer v. Kugler, 404 U.S. 1027 (1972)

Swann v. Charlotte-Mecklenburg Board of Education, 402 U.S. 1 (1971)

Sweatt v. Painter, 339 U.S. 629 (1950)

CHRONOLOGY

mid-1960s	Detroit civil rights activists advocate decentralization or "community control" of public schools (patterned after movement in New York City)
1965	Liberal-labor-black coalition takes control of Detroit Board of Education; hires pro-integration superintendent in 1966
1966	Sixth Circuit decides *Deal v. Cincinnati Board of Education* — rules that segregation of neighborhood schools is solely result of private housing choices
July 1967	Civil unrest in Detroit
1968	"Community control" bills introduced into Michigan House of Representatives but defeated; School board elections result in membership of four pro-integration liberals, two anti-integration conservatives, and one community control advocate
1969	Michigan Senate passes decentralization bill introduced by Coleman Young; bill passed by Michigan House, signed by Governor William Milliken
1970	
April 7	Detroit Board of Education decentralization plan approved — established limited plan for desegregating high schools
April–June	Public protests against desegregation plan; Michigan legislature votes to rescind April 7 Detroit board plan: passed decentralization without integration
July 7	Governor Milliken signs Act 48 into law — officially rescinds April 7 Detroit board plan; new law shortens terms of pro-integration board members
August 4	Pro-integration school board members recalled in first successful recall effort in the 128-year history of the school board
August 18	NAACP files suit in federal district court against school board and state officials, charging that Act 48 is unconstitutional; requested reinstatement of April 7 plan
August–September	Federal district judge Stephen Roth assigned to case; Roth rejects motion for restoration of April 7 plan; Roth also dismisses governor and attorney general as defendants

October 13	Sixth Circuit declares Act 48 unconstitutional and reinstates governor and attorney general as defendants; Roth again rejects integration plan and postpones start of trial
December 3	Roth approves voluntary magnet school plan offered by Detroit School Board

1971

February 22	Sixth Circuit upholds ruling on magnet schools but remands case to Roth for full trial on issue of segregation
April 6	Trial begins; forty-one-day trial held over four-month period
April 20	Supreme Court upholds busing as remedy for de jure segregation in *Swann v. Charlotte-Mecklenburg Board of Education*
July 22	End of trial
September 27	Roth rules that Detroit schools are segregated de jure; orders preparation of desegregation plans
October	Michigan Senator Robert Griffin introduces a constitutional amendment to ban busing as remedy for school segregation; Lewis Powell and William Rehnquist appointed to the Supreme Court to succeed Justices Hugo Black and John Marshall Harlan, respectively

1972

February	Detroit school board concedes on segregation claims and decides to support a metropolitan remedy
March–April	Roth rejects Detroit-only desegregation plans; admits suburbs as intervenors; holds hearings on metropolitan-wide desegregation plans
May	George Wallace wins Michigan Democratic presidential primary
June 5	Fourth Circuit reverses metropolitan remedy in *Bradley v. School Board of Richmond*
June 14	Roth issues ruling calling for a metropolitan remedy, including cross-district busing
November 4	President Nixon reelected; Roth suffers massive heart attack
December 8	Three-judge panel of Sixth Circuit affirms Roth's findings of (1) de jure segregation of Detroit public schools by school board and state of Michigan, and (2) desegregation limited

	to Detroit would be inadequate remedy; vacated other portions of ruling
1973	
March 21	Supreme Court decides *San Antonio Independent School District v. Rodriguez* — upholds property tax system for financing public education over claims that it violated Equal Protection Clause
May 21	Supreme Court splits 4-4 in Richmond case so appeals court ruling upheld
June 12	Sixth Circuit en banc reissues three-judge panel opinion in *Milliken* with minor revisions; vacated Roth's ruling on metropolitan plan; sent back to Roth to hear suburbs before ordering cross-district remedy
June 21	Supreme Court decides *Keyes v. School District of Denver* — makes distinction between de jure and de facto segregation
September 6	State and suburban defendants petition Supreme Court for review
November 19	Supreme Court grants cert in *Milliken*
1974	
February 27	Supreme Court hears oral arguments
July 10	Judge Roth suffers third heart attack; dies the next day
July 25	Supreme Court upholds ruling of de jure segregation of Detroit public schools, but strikes cross-district remedy; remands case to district court for development of Detroit-only remedy
1975	
January	Judge Robert DeMascio assigned as Roth's successor
April-August	DeMascio reviews desegregation proposals and orders new remedy — limited busing plan and ancillary relief
1976	
January	Peaceful implementation of busing/pupil reassignment plan
May	DeMascio orders state to pay portion of ancillary relief
August 4	Sixth Circuit affirms DeMascio rulings with some caveats; State subsequently appeals Sixth Circuit's decision to Supreme Court
November	Supreme Court grants review

1977

March 22   Supreme Court hears oral arguments in *Milliken II*

June 27   Supreme Court upholds ancillary relief and requirement of
                state payment for programs

1977-1980   Ancillary relief implemented

1979   Supreme Court decides *Columbus Board of Education v.
                Penick* and *Dayton Board of Education v. Brinkman II* —
                upholds systemwide desegregation remedies for public
                schools within the cities of Columbus and Dayton, Ohio

August 1980   DeMascio replaced by three-judge panel

1985   Case moves from three-judge panel to single judge, Avern
                Cohn

February 1989   Cohn closes case

1990   Supreme Court decides *Missouri v. Jenkins I* — upholds
                federal court order directing school board officials in
                Kansas City to increase taxes in order to help fund magnet
                school program aimed at promoting integration

1991   *Board of Education of Oklahoma City v. Dowell* — Supreme
                Court permits school district operating under a
                desegregation decree to end busing in favor of
                neighborhood schools, even if result is return to one-race
                schools

1992   Supreme Court decides *Freeman v. Pitts* — authorizes partial
                withdrawal of federal court supervision over DeKalb
                County, Georgia, school system although full compliance
                with desegregation order not yet achieved

1995   *Missouri v. Jenkins II* — Supreme Court overrules federal
                court order directing state to increase funding for staffing
                and operation of magnet school program

2007   *Parents Involved in Community Schools v. Seattle School District
                No. 1* and *Meredith v. Jefferson County Board of Education* —
                Supreme Court invalidates race-based student assignment
                plans voluntarily adopted by school districts in Seattle,
                Washington, and Louisville, Kentucky, to maintain
                integration

BIBLIOGRAPHICAL ESSAY

Note from the Series Editors: The following bibliographical essay contains the major primary and secondary sources the author consulted for this volume. We have asked all authors in the series to omit formal citations in order to make our volumes more readable, inexpensive, and appealing for students and general readers. In adopting this format, Landmark Law Cases and American Society follows the precedent of a number of highly regarded and widely consulted series.

Beyond Busing: Reflections on Urban Segregation, the Courts & Equal Opportunity (Ann Arbor: University of Michigan Press, 2005), by Paul R. Dimond, a member of the plaintiffs' legal team in *Milliken*, is the first source I discovered that provides a comprehensive discussion of the case from its beginnings through the Supreme Court's second decision in 1977. As noted in the preface, I also was fortunate enough to be able to interview Mr. Dimond and several other key figures: William Grant, former education writer for the *Detroit Free Press*; William Saxton, attorney for the suburban districts that challenged the metropolitan remedy; federal district judge Avern Cohn who eventually closed the case; former Michigan Attorney General Frank Kelley, one of the defendants; Alexander Ritchie, who represented the white Detroit parents who opposed the desegregation efforts; and Nathaniel Jones, lead counsel for the plaintiffs, who later was appointed to the Sixth Circuit Court of Appeals.

The LexisNexis Academic Service, available online through my university's library, was indispensable in obtaining the official rulings and opinions from all three court levels in *Milliken*, as well as opinions from other relevant cases. Party and amicus case briefs and a transcript of the oral argument in *Milliken I* are available in volume 80 of *Landmark Briefs and Arguments of the Supreme Court of the United States* (University Publications of America, 1975), edited by Philip B. Kurland and Gerhard Casper. Lewis Powell's amicus brief for the Commonwealth of Virginia in *Swann v. Charlotte-Mecklenburg Board of Education* (1971) is found in an earlier volume of the same series.

I spent several days at the Manuscript Division of the Library of Congress examining the collected papers of Justices William Brennan, William O. Douglas, Thurgood Marshall, and Harry Blackmun, who kept the most comprehensive and detailed records of the four. I discovered valuable behind-the-scenes information about conference deliberations, preparations for oral argument, and the negotiations that occurred during the opinion writing phase. While at the LOC, I also was able to look at the *Milliken* materials in the NAACP papers, which helped to shed additional light on important issues.

For information on the events leading up to the case, proceedings in the trial and appellate courts, and the political context, I benefitted from many sources. William Grant's "Community Control vs. School Integration — the case of Detroit," *Public Interest* 24 (1971): 62–79; "The Detroit School Case: An Historical Overview," *Wayne Law Review* 21 (March 1975): 854–866; and "Letter from Detroit: The Courts and the Schools," *Urban Review* 8 (1975): 145–152, all helped to illuminate important phases of the case. William Saxton shared with me the joint appendix, a set of documents sent to the Supreme Court by the attorneys for both sides that contains the most significant pleadings and motions filed by the parties, key excerpts from the trial transcripts, rulings by the judges, depositions, and other exhibits. Judge Avern Cohn initially made copies of selected documents from the second round of the case and later sent his complete file. Even more useful was a four-part series on *Milliken* that was spearheaded by Cohn and edited by John P. Mayer. These articles were published in 2008 and 2009 in *The Court Legacy*, the journal of The Historical Society for the United States District Court for the Eastern District of Michigan. They are Jennifer A. Huff, "The Only Feasible Desegregation Plan: *Milliken v. Bradley* and Judge Roth's Order for Cross-District Busing" 15 (May 2008): 1–11; John R. Runyan, "*Milliken v. Bradley I:* The Struggle to Apply *Brown v. Board of Education* in the North" 15 (September 2008): 1–16; Samuel C. Damren, "*Milliken v. Bradley I* on Remand: The Impossible Assignment" 16 (February 2009): 1–11; and U.S. District Judge Avern Cohn and John P. Mayer, "Winding Up *Bradley v. Milliken*" 16 (June 2009): 1–9.

Elwood Hain's "Sealing off the City: School Desegregation in Detroit," in *Limits of Justice: The Courts' Role in School Desegregation*, edited by Howard I. Kalodner and James J. Fishman (Cambridge, MA: Ballinger, 1978), detailed the case from its origins through Judge DeMascio's development of the Detroit-only remedy. Joseph Radelet took a longer-term look at the case, including implementation of the remedy, in "Stillness at Detroit's Racial Divide: A Perspective on Detroit's School Desegregation Court Order — 1970–1989," appearing in *Urban Review* 23 (1991): 173–190. Arthur Johnson, former Detroit schools assistant superintendent and director of the Detroit branch of the NAACP, provides an insider's perspective in Chapter 4 of his *Race and Remembrance: A Memoir* (Detroit: Wayne State University Press, 2008). Eleanor Wolf's *Trial and Error* (Detroit: Wayne State University Press, 1981) offers a disparaging account of the *Milliken* trial, with particular criticism of Judge Roth's conclusions regarding the connection between housing discrimination and school segregation.

For additional information concerning the attitudes of Michigan's public officials and Detroit-area residents about school desegregation and busing, David Riddle's "Race and Reaction in Warren, Michigan, 1971 to 1974: *Bradley v. Milliken* and the Cross-district Busing Controversy," *Michigan Historical Review* 26 (Fall 2000): 1–49, was particularly helpful. See also Michael

O'Brien's *Philip Hart: The Conscience of the Senate* (East Lansing: Michigan State University Press, 1995). I supplemented these sources with news articles and editorials from the *Detroit Free Press, Detroit News, Macomb Daily, Michigan Chronicle, New York Times, Washington Post,* and *Newsweek.* For discussion about attitudes toward busing on a broader level, see Gary Orfield's *Must We Bus: Segregated Schools and National Policy* (Washington, DC: Brookings Institution, 1978), Christine H. Rossell's "The Convergence of Black and White Attitudes on School Desegregation Issues," and Drew S. Days's *"Brown* Blues: Rethinking the Integrative Ideal," both published in *Redefining Equality,* edited by Neal Devins and Davison M. Douglas (New York: Oxford University Press, 1998). On the Boston busing controversy, see J. Anthony Lukas, *Common Ground: A Turbulent Decade in the Lives of Three American Families* (New York: Vintage Books, 1985), and Peter Irons, *Jim Crow's Children: The Broken Promise of the Brown Decision* (New York: Viking Penguin, 2002).

I consulted numerous writings on the history of race relations in Michigan generally and Detroit specifically, including race and public education. Roy Finkenbine's "A Beacon of Liberty on the Great Lakes: Race, Slavery, and the Law in Antebellum Michigan" and Paul Finkelman's "The Promise of Equality and the Limits of Law: From the Civil War to World War II" described the city's and state's racial histories from Michigan's territorial days until the middle of the twentieth century. These were included in *The History of Michigan,* edited by Finkelman and Martin J. Hershock (Athens: Ohio University Press, 2006). Chapters 1 and 3 of David M. Katzman's *Before the Ghetto: Black Detroit in the Nineteenth Century* (Urbana: University of Illinois Press, 1973) include an illuminating discussion of the development of public education for black children in Detroit from the 1840s until 1871. An essential resource was Jeffrey Mirel's *The Rise and Fall of an Urban School System: Detroit, 1907–1981* (Ann Arbor: University of Michigan Press, 1993), which traces the history of public education in Detroit, including descriptions of how controversies over desegregation, school board elections, school reform, and fiscal problems and other crises affected *Milliken.* The connection between segregated housing and segregated schools in Detroit is examined at length in two articles from a March 1975 symposium issue of the *Wayne Law Review*—Karl E. Taeuber's "Demographic Perspectives on Housing and School Segregation" (833–850) and "Population Trends and School Segregation in the Detroit Metropolitan Area" by Reynolds Farley (867–902).

Thomas Sugrue's *The Origins of the Urban Crisis: Race and Inequality in Postwar Detroit* (Princeton, NJ: Princeton University Press, 2005) is indispensable in understanding the development and maintenance of the racial divide in the Detroit metropolitan area. Other helpful contributions to this topic are *Detroit Divided,* by Reynolds Farley, Sheldon Danziger, and Harry J. Holzer (New York: Russell Sage Foundation, 2000), and *Detroit: Race and Uneven*

Development, by Joe T. Darden, et al. (Philadelphia: Temple University Press, 1987).

On the development of de facto segregation in urban and suburban communities in the North in general, I found several books useful. Among them were Alan B. Anderson and George W. Pickering, *Confronting the Color Line: The Broken Promise of the Civil Rights Movement in Chicago* (Athens: University of Georgia Press, 1986), Douglas S. Massey and Nancy A. Denton, *American Apartheid: Segregation and the Making of the Underclass* (Cambridge: Harvard University Press, 1993), Reynolds Farley and Walter R. Allen, *The Color Line and the Quality of Life in America* (New York: Oxford University Press, 1989), Charles M. Lamb, *Housing Segregation in Suburban America Since 1960: Presidential and Judicial Politics* (New York: Cambridge University Press, 2005), and Kenneth T. Jackson, *Crabgrass Frontier: The Suburbanization of the United States* (New York: Oxford University Press, 1985). Clement Vose's *Caucasians Only: The Supreme Court, the NAACP and the Restrictive Covenant Cases* (Berkeley: University of California Press, 1959) is a classic study of the significance of racially restrictive covenants in producing and maintaining segregated housing. James Loewen's more recent *Sundown Towns: A Hidden Dimension of American Racism* (New York: New Press, 2005) adds another dimension to understanding the patterns of racial segregation that pervade northern communities. The *Report of the National Advisory Commission on Civil Disorders* (New York: Bantam, 1968) is a poignant analysis of the racial disorder that exploded in American cities during the 1960s. For another examination of the situation in Detroit specifically, Peter Charles Hoffer's *Seven Fires* (New York: PublicAffairs, 2006) is an engaging resource.

Volumes have been written about *Brown v. Board of Education* and school desegregation in general. Richard Kluger's seminal work, *Simple Justice: The History of Brown v. Board of Education and Black America's Struggle for Equality* (New York: Vintage Books, 1975), explains the development and execution of the NAACP's legal strategy to overturn the "separate but equal" doctrine emanating from *Plessy v. Ferguson* (1896). Genna Rae McNeil's *Groundwork: Charles Hamilton Houston and the Struggle for Civil Rights* (Philadelphia: University of Pennsylvania Press, 1983) and Mark Tushnet's *Making Civil Rights Law: Thurgood Marshall and the Supreme Court, 1936–1961* (New York: Oxford University Press, 1994) provide additional insights, focusing on the architects of this strategy.

Mary Dudziak's *Cold War Civil Rights: Race and the Image of American Democracy* (Princeton, NJ: Princeton University Press, 2000) is at the forefront of the literature on the role of the Cold War and American foreign policy in prodding the executive branch to support efforts to end Jim Crow. See also *The Unsteady March: The Rise and Decline of Racial Equality in America* (Chicago: University of Chicago Press, 1999), by Philip A. Klinkner with

Rogers M. Smith. To learn about the civil rights movement more broadly, see Aldon D. Morris, *The Origins of the Civil Rights Movement: Black Communities Organizing for Change* (New York: The Free Press, 1984), Henry Hampton and Steve Fayer, *Voices of Freedom: An Oral History of the Civil Rights Movement from the 1950s through the 1980s* (New York: Bantam Books, 1990), and *The Eyes on the Prize Civil Rights Reader*, edited by Clayborne Carson et al. (New York: Penguin Books USA, 1991).

Gerald Rosenberg's *The Hollow Hope: Can Courts Bring about Social Change?* (Chicago: University of Chicago Press, 1991) questioned whether *Brown*'s effects were as widespread and profound as many had assumed, prompting others to enter this debate, including James T. Patterson, *Brown v. Board of Education: A Civil Rights Milestone and Its Troubled Legacy* (New York: Oxford University Press, 2001); Derrick Bell, *Silent Covenants: Brown v. Board of Education and the Unfulfilled Hopes for Racial Reform* (New York: Oxford University Press, 2004); and Charles J. Ogletree, *All Deliberate Speed: Reflections on the First Half Century of Brown v. Board of Education* (New York: W. W. Norton, 2004). The most comprehensive recent work on this topic is Michael J. Klarman's, *From Jim Crow to Civil Rights: The Supreme Court and the Struggle for Racial Equality* (New York: Oxford University Press, 2004). Paul Finkelman's review of Klarman's book, "Civil Rights in Historical Context: In Defense of *Brown*," *Harvard Law Review* 118 (January 2005: 973–1029), takes a contrary view. A host of other scholars commented on the case's legacy on its fiftieth anniversary, in *Black, White, and Brown: The Landmark School Desegregation Case in Retrospect* (Washington, DC: CQ Press, 2004), edited by Clare Cushman and Melvin I. Urofsky for the Supreme Court Historical Society.

Others have written about the struggle to implement *Brown* in the South. J. W. Peltason's classic work, *Fifty-Eight Lonely Men: Southern Federal Judges and School Desegregation*, (New York: Harcourt, Brace & World, 1961), examines the conflicts faced by the judges directly responsible for supervising desegregation. The importance of the Civil Rights Act of 1964 and guidelines issued by the executive branch to force compliance are discussed by James R. Dunn in "Title VI, the Guidelines and School Desegregation in the South," *Virginia Law Review* 53 (December 1967: 42–88) and by Harrell R. Rodgers and Charles S. Bullock in "School Desegregation: A Policy Analysis," *Journal of Black Studies* 2 (June 1972: 409–437). See also Gary Orfield's *The Reconstruction of Southern Education: The Schools and the 1964 Civil Rights Act* (New York: Wiley-Interscience, 1969).

Gary Orfield, along with his colleagues at The Civil Rights Project, have authored numerous studies of the effects of *Brown* on public schools throughout the country. Two significant recent analyses are "*Brown* at 50: King's Dream or *Plessy*'s Nightmare?" (January 2004) and "Racial Transformation and the Changing Nature of Segregation" (January 2006). The most comprehensive treatment of segregation in public schools in the North prior to *Brown* is Davison M. Douglas's excellent work, *Jim Crow Moves North: The Battle over Northern School Segregation, 1865–1954* (New York: Cambridge University Press, 2005).

The impact of other federal court decisions on school desegregation has been studied by J. Harvie Wilkinson in *From Brown to Bakke: The Supreme Court and School Integration, 1954–1978* (New York: Oxford University Press, 1979) and by Gary Orfield and Susan E. Eaton in *Dismantling Desegregation: The Quiet Reversal of Brown v. Board of Education* (New York: New Press, 1996). Paul A. Sracic's San Antonio v. Rodriguez *and the Pursuit of Equal Education: The Debate over Discrimination and School Funding* (Lawrence: University Press of Kansas, 2006) includes an excellent discussion of the link between racial segregation and unequal funding in public education, focusing particularly on Justice Douglas's dissenting opinion in *Milliken*. Sources concerning the effects of school desegregation on educational achievement and race relations include James S. Coleman et al., *Trends in School Segregation, 1968–1973*, 76–80 (Urban Institute Paper No. 722-03-01, 1975); David Armor, *Forced Justice: School Desegregation and the Law* (New York: Oxford University Press, 1995); and Jennifer L. Hochschild and Nathan Scovronick, *The American Dream and the Public Schools* (New York: Oxford University Press, 2003).

Finally, David O'Brien's *Storm Center: The Supreme Court in American Politics*, 8th ed. (New York: W. W. Norton, 2008) provides an excellent scholarly analysis of the inner workings of the Supreme Court, while *The Brethren: Inside the Supreme Court* (New York: Avon Books, 1979) by Bob Woodward and Scott Armstrong offers a journalistic perspective on the subject. Henry J. Abraham's *Justices, Presidents, and Senators: A History of U.S. Supreme Court Appointments from Washington to Bush II*, 5th ed. (Lanham, MD: Rowman & Littlefield, 2008) is widely heralded as the definitive book on Supreme Court appointments. Abraham L. Davis and Barbara Luck Graham present an engaging examination of the Court's treatment of race and the law, including case excerpts, in *The Supreme Court, Race, and Civil Rights* (Thousand Oaks, CA: Sage Publications, 1995). Useful summaries of significant cases are provided in *Landmark Decisions of the United States Supreme Court*, 2d ed. (Washington, D.C.: CQ Press, 2008), by Paul Finkelman and Melvin I. Urofsky. *100 Americans Making Constitutional History: A Biographical History* (Washington, DC: CQ Press, 2004), edited by Urofsky, includes helpful profiles of the litigants involved in some of the Court's most notable cases.

INDEX

Boundaries
  attendance, 65, 66, 78, 82, 107, 110, 123, 151
  housing, 35
  neighborhood, 106
  racial, 29, 35
  regional, 77, 78, 82, 184
Boycotts, 51, 52, 64, 79
Boyle, Patricia, 189
Bradley, Ronald, 86, 175
Bradley, Verda, 175, 209
Bradley v. School Board of Richmond
  (1974), 122, 139, 148, 157–158
Brennan, William, xiii, 156, 192, 201
  Green and, 47
  Keyes and, 140–141
  Milliken and, 142, 155, 158, 169
  Richmond and, 157
Breyer, Stephen, 202, 205
Briggs v. Elliott (1954), 12
Broomfield, William, 130
Brown, Henry, 1, 2
Brownell, Samuel, 62, 64, 65, 67, 69, 70
Brown v. Board of Education (1954), x, xi,
  xii, 11, 12–15, 87, 94, 105, 120, 121, 127,
  136, 142, 145, 149, 156, 165, 179, 188,
  191, 192, 193, 194, 203, 209
  all deliberate speed and, 15, 17, 43, 48
  implementing, 15, 43–49
  integrative ideal and, 200
  Milliken and, 194
  resistance to, ix, 15–17, 43, 83, 205
Brown v. Board of Education II (1955), 15,
  47, 104, 123, 188
Buchanan v. Warley (1917), 27
Bureau of Statistics and Reference, data
  from, 67
Burger, Warren, 192
  Alexander and, 157
  busing and, 166, 179
  due process rights and, 162
  Keyes and, 140, 157
  Marshall and, 171
  Milliken and, 142, 158, 159, 161–167, 171,
    178, 188
  on pupil assignment, 188
  racial balance and, 161, 163, 164
  Richmond and, 157, 158
  Swann and, 104–105, 157, 167

Bush, George H. W., 201
Bush, George W., 206
Bush, Jim, 103
Bushnell, George, 85, 87, 88, 90, 96, 102,
  103, 109–111, 132
Busing, ix, 104, 109, 152, 156, 160, 166, 167,
  172, 199
  alternatives to, 198–199, 208
  Boston and, 160, 181, 199
  constitutional amendment to ban (pro-
    posed), 119, 131, 157, 193
  Denver *(Keyes)* and, 144, 156, 157
  implementation of, 186–187
  Louisville and, 199, 204
  opposition to, 64, 113–114, 119–120, 122,
    126, 127, 130–133, 144, 172, 173, 174,
    176–177, 179, 182, 187, 198, 199, 208
  as political issue, 113, 119, 126–127,
    130–131, 133, 174–175, 193, 198
  Pontiac, Michigan and, 109, 113–114
  Roth, rulings on, 127–130, 132
  Sixth Circuit Court of Appeals and,
    136
  Swann and, 104, 105, 142, 156, 157, 167
  U.S. Supreme Court in *Milliken* and,
    144, 145, 147, 148, 152, 162, 166, 167
  See also Antibusing movement;
    Interdistrict remedy; Metropolitan
    remedy

CAC. *See* Citizens Advisory Committee on
  School Needs
Caldwell, William, 106
Carmichael, Stokely, 71, 72
Carter, Jimmy, 198
Carter, Robert, 87
Carver High School, 143, 148
Cass County, 57
Cass Tech High School, 60
Cavanagh, Jerome, 39–40
CCBE. *See* Citizens' Committee for Better
  Education
Central High School (Detroit), 65
Central High School (Little Rock), 16, 17
Chachkin, Norm, 122
Chadsey High School, 65
Chicago Movement, 19
Chrysler, 24

{ *Index* }